Flämische Barockmalerei

Meisterwerke
der Alten Pinakothek München

Flemish Baroque Painting

Masterpieces
of the Alte Pinakothek München

Flämische Barockmalerei

Meisterwerke
der Alten Pinakothek München

Flemish Baroque Painting

Masterpieces
of the Alte Pinakothek München

Eine Publikation des MARC-Projektes,
gefördert von der Europäischen Kommission

Publication of the MARC Project,
with the support of the European Commission

Andreas Burmester, Lars Raffelt, Konrad Renger, George Robinson
und Susanne Wagini

HIRMER VERLAG MÜNCHEN

Redaktion: Susanne Wagini

Übersetzung ins Englische:
Michael D. Price und Nicholas Dorman
(Vorwort, Beitrag A. Burmester, L. Raffelt, G. Robinson, S. Wagini)
Peter Green (Beitrag K. Renger, Katalogtexte und Biographien)

MARC-Aufnahmen und digitale Bearbeitung:
Bayerische Staatsgemäldesammlungen (Lars Raffelt)

Schwarzweiß-Aufnahme: Bayerische Staatsgemäldesammlungen

Umschlag: Peter Paul Rubens, Amazonenschlacht (Detail)

Die Deutsche Bibliothek – CIP-Einheitsaufnahme
Flämische Barockmalerei : Meisterwerke der Alten Pinakothek
München ; eine Publikation des MARC-Projektes – Flemish
baroque painting / [Hrsg.: Bayerische Staatsgemäldesammlungen].
Andreas Burmester . . . [Red.: Susanne Wagini. Übers. ins Engl.:
Peter Green, Michael D. Price und Nicholas Dorman]. –
München : Hirmer, 1996
   ISBN 3-7774-7030-9
NE: Burmester, Andreas; Wagini, Susanne [Red.]; Bayerische
Staatsgemäldesammlungen < München >; Flemish baroque painting

Herausgeber: Bayerische Staatsgemäldesammlungen

© 1996 by Hirmer Verlag München
und Bayerische Staatsgemäldesammlungen München

Satz: Setzerei Max Vornehm GmbH, München
Lithos: Lars Raffelt und mt-color (München)
Druck: Buchdruckerei Holzer, Weiler/Allgäu
Papier: HÅFRESTRÖMS AB Arctic natura

Printed in Germany

ISBN 3-7774-7030-9

INHALT

CONTENTS

MARC

(Esprit Nr. 6937)

Europäische Kommission DGIII/F6
Dominique Gonthier

Projektgutachter
Chris Lloyd, Jan van Daele

Projektleitung

Thomson Broadcast Systems, Rennes (F):
Hervé Derrien, Olivier Dehoux, Philippe Letellier,
Denis Boillon

Projektpartner

CCD Videometrie, München (D): *Dr. habil. Reimar Lenz,*
Dr. Udo Lenz, Dipl.-Ing. Roland Beutlhauser

The National Gallery, London (GB): *Dr. David Saunders,*
Dr. John Cupitt

Birkbeck College, London (GB): *Dr. Kirk Martinez*

Crosfield Electronics Ltd., Hemel Hempstead (GB):
Lindsay MacDonald, Dax Rughani, Jacqui Deane

Bayerische Staatsgemäldesammlungen, München (D):
Dr. Andreas Burmester, Dipl.-Phys. Florian Bayerer,
Klaus Büchel, Sibylle Forster, Bruno Hartinger,
Georg Hayde, Dr. Manfred Müller,
Veronika Poll-Frommel, Dipl.-Ing. Lars Raffelt,
Dr. Konrad Renger, George Robinson,
Dr. Martin Schawe, Jan Schmidt, Gottfried Schneider,
Dr. Susanne Wagini

Schwitter AG, Allschwil (CH): *Jan Schwitter,*
Thierry Ritzenthaler

Hirmer Verlag, München (D): *Albert Hirmer*

Das MARC-Konsortium dankt den Firmen
mt-color, München (D)
und Buchdruckerei Holzer, Weiler im Allgäu (D)

MARC

(Esprit No. 6937)

European Commission DGIII/F6
Dominique Gonthier

Project Reviewers
Chris Lloyd, Jan van Daele

Project Management

Thomson Broadcast Systems, Rennes (F):
Hervé Derrien, Olivier Dehoux, Philippe Letellier,
Denis Boillon

Project Partners

CCD Videometrie, München (D): *Dr. habil. Reimar Lenz,*
Dr. Udo Lenz, Dipl.-Ing. Roland Beutlhauser

The National Gallery, London (GB): *Dr. David Saunders,*
Dr. John Cupitt

Birkbeck College, London (GB): *Dr. Kirk Martinez*

Crosfield Electronics Ltd., Hemel Hempstead (GB):
Lindsay MacDonald, Dax Rughani, Jacqui Deane

Bayerische Staatsgemäldesammlungen, München (D):
Dr. Andreas Burmester, Dipl.-Phys. Florian Bayerer,
Klaus Büchel, Sibylle Forster, Bruno Hartinger,
Georg Hayde, Dr. Manfred Müller,
Veronika Poll-Frommel, Dipl.-Ing. Lars Raffelt,
Dr. Konrad Renger, George Robinson,
Dr. Martin Schawe, Jan Schmidt, Gottfried Schneider,
Dr. Susanne Wagini

Schwitter AG, Allschwil (CH): *Jan Schwitter,*
Thierry Ritzenthaler

Hirmer Verlag, München (D): *Albert Hirmer*

The MARC consortium thanks
mt-color, München (D)
and Buchdruckerei Holzer, Weiler im Allgäu (D)

VORWORT

MARC ist nach VASARI bereits das zweite große europäische Forschungsvorhaben, an dem die Bayerischen Staatsgemäldesammlungen und das Doerner-Institut als Teil dieses Hauses maßgeblich beteiligt waren. Das Projekt *Methodology of Art Reproduction in Colour* (MARC) hat sich das scheinbar einfache, technisch jedoch höchst anspruchsvolle Ziel gesetzt, die Qualität von Farbabbildungen in Kunstkatalogen und Kunstbüchern zu verbessern. Der mit der Problematik Vertraute wird dies begrüßen, gleicht doch manche Abbildung in ihrer Farbigkeit nur noch einem Zitat des Originals. Für das Publikum wie den Fachwissenschaftler ein Ärgernis, dem jedoch mit konventionellen photographischen wie drucktechnischen Verfahren nicht beizukommen ist. Die Einführung digitaler Techniken verspricht hier umwälzende Neuerungen, die wir als große Chance ansehen. Neben zahlreichen Verbesserungen und Vereinfachungen, die sich auf den Ablauf der Katalog- und Buchproduktion und letztendlich auf die Kosten auswirken werden, hoffen wir, die digitale MARC-Aufnahmetechnik so zu nutzen, daß sich wiederholtes Photographieren erübrigt und damit Belastungen für die Gemälde reduziert werden. Allein deshalb ist das MARC-Projekt zu begrüßen und begründet das Engagement des Doerner-Institutes. Zudem wird das digitale Bild für vielfältige andere Zwecke nutzbar sein und das Reproduktionswesen unseres Hauses nachhaltig bereichern.

Wie die Bayerischen Staatsgemäldesammlungen litt auch das MARC-Projekt unter der Schließung der Alten Pinakothek. Nicht alle sich daraus ergebenden Schwierigkeiten konnten gelöst werden. Darüber hinaus machten technische Probleme es notwendig, die Anzahl der ursprünglich für den Bildband vorgesehenen Gemälde zu reduzieren. Dennoch ist die Auswahl umfassend genug, dem Leser ein „Bild" vom Reichtum flämischer Barockmalerei in der Alten Pinakothek zu geben. Als Beleg für die in MARC geleistete Arbeit kann heute dieser Band flämischer Meisterwerke aus der Alten Pinakothek vorgelegt werden. Ungeachtet der Tatsache, daß er nach unserem Wissen der erste, ausschließlich auf der Basis hochaufgelöster und kolorimetrisch farbgetreuer digitaler Bilder produzierte Bildband ist, mag die Farbgenauigkeit und der Detailreichtum Stoff für rege Diskussionen darüber liefern, ob MARC seine Ziele erreicht hat.

Die Bayerischen Staatsgemäldesammlungen danken der Europäischen Kommission, die diese Arbeit unter dem Schwerpunkt Esprit (No. 6937) großzügig gefördert und unterstützt hat. Die treibende Kraft für die Beteiligung der Bayerischen Staatsgemäldesammlungen, für die Antragstellung wie auch die örtliche Projektführung, war Dr. Andreas Burmester. Neben ihm verdanken wir George Robinson und Dipl.-Ing. Lars Raffelt – die die technische Arbeit übernahmen –, Dr. Susanne Wagini und Dr. Konrad Renger – die die kunsthistorischen Texte dieses Bildbandes verfaßten –, Klaus Büchel, Veronika Poll-Frommel und Jan Schmidt – die die restauratorische Betreuung übernahmen – sowie den Photographen unter Leitung von Gottfried Schneider und vielen anderen Mitarbeitern unseres Hauses die Entstehung dieses Bildbandes. Unsere europäischen Partner waren Thomson Broadcast Systems, Rennes (F), CCD Videometrie, München (D), The National Gallery, London (GB), Birkbeck College, London (GB), Crosfield Electronics Ltd., Hemel Hempstead (GB), Schwitter AG, Allschwil (CH) und Hirmer Verlag, München (D), ohne die dieser Bildband nie entstanden wäre.

Johann Georg Prinz von Hohenzollern
Generaldirektor

8

PREFACE

After VASARI, the MARC project is the second major European research programme to involve the Bayerische Staatsgemäldesammlungen and the Doerner-Institut, which is part of this organization. The seemingly straightforward, but at the same time ambitious, aim of the project *"Methodology of Art Reproduction in Colour"* (MARC) was to improve the quality of reproductions in art catalogues and books. Those who are familiar with the nature of the problem will be pleased to hear this, because the colour of reproductions often bears little resemblance to that of the original paintings. For the general public, as well as for the scholar, this has been an annoying, but nevertheless unavoidable characteristic of conventional photographic and printing techniques. With the advent of digital technology, came about the promise of revolutionary innovations which we regarded as a great challenge. Besides the numerous improvements and simplifications offered by digital techniques, we hope to be able to make use of the MARC digital image acquisition technology in order to replace the repeated photographing of paintings, thereby significantly reducing the burden placed upon them. This consideration alone was reason enough for the Doerner-Institut to want to become involved in this project. The MARC concept will also have considerable effects on the production and the cost of art catalogues. Besides this, the digital image will be useful for many other purposes, and the reproduction department of the Bayerische Staatsgemäldesammlungen will subsequently benefit from this.

The Bayerische Staatsgemäldesammlungen as well as the MARC project were considerably affected by the temporary closure of the Alte Pinakothek. Not all of the resultant problems could be resolved and, in the end, the closure of the gallery together with specific technical problems meant that the number of paintings to be reproduced in this catalogue had to be reduced some-what. We feel, however, that the final selection includes sufficient a number works to give the reader an insight into the wealth of Flemish Baroque painting in the Alte Pinakothek. This catalogue alone constitutes proof enough of the work carried out on the MARC project, not forgetting the fact that, as far as we know, this is the first catalogue ever which is comprised exclusively from reproduced colorimetric high-resolution digital images. We are certain that the colour accuracy and richness of detail will give rise to numerous discussions as to whether or not MARC fulfilled its aims.

The Bayerische Staatsgemäldesammlungen would like to thank the European Commission for generously promoting and supporting this project under "Esprit" (No. 6937). Dr. Andreas Burmester, who was the driving force for the participation of the Bayerische Staatsgemäldesammlungen, was in charge of the local project management. Besides Dr. Burmester, we would like to thank George Robinson and Dipl.-Ing. Lars Raffelt who were responsible for the technical work, Dr. Susanne Wagini and Dr. Konrad Renger who wrote the art historical text for the catalogue, Klaus Büchel, Veronika Poll-Frommel and Jan Schmidt who dealt with the conservation concerns, Gottfried Schneider who was in charge of the team of photographers, and many others at our museum who helped with the production of this catalogue. Our European partners were Thomson Broadcast Systems, Rennes (F), CCD Videometrie, München (D), The National Gallery, London (GB), Birkbeck College, London (GB), Crosfield Electronics Ltd., Hemel Hempstead (GB), Schwitter AG, Allschwil (CH) and Hirmer Verlag, München (D) without whom this catalogue could never have been produced.

Johann Georg Prinz von Hohenzollern
General Director

9

DAS MARC-PROJEKT:
VON DER ANALOGEN ZUR DIGITALEN REPRODUKTION

Andreas Burmester, Lars Raffelt, George Robinson und Susanne Wagini

Die Vorgeschichte

In unserem Haus dreht sich alles um Bilder – ob als Original oder in Reproduktion. Als 1987 die Frage an uns herangetragen wurde, ob digitale Bilder für die Bayerischen Staatsgemäldesammlungen nützlich sein könnten, war nicht abzuschätzen, wie rasant die Entwicklung in diesem Bereich voranschreiten würde. Wohl war absehbar, daß über kurz oder lang alle Texte auf dem Personalcomputer geschrieben würden, aber daß digitale Bilder in diese Texte eingebunden werden könnten, erschien undenkbar. Heute, acht Jahre später, ist unsere Skepsis der Überzeugung gewichen, daß digitalen Bildern über kurz oder lang die Zukunft gehören wird. Doch hiermit greifen wir der Entstehungsgeschichte dieses Bildbandes weit voraus.

Ihren Anfang nahm die Geschichte bei dem Forschungsprojekt VASARI, das erstmals digitale Bilder nutzte, um Veränderungen von Gemäldeoberflächen durch Transporte festzustellen und zu dokumentieren. Aus diesem Projekt wurde 1991 die Idee geboren, Gemälde in hoher Auflösung und in höchster Farbgenauigkeit digital aufzunehmen und für die Produktion von Kunstkatalogen und Kunstbüchern zu nutzen. Eigentlich ist dies der Punkt, an dem das Doerner-Institut zu seinen Aufgaben, zu Fragen der Konservierung, Restaurierung und der Untersuchung von Kunstwerken hätte zurückkehren können, statt sich um Reproduktionsfragen zu kümmern. Doch seit geraumer Zeit wird museumsinternen Belastungen der Kunstobjekte kritisches Augenmerk geschenkt. Diese Belastungen sind eine Tatsache, die nur ungerne zur Kenntnis genommen wird. Hierzu gehört auch das Photographieren der uns anvertrauten Objekte, das zudem immer wieder notwendig wird, da die verwendeten Filme altern, ihre Farbe verlieren, beschädigt werden oder – was weitaus häufiger ist – da immer wieder neue Details erwünscht sind.

Die Idee: Um die Belastung zu verringern, soll wiederholtes Photographieren der Gemälde und das damit verbundene „handling" möglichst vermieden werden. Selteneres Abhängen, Ausrahmen, weniger Transporte, etc. bedeuten eine Verkleinerung des Risikos. Erreichbar wäre dies durch eine einzige digitale Aufnahme in höchster Auflösung und Farbtreue, die sich dann beliebig oft und ohne Qualitätsverlust kopieren ließe, was bekanntlich mit konventionellem Filmmaterial nicht möglich ist. Dank der hohen Auflösung ließe sich zudem jedes beliebige Detail herausvergrößern. Das digitale Bild würde nicht altern und es würde seine Farbe nicht verlieren. Eine Fülle vielversprechender Möglichkeiten, zugleich aber auch Bedenken hinsichtlich des Copyrights: Wer hindert Außenstehende, diese digitalen Bilder ohne Genehmigung zu kopieren, zu verbreiten, in Datennetze einzuspeisen? So war die Befürchtung, die Kontrolle über unser Bildmaterial zu verlieren, die meistgenannte. Dann der Irrglaube, mit dem Auge die Farbtreue objektiv beurteilen zu können, ja besser als dies physikalische Messungen vermögen. Und Hoffnungen, mit digitalen Bildern alle Arten von Ausgabemedien bedienen zu können – vom Kleinbilddia bis hin zum Farbabzug, von der Schwarzweißaufnahme hin zur Farbreproduktion. Wie werden sich digitale Techniken auf die eingefahrenen Wege der Katalog- und Buchherstellung auswirken?

Aus diesen Fragen, Erwartungen und Zweifeln entstand MARC. Ein tieferes Eintauchen in die Thematik von Reproduktionen machte allerdings bald deutlich, daß die Neuerung nicht einzig im digitalen Bild, sondern in einer neuen Methodik zur Herstellung von Farbreproduktionen liegen müßte – was sich sprachlich zu *Methodology of Art Reproduction in Colour* (MARC) verknappte. Hierbei zeichneten sich vier Problemkreise ab:

1. Ohne nähere Erläuterung war bereits mehrfach von digitalen Bildern die Rede. Was heißt eigentlich digital

in diesem Zusammenhang? Das, was wir beim Betrachten einer Schwarzweiß-Photographie als Bild mit dem Auge wahrnehmen, ist eine flächige Verteilung von Grauwerten. Grauwertsprünge bilden den Kontrast, Flächen ähnlichen Kontrastes Formen. Die Formgebung folgt keinem geometrischen Grundmuster. Anders bei einem digitalen Bild: Hier wird dem Bild ein äußerst feines Raster übergelegt, das Dargestellte also in Rasterpunkte zerlegt. Die Besonderheit ist nun, daß jeder Rasterpunkt als ein Zahlenwert behandelt wird. Digitale Bilder sind also eine Vereinfachung der Wirklichkeit, denn die Konturen der Rasterpunkte folgen nicht dem Verlauf der tatsächlichen Formen – ein allerdings mit dem Auge nicht wahrnehmbarer Effekt. Digitale Bilder sind Zahlenfelder, mit denen sich rechnen läßt, sie lassen sich kopieren, speichern etc.

Betrachten wir einen einzelnen Punkt des digitalen Bildes, einen Zahlenwert. Wie kommt es zu diesem Zahlenwert? Hier liegt der zweite große Unterschied zur konventionellen Photographie. Fällt dort Licht auf den Film, so wird er belichtet. Je mehr Licht auf eine Stelle fällt, desto schwärzer wird der Film. Die Bandbreite reicht dabei von unbelichtet bis zur Sättigung – mehr Licht würde keine Veränderung mehr hervorrufen. Die bei der Filmentwicklung erzeugten Grauwerte umfassen ohne Abstufung alle Helligkeitswerte von Weiß bis Schwarz. Rein theoretisch sind auf diese Weise unendlich viele Grautöne darstellbar. Ein derartiges Verhalten ist charakteristisch für ein sogenanntes analoges Signal. Jedes digitale Signal beruht nun auf einem analogen. Auf elektronischem Weg wird den unendlich vielen Grautönen des analogen Signals eine begrenzte Anzahl von Zahlenwerten zugewiesen. Im Falle einer sogenannten 8-Bit-Darstellung 0 für Schwarz und 255 für Weiß. Jeder einzelne der dazwischen liegenden Grautöne wird genau einem der Zahlenwerte 1 bis 254 zugeordnet. Die solchermaßen darstellbaren 256 Grauwerte sind im übrigen weit mehr als die rund 40 Grautöne, die unser Auge unter optimalen Bedingungen unterscheiden kann. Doch zurück zum Thema: Ein digitales Signal ist also eigentlich nur ein Zahlenwert. Und da mehrere Grautöne unter einem Zahlenwert zusammengefaßt werden, geht auch Information verloren. Dies wird dadurch wettgemacht, daß man mit Zahlenwerten rechnen, diese in Computern verarbeiten, sie beliebig oft und ohne Qualitätsverlust kopieren und vor allem auf geeigneten Speichermedien abspeichern kann.

Zur Aufnahme digitaler Bilder benötigt man spezielle Kameras. In günstigen Fällen liefern sie Aufnahmen, die – wie im Fall der im VASARI-Projekt verwendeten Kamera – in ihrer Auflösung mit der eines Kleinbilddias zu vergleichen sind. Landläufige Erfahrung ist jedoch, daß ein Kleinbilddia nicht ausreicht, um eine qualitativ befriedigende Reproduktion zu erzeugen. Eine Möglichkeit wäre – wie dies im VASARI-Projekt geschah – die Auflösung der Kamera dadurch zu vergrößern, daß das Gemälde in kleinen Ausschnitten digital aufgenommen wird und diese dann zu einer Gesamtaufnahme zusammengesetzt werden. Ein umständliches Verfahren, für das MARC einen grundsätzlich neuen Weg finden mußte.

2. Filme oder Photomaterialien verändern ihre Farbe. Sie sind vergänglich. Die Qualität der Farbwiedergabe, auch der besten Filme, ändert sich zudem von Hersteller zu Hersteller, zuweilen von Lieferung zu Lieferung, und immer von einer naßchemischen Entwicklung zur nächsten. Wie unsere Fernsehgeräte zeigen auch Photographien häufig zu gesättigte Farben, was das Farbempfinden weiter Kreise der Bevölkerung bereits nachhaltig geprägt hat. Die Farbabweichungen sind zudem unsystematisch: Hat ein Film eines Fabrikates eine zu warme Farbwiedergabe, zeigt der eines anderen Herstellers eine klare Überbetonung der Blauwerte. Dies erklärt zum Teil, daß Kunstreproduktionen häufig nicht nur in der Farbwiedergabe falsch, sondern zudem noch inhomogen sind, ja sein müssen. Die Reproduktion auf der einen Buchseite mag man als gelbstichig, die auf der gegenüberliegenden Seite als zu grünlich empfinden. All diese Effekte sind jedoch nicht einzig der Photovorlage anzulasten, vielmehr kommen später in der Reproanstalt und beim Druck weitere Farbverschiebungen hinzu, ein nicht kontrollierbarer Prozeß.

In der Summe ist dies für Kunstreproduktionen fatal. Beim Vergleich eines Dias, einer Postkarte, einer Abbildung im Saalführer mit dem Gemälde selbst erreicht keine der Reproduktionen in ihrer Farbigkeit das Original.

MARC stand also vor der Aufgabe, zum einen eine Farbwiedergabe gleichbleibender Qualität zu garantieren und zum zweiten die Farbabweichung vom wirklichen, physikalisch meßbaren Wert so gering als möglich zu halten. Homogen und kolorimetrisch farbgetreu, zwei ehrgeizige Ziele. Vor diesem Hintergrund ist leicht einsichtig, daß die digitale MARC-Aufnahme direkt vom Original erfolgen muß. Dies ist eine Neuerung, denn in manchen Museen werden digitale Aufnahmen durch die Digitalisierung einer Reproduktionsvorlage, sei es eines Ektachromes oder eines Diapositives, aber nicht des Originals, gewonnen. Die Fehlfarben der analogen

Vorlage werden auf diesem Wege in die digitale Welt geschleppt, was nicht die Absicht von MARC sein konnte.

3. 150 Jahre Photographie heißt zugleich fast 150 Jahre photographische Wiedergabe von Kunstobjekten. Eine lange Tradition, die auch in unserem Hause fest verwurzelt ist. Photographische Fertigkeiten und von Mund zu Mund weitergereichte praktische Erfahrungen finden ihren Beleg in Abertausenden von Kunstreproduktionen. MARC setzte sich deshalb zum Ziel, die digitalen Techniken dicht an der photographischen Praxis zu entwickeln, um diese handwerklich-technischen Kenntnisse bestmöglich zu nutzen.

4. Der Weg von einer Vorlage zur fertig gedruckten Abbildung ist heute weitgehend von traditionellen, analogen Techniken geprägt. Was sollte also eine kolorimetrisch farbgetreue MARC-Aufnahme nutzen, wenn in einem der nachfolgenden Schritte – sei es in der Reproanstalt, sei es in der Druckerei – diese hohe Wiedergabequalität verfälscht oder verändert würde? Bislang erfolgten Farbkorrekturen nach Gutdünken, nach Erfahrungswerten und nach Wunsch des Kunden – oder sie unterblieben aus Kostengründen. MARC mußte sich deshalb zum Ziel setzen, die Anzahl der Eingriffsmöglichkeiten für Lithograph oder Drucker zu reduzieren, Korrekturen nach dem Auge zu unterbinden und die Wegstrecke zwischen der digitalen Aufnahme und der gedruckten Reproduktion zu verkürzen. Von Anbeginn war klar, daß sich ein derartiger Prozeß nur dann durchsetzen könnte, wenn dadurch zugleich auch die Kosten gesenkt würden.

Aber steht unserem Bemühen um eine physikalisch getreue Farbwiedergabe nicht eine grundsätzliche Schwierigkeit entgegen? Es ist einleuchtend, daß ein Drucker mit zwei Druckfarben – wie zum Beispiel Gelb und Schwarz – nicht alle Farben drucken kann. Selbst wenn er, wie für einen normalerweise im Vierfarbdruck hergestellten Kunstkatalog, noch Blau (Cyan) und Rot (Magenta) hinzunimmt, gibt es immer noch eine ganze Reihe von Farben, die auf drucktechnischem Wege nicht darstellbar sind. Mit zusätzlichen Farben zu drucken, also z. B. zu einem Siebenfarbdruck überzugehen, mag die Palette druckbarer Farbtöne erweitern, erhöht aber die Kosten erheblich. Verzichtet man jedoch auf eine richtige Darstellung einiger Farbtöne, so wird sich dies dem Auge sofort bemerkbar machen. Bei der einen Reproduktion mehr, bei der anderen weniger. Wird MARC dieses Dilemma lösen können?

Eine Fülle von Fragen und Ideen, zähe Entwicklungsarbeit vor dem Computer, technische Treffen in Rennes, Basel, London oder München, Zweifel, endlose Faxe, Ärgerliches und vergnügte Abende. MARC führte sehr verschiedene Partner an einen Tisch: Museumsleute, Ingenieure, Softwareentwickler, Verleger und Spezialisten für Reproduktionen. Verschiedene Welten, neben Englisch, Deutsch und Französisch keine gemeinsame technische Sprache. Dem Leser soll all dies erspart bleiben, technische Details sind anderen Publikationen vorbehalten. Es erschien uns vielmehr angezeigt, am Beispiel der Produktion des vorliegenden Bildbandes aufzuzeigen, wo die wesentlichen Unterschiede des digitalen zum analogen Verfahren liegen und welche Erfolge und auch Mißerfolge MARC verzeichnen konnte.

Zwischen Umzug und Photoatelier

Sichtbarer Beleg für die Erfolge des MARC-Projektes sollte also ein Bildband sein. Dafür wurde aus dem umfangreichen und bedeutenden Bestand der flämischen Barockmalerei der Alten Pinakothek eine Auswahl getroffen, die einen repräsentativen Überblick über die Malerei dieser Epoche und Landschaft gibt. Obgleich Verzögerungen in der technischen Entwicklungsarbeit den Umfang schrumpfen ließen, bietet der vorliegende Band einen eindrucksvollen Überblick über die Künstler des flämischen Barock und ihre Werke.

Die eigentliche Aufnahme der Gemälde wurde durch praktische Aspekte bestimmt. Ihr Ablauf unterschied sich nur wenig von der einer konventionellen Aufnahme. Auch hier galt unsere konservatorische Sorge den Gemälden, ihren Belastungen vielfältiger Art. So mußten sie entweder aus der Galeriehängung genommen oder aus dem Depot geholt werden, was immer und erst recht bei großformatigen, empfindlichen und oft schweren Holztafeln Risiken in sich birgt. Nach Ausrahmen und Ausglasen kamen die Gemälde ins Photostudio, wo MARC-Kamera und Beleuchtung vorbereitet warteten. Nach der digitalen Aufnahme nahm der Vorgang seinen umgekehrten Weg. Unser aller Wunsch, die Galeriehängung so wenig wie möglich zu beeinträchtigen, die Auslastung des Photostudios und die Kapazität des MARC-Computers begrenzten die Aufnahmeaktion auf zwei Tage pro Woche, auf die verteilt insgesamt fünf Gemälde aufgenommen wurden. Ein organisatorisch verzwickter Ablauf, der oft mehr Hände erforderte, als wir zur Verfügung hatten.

Bei Planung des MARC-Projektes ahnten wir noch nicht, daß die Sanierung der Alten Pinakothek Wirklichkeit würde. Als die Galerie dann am 5. April 1994 ihre Tore schloß, zeigte sich, daß dies massive Auswirkungen auf den Projektverlauf haben würde, was nicht nur unsere Arbeit, sondern auch die aller Projektpartner beeinträchtigte. So wurde bald deutlich, daß großformatige Gemälde, wie das monumentale „Große Jüngste Gericht" von Peter Paul Rubens mit 606 cm Höhe und 460 cm Breite ein außergewöhnliches Großformat, nach dem Auszug nicht gezeigt werden könnten. Dies zwang uns, kurz vor der Schließung der Alten Pinakothek erste MARC-Aufnahmen zu machen, zu einem Zeitpunkt, an dem die technische Entwicklung bei weitem noch nicht an dem Punkt angelangt war, der zur Bewältigung dieser Aufnahmen notwendig gewesen wäre. Zu den technischen Schwierigkeiten mit der MARC-Kamera und Software kamen das riesige Format, Probleme mit der Ausleuchtung, Schattenwürfe vom Rahmen, riesige Lampen (woher sollte der viele Strom kommen?), Angst vor dem maroden Elektronetz der Alten Pinakothek, Reflexe auf dem Rahmen, eine sperrige Hebebühne für die MARC-Kamera, Sicherheitsprobleme und konservatorische Bedenken. Alle vier Aufnahmetermine konnten erst nach der abendlichen Schließung der Galerie stattfinden, nachdem das Tageslicht der Dunkelheit gewichen war. Diese nächtlichen Aufnahmen in der Alten Pinakothek stellten in jeder Hinsicht eine Ausnahmesituation dar und boten reichlich Gelegenheit, Erfahrungen zu sammeln, die dem weiteren Verlauf des Projektes nützlich waren. Spätere Aufnahmen fanden unter geeigneteren Rahmenbedingungen statt.

Die Aufnahme

Ängste vor neuen Techniken sind in der Regel größer als die mit ihrer Einführung verbundenen Neuerungen. Dies bestätigte sich wieder einmal mehr auch im MARC-Projekt. Entgegen allen Befürchtungen zeigte sich bereits beim „Großen Jüngsten Gericht", daß sich die Aufnahme eines digitalen Bildes nicht grundsätzlich von der eines Photos unterscheidet. So entsprach die Ausleuchtung und das Einrichten der Kamera dem photographischen Alltag. Ebenso wie auch in der konventionellen Photographie schufen die Lampen im Studio eine Kunstlichtsituation, die stark vom Tageslicht in der Galerie abweicht. Aber auch andere Faktoren, auf die weiter unten noch einzugehen sein wird, lassen die Gemälde „in anderem Licht" erscheinen. Und doch

brachte MARC umwälzende Neuerungen für den Photographen mit sich: Der Computer zog in das Studio ein und die Arbeiten in der Dunkelkammer entfielen. Statt des Filmes lieferte ein lichtempfindlicher Halbleitersensor (CCD) ein Bild, statt der naßchemischen Entwicklung erfolgte eine rechnerische Bearbeitung des digitalen Bildes. Neben letzterem, aus ökologischer Sicht sehr erfreulichen Aspekt, wurde bald deutlich, daß das MARC-Aufnahmeverfahren eine Kinderkrankheit aufweist, die innerhalb der Projektlaufdauer nicht zu beheben war: Aus konservatorischen Gründen galt die übliche Vorgabe, daß die Aufnahmedauer so kurz und die Beleuchtungsstärken so niedrig wie möglich gehalten werden und nicht mehr als 2500 lux betragen sollten. Zudem mußten ultraviolette Strahlungsanteile und die Wärmestrahlung der Lichtquellen ausgefiltert werden. Während letztere beide Forderungen einfach zu erfüllen waren, stellte sich bald heraus, daß auf Grund des relativ unempfindlichen CCD-Sensors der MARC-Kamera die durchschnittlichen Beleuchtungsstärken bei circa 2500 lux liegen mußten. Aber auch dieser Wert konnte nur bei langen Belichtungszeiten erreicht werden. Aufgrund langer Belichtungszeiten tauchten bei dunklen Gemälden dann neue Schwierigkeiten auf, die hier jedoch nicht weiter erläutert werden sollen. Außerdem mußte die Blende des Objektives auf 5.6 geöffnet werden: ein aus photographischer Sicht unakzeptabler Wert, da jegliche Tiefenschärfe verlorengeht. Gemessen an den Vorteilen, die die MARC-Aufnahme bietet, ist dies jedoch ein unwesentlicher Aspekt, der durch eine technische Änderung zu beheben sein wird. Unüblich im Vergleich zu dem analogen Verfahren war außerdem, daß die Ausleuchtung des Gemäldes möglichst homogen sein sollte, um das digitale Rechenverfahren zu unterstützen.

Andere Schwierigkeiten betreffen analoge wie auch digitale Aufnahmen in gleichem Maße: Während wir in der Galerie in der Regel diffuse Beleuchtung antreffen, werden bei der Aufnahme von Gemälden im Atelier Photoleuchten eingesetzt. Dadurch entstehende störende Reflexe auf den gefirnisten Gemäldeoberflächen werden durch Polarisationsfilter weggefiltert. Dies hat den unangenehmen Nebeneffekt, daß die Farben des Gemäldes und insbesondere die dunklen Partien gesättigter und somit noch dunkler erscheinen, was bedeutet, daß das Gemälde zwangsläufig anders aussehen muß als es uns aus der Galerie vertraut ist. Zudem wurden die Gemälde ohne die schützende entspiegelte Verglasung aufgenommen. Durch die Verglasung erscheint das Gemälde aber sowohl gesättigter als auch blaugrünlicher. Ein weiterer Unterschied ist, daß die Gemälde unter Tageslicht mit einer Farbtemperatur von 4100 bis 6500 K ausgestellt sind, aber für die MARC-Aufnahme HMI Lampen mit einer Farbtemperatur von rund 5600 K verwendet wurden. Für die hochgesteckten Ziele des MARC-Projektes hat all dies eine Konsequenz: Es ist in keinem Fall zu erwarten, daß die in diesem Bildband vorgelegten Reproduktionen völlig das wiedergeben werden, was wir in der Galerie sehen. Der Vergleich all der in diesem Katalog vorgelegten Abbildungen mit den Originalen in der Galerie ist folglich nur bedingt möglich.

Der eigentlichen MARC-Aufnahme sind mehrere Arbeitsschritte vorgeschaltet, von denen jedoch nur einige Erwähnung finden sollen. Bei Motivsuche und Fokussieren hat sich zum einen der sogenannte Preview-Modus der MARC-Aufnahmesoftware als hilfreich erwiesen, der eine rasche, jedoch niedrig aufgelöste Wiedergabe des gewählten Ausschnittes auf dem Computermonitor gestattet. Der eigentlichen Aufnahme ist zum anderen die Aufnahme mehrerer Farbkontrollkarten vorangestellt. Im Gegensatz zum analogen Verfahren, wo ebenfalls ein Grau- und ein Farbkeil mit aufgenommen werden, umfassen die für MARC verwendeten Farbkontrollkarten weitaus mehr Grau- und zahlreiche Farbtöne. Die Karten sind für die nachfolgende Kalibrierung von zentraler Bedeutung: Da die genauen Farbwerte jedes einzelnen dieser Grau- und Farbtöne bekannt sind, lassen sich bei der MARC-Aufnahme unweigerlich eingeschleppte Abweichungen korrigieren. Im herkömmlichen Verfahren ist es dagegen der Erfahrung des Photographen überlassen, inwieweit er Grau- und Farbkeile nutzt, um nach der naßchemischen Entwicklung des Filmes die Farbigkeit zu beurteilen. Korrekturen sind jedoch nicht möglich, und jede Neuaufnahme bedeutet eine zusätzliche Belastung für das Gemälde. Im MARC-Verfahren erfolgen Korrekturen rein rechnerisch und sind der analogen Abschätzung durch das Auge des Photographen überlegen. Muß die Farbkalibrierung wiederholt werden, kann immer wieder auf denselben digitalen Rohdatensatz zurückgegriffen werden, eine Neuaufnahme ist also nicht nötig! Hierin liegt ein wesentlicher Vorteil des MARC-Verfahrens.

Nachdem die Farbkontrollkarten weggenommen wurden, wird noch einmal sorgsam fokussiert. Die eigentliche Aufnahme kann beginnen. Während diese nun läuft, was zwischen 20 und 45 Minuten dauert, erscheint es reizvoll, mehr über den Aufbau der MARC-Kamera zu erfahren.

Aus eingangs erwähnten Beweggründen stand für MARC eine äußerst genaue Wiedergabe der gesamten Gemäldeoberfläche bis hin in das Craquelé im Vordergrund, was weder mit Kleinbildkameras noch herkömmlichen CCD-Kameras möglich ist. Während der Photograph derzeit zur handelsüblichen Mittel- oder Großformatkamera greift, mußte für das MARC-Vorhaben eine neue, digitale Lösung gefunden werden. Die unter diesen Vorgaben in den ersten 18 Monaten des MARC-Projektes entworfene Kamera erlaubt, digitale Bilder mit bis zu 20 000 mal 20 000 Bildpunkten aufzunehmen. Dies ist allerdings ein theoretischer Wert, da er an der Grenze dessen liegt, was die verwendete Optik überhaupt abbilden kann und sich zudem bei derartig hohen Auflösungen Abbildungsfehler störend bemerkbar machen. In der Praxis erschien aus vielerlei Gründen – für diesen Bildband und unabhängig von der Größe der aufgenommenen Gemälde – ein Format von 10 000 mal 10 000 Bildpunkten sinnvoll. Aber auch diese Größe ist nur vorstellbar, wenn man sich vor Augen führt, daß auf gängigen PC-Bildschirmen heute selten mehr als 1024 mal 768 Bildpunkte oder entsprechend große digitale Bilder darstellbar sind. Ein MARC-Bild würde somit rund 140 PC-Bildschirme füllen. Oder: 10 000 mal 10 000 Bildpunkte bedeuten bei einem ein Quadratmeter großen Gemälde eine Auflösung eines Quadratzentimeters auf der Gemäldeoberfläche in 10 000 digitale Bildpunkte.

Die volle Auflösung der MARC-Kamera wird durch zwei technische Kniffe erreicht: Zum einen wird der CCD-Farbsensor mittels Schrittmotoren um Bruchteile des Abstandes zwischen zweien seiner lichtempfindlichen Flächen bewegt. Durch derartige Mikroverschiebungen in zwei Achsen ist eine Bildgröße von 3000 mal 2300 Bildpunkten zu erreichen. Dies entspricht der Auflösung besagten Kleinbilddias und ist somit nicht ausreichend für eine qualitativ hochwertige, großformatige Kunstreproduktion. Deshalb wird – und das ist die zweite technische Besonderheit – der gesamte Sensor innerhalb des Kameragehäuses bewegt, um so das gesamte Bildfeld des Objektives zu erfassen. Hierbei wird der Sensor Stück für Stück in der Kamera versetzt. Oder anders ausgedrückt: Ein Gesamtbild setzt sich aus bis zu 63 Teilbildern – Kacheln, wie wir anschaulich sagen – zusammen, die aneinander „genäht" das ganze digitale Bild ergeben. Da sich MARC neben der hohen Auflösung einer kolorimetrisch farbgetreuen Wiedergabe verpflichtet hat, ist ausschlaggebend, wieviele Farbtöne und -abstufungen mit der Kamera darstellbar sind. Ohne darauf näher eingehen zu wollen, wurde aus technischen Gründen eine

12-Bit-Darstellung pro Farbkanal gewählt, was theoretisch 68 Milliarden darstellbaren Farbtönen entspricht, aber in der Praxis deutlich darunter liegt. Frühzeitig wurde erkannt, daß der anfallende Datenstrom so riesig sein würde, daß einer raschen Übertragung der Daten von der Kamera in den angeschlossenen Computer große Bedeutung zukommen wird. Das im Hinblick hierauf speziell entwickelte MARC-Interface erlaubt derzeit Übertragungsgeschwindigkeiten von maximal 15 MB pro Sekunde.

Eine der zentralen Aufgaben war von Anbeginn, die für die Aufnahme benutzte Software derart zu gestalten, daß sie nach Abschluß der Entwicklungsarbeiten von einem Photographen ohne tiefergehende Kenntnisse der Architektur oder Programmiersprachen des verwendeten Computers bedient werden kann.

Die Farbkalibrierung

Inzwischen ist die Aufnahme abgeschlossen. Während der Photograph jetzt in der Dunkelkammer verschwinden würde, um den konventionell belichteten Film zu entwickeln, schließt sich bei MARC eine rechnerische Bearbeitung der Rohdaten an, die im wesentlichen einer Farbkalibrierung dient. Bevor dieser wichtige Schritt jedoch eingeleitet wird, werden die Daten ortsabhängig zugeordnet: So entsteht das MARC-Bild. Geometrische Verzerrungen werden herausgerechnet, Fehlstellen auf dem Sensor sowie systematische Signalstörungen berücksichtigt und ein Abfallen der Durchlässigkeit des verwendeten Objektives zum Rand hin korrigiert. Die eigentliche Farbkalibrierung beginnt mit einer Umsetzung der Rohdaten (RGB) in einen standardisierten Farbraum (XYZ). Solch ein Farbraum ist nichts anderes als ein Hilfsmittel zur griffigen Beschreibung des komplexen Phänomens Farbe. Ein Soll-Ist-Vergleich der Farbwerte der mitaufgenommenen Kontrollkarten sowie eine Umrechnung der Beleuchtungsart ergibt gleichzeitig die Farbkorrektur. Abschließender Schritt ist eine Umsetzung in den sehr gängigen CIELAB-Farbraum, einen an die Gegebenheiten des menschlichen Auges angepaßten Farbraum. Nun muß nur noch das hochaufgelöste, kolorimetrisch farbgetreue Bild auf geeignete Massenspeicher wie Magnetbänder (Exabyte und DAT) oder optische Platten (CD/ROM) archiviert werden.

So elegant und so reibungslos sich dies anhört, gab es bei der Aufnahme und rechnerischen Bearbeitung

jedoch eine Fülle von technischen Schwierigkeiten, die nicht verschwiegen werden sollten. Insbesondere hat sich die Farbkalibrierung als fehlerhaft erwiesen und nach mühsamer Fehlerbehebung mußten deshalb alle Bilder nachkalibriert werden. Der Kernpunkt von MARC: Denn im Gegensatz zur Photoemulsion, die – einmal entwickelt – nicht mehr in ihren Farbwerten korrigierbar ist und deshalb eine Neuaufnahme unumgänglich macht, ist eine zweite und dritte und jede zukünftige rechnerische Nachbearbeitung der MARC-Bilder möglich. Deshalb war es auch völlig unproblematisch, ganz am Ende unseres Vorhabens zusätzlich auftauchende Bildfehler zu korrigieren.

Der Druck

Hinter den ersten beiden großen Schwierigkeiten – der MARC-Kamera und der Farbkalibrierung – verbargen sich weitere Probleme. Bedenken, wie die digitalen Bilder beim Druck umgesetzt werden könnten, wurden anfänglich mit dem Hinweis auf den digitalen Druck der Zukunft zerstreut. Wie sich jedoch herausstellte, bot MARC – da der technischen Entwicklung weit voraus – sein Bildmaterial offensichtlich zu einem Zeitpunkt an, der für die Reproduktions- und Druckindustrie verfrüht war. Am Ende entwickelte sich deshalb der Druck der digitalen Bilder mit analogen Techniken zum eigentlichen Engpaß des MARC-Projektes.

Um eine Vorstellung von den Schwierigkeiten zu bekommen, muß der Weg von der Bildvorlage zur gedruckten Reproduktion Schritt für Schritt nachvollzogen werden. Denn kaum einer, der einen Kunstkatalog in die Hand nimmt, hat eine Vorstellung davon, wieviele Vorgänge notwendig sind, um aus einem Photo, einem Kleinbilddia oder einem Ektachrome eine „schöne" Abbildung zu machen. Wie entsteht eine Abbildung, was war bisher vonnöten, welche Neuerungen und Vorteile bringt MARC?

Der konventionelle Weg nimmt, stark vereinfacht dargestellt, seinen Ausgang bei einer Photovorlage, die in der Lithoanstalt – auf einen Trommelscanner aufgespannt – abgetastet und auf diesem Wege in ein digitales Bild umgewandelt wird. Dies entspricht gleichzeitig einer Trennung in die Farben Cyan (c), Magenta (m), Gelb (y) und Schwarz (k) – die verwendeten Druckfarben. Diese Druckfarben sind nicht streng standardisiert und somit von Lithoanstalt zu Lithoanstalt anders. Zudem wird eine Korrektur vorgenommen, die vermutete Fehlfarben auf der Photovorlage ausgleichen soll und nach Erfahrungswerten erfolgt. Weiterhin werden die Helligkeitswerte jedes einzelnen Bildpunktes in mehr oder weniger dicht verteilte Punktwolken übersetzt. Wie bereits weiter oben angesprochen sind im Vierfarbdruck, ja selbst im Siebenfarbdruck, nicht alle vorkommenden Farbtöne druckbar. Deshalb werden nichtdruckbare Farben durch druckbare ersetzt, was nur dadurch geschehen kann, daß der Farbraum des Originals auf den Farbraum des Vier- bzw. Siebenfarbdruckes verkleinert wird. Dies beeinflußt alle Farbtöne.

Das Bild wird dann im Lithobelichter, nach Farbauszügen getrennt, auf Filme (Lithos) belichtet. In Vorbereitung für den Andruck werden die Lithos zusammen mit (Farb-)Kontrollstreifen auf Aluminiumplatten ausbelichtet und letztere entwickelt. Aus den vier montierten Aluminiumplatten entsteht dann der sogenannte Andruck auf einer kleinen Druckmaschine. Farbabweichungen werden über den mitgedruckten Kontrollstreifen erfaßt und korrigiert. Der Andruck dient dem Auftraggeber, die Reproduktionsqualität und insbesondere die Farbwiedergabe zu beurteilen. Wünsche nach Änderung lauten „weniger Gelb" oder ein „klein bißchen mehr Blau".

Es ist leicht nachzuvollziehen, daß diese „analogen" Angaben naturgemäß nicht immer zu Verbesserungen führen werden, nicht zuletzt, da der Auftraggeber häufig das Original, das vielleicht erst für die Ausstellung ins Haus kommen wird, nur von kurzen Besuchen und natürlich von (fehlfarbenen Farb-)Reproduktionen kennt. Ein Vergleich vor dem Original ist also in vielen Fällen nicht einmal für den Auftraggeber, geschweige denn für die Reproanstalt oder den Verlag möglich. Werden Korrekturen als notwendig erachtet, werden die Lithos korrigiert bzw. neue erstellt. Aus Kosten- und Zeitgründen entfällt jedoch in der Regel ein zweiter Andruck. Ist dieser zeitaufwendige Prozeß von der Bildvorlage bis zum Andruck durchlaufen, werden die Lithos ausgeliefert, und der Druck kann beginnen. Da auch der Drucker das Original nicht kennt, orientiert er sich an den Andrucken.

All dies macht deutlich, daß die Farbwiedergabequalität bislang eigentlich nicht kontrollierbar war und erklärt, warum konventionelle Abbildungen in Kunstkatalogen und -büchern oft so schlechte Farben zeigen. Der bisherige Weg – von der analogen Photovorlage bis hin zur gedruckten Abbildung – weist eine Fülle von Farbkorrekturen auf und wird trotz vieler Kontroll- und Eingriffsmöglichkeiten nie kolorimetrisch farbgetreu sein können.

In Ermangelung digitaler Drucktechniken mußte sich MARC zwangsläufig einer Verbesserung des analogen Druckverfahrens stellen. Dies war eine von allen Partnern unterschätzte Aufgabe. Von zentraler Bedeutung schien zu sein, das Einscannen von Filmen zu vermeiden, also den Trommelscanner zu umgehen und damit auch den Weg abzukürzen, und dann vor allem alle Maschinen und Materialien, die während des Druckes verwendet werden, physikalisch zu charakterisieren. Hierzu zählen das Belichtungsgerät, Bildschärfungs- und Verkleinerungsfunktionen, die Papiersorte, Druckfarben und die Druckmaschine. Für diese Charakterisierung erwies sich ein synthetischer Farbdatensatz als überaus nützlich. Dieser Farbdatensatz durchläuft den gesamten Kreislauf. Einmal gedruckt, werden die Farbflächen kolorimetrisch vermessen und die Abweichung gegenüber den Originaldaten als Korrekturfaktoren benutzt. Dies liefert zum einen Informationen darüber, wie cmyk Werte – von denen oben im Zusammenhang mit den Druckfarben die Rede war – in gedruckte Farbtöne umgesetzt werden. All dies gilt jedoch streng genommen nur für obigen Farbdatensatz, der so gewählt wurde, daß er ausschließlich druckbare Farbtöne umfaßt. Ein Gemälde mit entsprechenden Farbtönen könnte also zu unser aller Zufriedenheit gedruckt werden. Nun zeigt die Künstlerpalette glücklicherweise weitaus mehr Farbtöne, doch befinden sich darunter leider auch solche, die sich selbst durch Kombination zweier oder mehrerer Farbtöne nicht drucken lassen. Hiermit stoßen wir auf ein Problem, das uns bereits beim konventionellen, analogen Verfahren Kopfzerbrechen bereitet hat. MARC sucht dieser Situation zu begegnen, indem die nicht druckbaren Farben in nächstliegende druckbare Werte umgewandelt werden. Im Gegensatz zum konventionellen Verfahren werden jedoch druckbare Farben zum Großteil unverändert gelassen.

Nach dieser letzten Korrektur dürfen entgegen der drucktechnischen Tradition keine weiteren Farbkorrekturen nach dem Auge erfolgen. Hiervon ausgenommen ist der letzte Schritt, ein der MARC-Idee zuwiderlaufendes Zugeständnis: Aus praktischen Gründen erfolgt die Charakterisierung der Druckmaschine bezüglich ihrer Farbwiedergabe immer einige Zeit vor dem endgültigen Druck. Hierdurch können sich in der Praxis geringfügige Abweichungen ergeben, die der Drucker jedoch an Hand einer Kontrollfarbkarte, die er im Original in die Hand bekommt, analog korrigiert. Gleichzeitig wird die digitale Aufnahme einer Kontrollkarte auf jedem Bogen mitgedruckt, was dann einen einfachen Farbabgleich mit dem Auge erlaubt.

17

Ausblick

Zum Zeitpunkt, während dieser Beitrag entstand, waren wir noch mitten in den ersten Druckläufen, immer neue Fehlerquellen und Überraschungen ließen an Dramatik nichts zu wünschen übrig. Technische Schwierigkeiten und der straffe Zeitplan, ganz zu schweigen von oben angeführten prinzipiellen Überlegungen, ließen ungewiß, wie gut oder wie schlecht die gedruckten MARC-Bilder am Ende sein würden. Eine abschließende Wertung muß deshalb unterbleiben. Bleibt das Gelingen des Vorhabens also offen, lassen sich doch bereits konkrete Ergebnisse verzeichnen:

1. Die MARC-Kamera hat sich in der unter außerordentlichem Zeitdruck stehenden ersten Anwendung – der Produktion der digitalen Bilder für diesen Bildband – vorzüglich bewährt. Einziges verbliebenes, jedoch technisch zu behebendes Problem ist der unempfindliche CCD-Sensor, der zu photographischen Zugeständnissen zwingt. Die für die Aufnahme entwickelte Software erlaubt auch einem mit dem Computer wenig vertrauten Laien eine einfache Handhabung. Die für Farbkalibrierung und Umsetzung auf die Druckmaschine zur Verfügung gestellten „Werkzeuge" haben ihre Funktionalität bewiesen, bedürfen jedoch noch mancher Verbesserungen.

2. Doch einzig das Ergebnis zählt: Die zum Druck überreichten digitalen MARC-Bilder zeigen überraschend geringe Farbabweichungen und übersteigen unsere Erwartungen bei weitem. Im Soll-Ist-Vergleich liegt die durchschnittliche Farbabweichung der jeweils mit den 56 Originalen aufgenommenen Farbkontrollkarten bei $\Delta E = 2,37$ mit einem minimalen Wert von 1,72 und einem maximalen von 3,56. Das, dem CIELAB-Farbordnungs-system entnommene, in der praktischen Arbeit sehr nützliche Qualitätsmaß ΔE wird dann greifbar, wenn man weiß, daß mit $\Delta E = 1$ ein für das Auge gerade erkennbarer Farbunterschied angegeben wird. Oder: Eine aus dem Büroalltag vertraute Klarsichthülle aus transparentem Kunststoff erzeugt, auf ein Blatt weißes Papier gelegt, bereits eine Farbverschiebung von rund $\Delta E = 5$ bis 6. An diesen beiden Werten mag der Leser ermessen, wie nahe die digitalen MARC-Bilder am Original liegen!

3. Sind die ersten Schwierigkeiten einmal überwunden, sind die MARC-Aufnahme und letztendlich auch der nachfolgende Druckvorgang wesentlich einfacher, weniger störungsanfällig und schneller als der konventionelle Weg. Das digitale Verfahren erübrigt vor allem Wiederholungsaufnahmen. Aber nicht nur dies: Es entfallen die naßchemische Filmentwicklung, der Trommelscanner, der Andruck und alle „analogen" Farbkorrekturen. Die verbesserte Farbwiedergabe ist allerdings nur mit einer rechenzeitaufwendigen Farbkalibrierung und einer Charakterisierung der im Druckprozeß eingesetzten Maschinen und Materialien zu erkaufen. Ein Prozeß, der einmal eingespielt, aus unserer Erfahrung unproblematisch ist.

Allen, die an der Entstehung dieses Bildbandes mitgewirkt haben, ist bewußt, daß wir mitten in einer das Reproduktionswesen unserer Museen umwälzenden Entwicklung stehen. Mit dieser Umstellung von analogen, in der Tradition verwurzelten Techniken auf digitale Verfahren sind technische, organisatorische und juristische Schwierigkeiten und Ablösungsprozesse, ja die Änderung ganzer Berufsbilder verknüpft. Mit MARC ist ein Anfang gemacht.

THE MARC PROJECT:

FROM ANALOGUE TO DIGITAL REPRODUCTION

Andreas Burmester, Lars Raffelt, George Robinson and Susanne Wagini

The Previous Situation

Within our museum, everything revolves around paintings, not only the original works of art themselves but also reproductions of them. In 1987, as we were faced with the question as to whether digital images could be of use for the Bayerische Staatsgemäldesammlungen, it was not yet possible to estimate how rapidly this area of technology would evolve. Of course, it was foreseeable that sooner or later every text would be written on personal computers, but it seemed unthinkable that digital images might be integrated into these texts. Today, eight years later, our scepticism has given way to the firm conviction that the future belongs to digitalized images. We are, however, getting a little ahead of ourselves with regard to the origins of this catalogue.

The story began with the VASARI research project, whereby digital images were first used to document the changes which come about in the surface of a painting through transportation. As a result of this project, it occurred to us in 1991 that paintings could be imaged digitally with high resolution together with the highest colour accuracy and that these images might be suitable for the production of art catalogues and books. At this point, the Doerner-Institut could have returned to the problems and questions facing the conservation, restoration and examination of works of art instead of becoming involved with questions pertaining to the reproduction of paintings. For some considerable time, however, the burden placed upon art works by the demands within the museums themselves has been observed quite critically. This burden is a fact which is not universally readily accepted. In addition to this, the repeated photographing of art works also places a significant strain upon them. It is necessary to photograph paintings numerous times because the films age and lose their colour or become damaged – which frequently happens – and because new details are also required time and again.

The driving concern behind this project was to reduce the burden on the paintings. This meant that the handling caused by the repeated photography should be avoided, or limited, as much as possible. Less taking paintings down from the gallery walls and removing them from their frames, less frequent transport, etc., would all result in fewer risks and a concrete reduction in wear and tear. We decided that such a decrease in the amount of handling within the museum might best be achieved by having one single digital image possessing the highest degree of resolution and colour accuracy. It would then be possible to copy the digital image as often as necessary without any loss of quality, which, as is well known, is not possible with conventional photographic material. With the high degree of resolution characteristic for such a system, each detail could be isolated and enlarged. The digital image would not age and would not lose its colour. An abundance of promising possibilities were envisaged but at the same time numerous doubts arose. For instance, considerations about the copyrights: who could hinder an outsider from copying the digital images without permission, from distributing them and storing them on a data base? The main fear was that of losing control over our reproductions. In addition to this concern, we needed to take into account the deep-seated belief that one's eye is more accurate in colour judgements than is an objective physical measuring system. The potential flexibility afforded by the digital image system is, however, far greater than is the case with traditional methods. One could use this image as the source for slides, colour photographs, black and white photographs and colour reproductions. Which effects might the digital technique have on the traditional way of producing a catalogue?

The MARC project arose out of these questions, expectations and doubts. Through the process of becoming steadily more acquainted with the subject of art catalogue reproduction it soon became clear that innovation was not only necessary with regard to the acquisition of the digital image, but also with a new method of producing colour reproductions. This gave rise to *Methodology of Art Reproduction in Colour,* abbreviated as MARC. The following four problem areas became apparent:

1. Without any further explanation so far, we have used the term digital image. What does digital actually mean? When we look at a black and white photograph, the eye perceives a surface distribution of grey values. The differences in the magnitudes of grey create the contrast which in turn defines the form. The resultant shapes do not follow any geometrical pattern. This is different with the digital image where, instead, the image is broken down into extremely small, evenly distributed points, each of which is treated as a numerical value. Digital images are therefore a simplification of reality since the contours of the points do not follow the course of the actual form, although this effect can hardly be perceived by the naked eye. Digital images are in fact numerical matrices, which can be calculated, copied and stored.

Let us look at one single point of a digital image, a numerical value. How do we arrive at this number? This is where the second fundamental difference to conventional photography lies. The photographic film becomes exposed where the light falls on it. Where more light falls on one area, the film becomes correspondingly darkened at that point. The scope of exposure possibilities ranges from the unexposed film to the saturated state whereby more light would no longer create any change. The grey values generated through the development of the film are comprised of light values from white to black without any gradation, theoretically constituting an endless number of potential grey tones. This is typical for the so-called analogue signal. Each digital signal is based on such an analogue signal. Via an electronic process, an infinite number of analogue grey tones are given a limited number of numerical values. In the case of an 8 bit representation, black is 0 and white is 255. Each individual grey tone that lies in-between is given a value from 1 to 254. These 256 grey tones are actually far more than the approximately 40 grey tones that the eye can differentiate under optimal conditions. A digital signal is, however, no more than a numerical value. Since a number of grey tones are collected under one numerical value, some of the information is inevitably lost. This loss is compensated for by the fact that one can calculate with numerical values, they are processed in computers and can be copied as often as required without any loss of quality and, most importantly, they can be stored on suitable storage media.

For the acquisition of digital images, one requires a special camera. Under favourable conditions, such a camera produces images in which the degree of resolution is comparable to that of a 35 mm slide. This was the case with the camera used in the VASARI project. Nevertheless, common experience has shown that slides are inadequate for reproductions of sufficiently high quality, such as is required for our purposes. Another possibility might have been – as in the VASARI project – to increase the resolution by imaging the painting in small sections then assembling the composite image afterwards like a mosaic. For the MARC project, however, we chose to seek out a completely new solution in order to bypass this complicated procedure.

2. Films and photographic material are subject to changes in colour over time. They are transitory. The quality of the colour reproduction, even with the best films, changes from one manufacturer to another, from one delivery to the next, and particularly from one wet-chemical photographic development to the next. As with colour televisions, photographs often have colours which are too saturated, and this has had a long-lasting effect upon the general public's perception of colour. Besides this, the deviations of colour are not systematic. If a film of one manufacturer reproduces all colours too warm, then one from another producer shows a clear exaggeration of the blue values. This partly explains why art catalogues not only have incorrect colour reproduction, but are also inconsistent. Such inconsistency is unavoidable. The reproduction on one page of the catalogue may be too yellow whereas on the adjacent page it may seem to be a shade too green. All of the blame for such effects, however, cannot be attributed to photographic material alone. A considerable number of colour changes and deformations arise as a result of printing, a series of processes which are impossible to regulate consistently.

The results of the aforementioned chain of inconsistencies become particularly evident before reproductions of art works. When comparing a slide, a postcard or a museum guide with an actual painting it is normally the case that none of them even comes close to the colour of the original work of art.

The primary objective of the MARC project has been to guarantee a consistent colour quality, the next aim being to keep deviations from actual physically measurable colour values as low as possible. Homogeneity from one reproduction to another and colorimetrical accuracy – two ambitious aims. Bearing in mind the background to this situation, it is easy to understand why the digital MARC image has to be recorded before the original painting. This is an innovation, since in many museums digital "photographs" are made by digitizing a reproduction, either a transparency or a 35 mm slide. The incorrect colours of the analogue photographic material are thereby carried over into the digital world; this is not the intention of MARC.

3. 150 years of photography means at the same time almost 150 years of photographic reproduction of art treasures. This is clearly a long tradition, and it is one which is also deeply rooted within our institution. Photographic skills and practical experience passed on by word of mouth find their testimony in thousands of art reproductions. Another objective of MARC has therefore been to develop digital reproduction techniques sufficiently compatible with established photographic practices in order to make the best possible use of this craft and technical tradition.

4. Nowadays, the well trodden path from a copy to the finished and printed reproduction in an art catalogue is essentially one of traditional analogue technology. What would be the use of having a colorimetric high resolution MARC image when in one of the following steps – whether at the lithographer's or at the printer's – this high reproduction quality were adulterated or changed? Up to the present time, colour corrections have either been carried out at the printer's discretion, or according to the experience of the customer – often they were not carried out at all because of the expense. With this in mind, through MARC we sought to restrict the number of operations for the lithographer and printer so as to eliminate the correction with the eye and to shorten the process from acquiring the digital image to the printed reproduction. It was obvious from the outset that a process of this kind could only succeed if the costs were to be reduced at the same time.
By trying to reproduce colours accurately, are we not aiming for the impossible? Obviously, a printer with two colours, for example yellow and black, cannot print every colour. Even with the addition of blue (cyan) and red (magenta) for the normal four-colour print, there is still a whole range of colours which technically cannot be represented through the printing process. By printing with additional colours, for example, to change to a seven-colour printing process, the palette of colours would be increased, but the costs would rise enormously. If one relinquishes the idea of having the correct representation of certain tones, it will immediately be apparent to the eye. With one reproduction it would be more obvious, with another less. Would MARC find a solution to this dilemma?

Numerous questions and ideas, concentrated development work with the computer, technical meetings in Rennes, Basel, London and Munich, doubts, an endless number of faxes, annoying and entertaining evenings. MARC brought very different partners together at one table: people from museums, engineers, software developers, publishers and reproduction specialists. Completely different worlds converged despite the fact that no common technical language was shared between the English, French and German-speaking working partners. The technical details which will be published elsewhere are not the concern of the reader here. Instead, it seemed far more sensible to us to make use of the present catalogue as an opportunity to demonstrate where the essential differences lie between the digital and analogue procedures, to provide an example of the results of MARC and to provide a possibility for the evaluation of the degree of success or failure which we were able to achieve through MARC.

From the Galleries to the Photo Studio

The catalogue was to be the tangible evidence for the success of the MARC project. For this, a selection of Flemish Baroque paintings from the extensive and important collection in the Alte Pinakothek was chosen in order to give a representative cross-section of the art of this epoch. Although delays in the development work reduced the number of paintings somewhat, the completed catalogue presents an impressive display of the works of the artists of the Flemish Baroque.
The actual acquisition of the digital images was determined by practical aspects. There was only a slight difference to the method of taking a conventional photograph. Here also, from the point of view of conservation, there was concern about the paintings and the burden from different sources. The paintings either had to be removed from the gallery rooms or out of the storage depository, tasks which can involve considerable risks for the works, particularly where large and very delicate, or sometimes heavy wooden panels are concerned. The paintings were taken out from their frames and brought into the photo studio where the MARC camera and lighting had already been prepared. After the digital

image had been acquired, the paintings were returned. We all wanted the hanging of the works in the gallery room to be affected as little as possible. With this in mind, together with the limited availabity of the photo studio and the limited capacity of the MARC computer, it was only possible to acquire five digital images per week spread over a period of two days in each week. The logistics of coordinating the project, without disrupting the day-to-day work in the museum too much, required fairly elaborate organization, a challenge which was compounded by the fact that more personnel were required than were available.

While planning the MARC project, we had no idea that the renovation of the Alte Pinakothek would become a reality. Then as the gallery was closed on 5 April 1994, it became apparent that this would have enormous consequences on the MARC project. Not only was our work affected, but also that of all our partners working on the project. It soon became obvious that large paintings such as the monumental "The Great Last Judgement" by Rubens measuring 6.06 metres in height and 4.60 metres in width, an unusually large format, would have to be put into storage for the duration of the gallery renovations. Shortly before the closure of the Alte Pinakothek, we were therefore forced to acquire some MARC images somewhat prematurely, before we had the chance to overcome all of technical difficulties which we were to encounter. Besides the problems with the technical development of the MARC camera and software, there was the huge format, difficulties with the lighting casting shadows and reflections from the frames, enormous lamps (where should the electricity come from?), fear of the inadequate electrical installation in the Alte Pinakothek, a bulky scaffold for the camera, security problems and last but not least, conservation concerns. All four acquisition sessions could only take place after the evening closure of the gallery and after nightfall. These evening acquisition sessions in the Alte Pinakothek were an exception in every respect, but they gave us a valuable and unique opportunity to learn from our experience, which was to prove useful for the continuation of the project.

Image Acquisition

Fears connected with new technologies are usually greater than the actual changes created by them. This was also the case with the MARC project. Contrary to all misgivings, it became apparent with "The Great Last Judgement" that acquiring a digital image of a painting was basically not so different from taking a conventional photograph. The lighting and the setting up of the camera corresponded with the everyday situation in a photographic studio. Just as with conventional photography, the lights in the studio created an artificial light situation which differs considerably from the daylight in the gallery. There were, however, additional factors, which we will go into later, which caused the paintings to appear "in a different light". The MARC system was also to bring revolutionary innovations for the photographers. The computer moved into the studio and there was no need for work in the darkroom. Instead of a film, the light-sensitive CCD semi-conductor sensor produced the image, and the wet-chemical development process was replaced by image-processing on the computer. Although the latter aspect was pleasing from an ecological point of view, it soon became apparent that the MARC procedure of acquiring an image was having some problems which, as it turned out, were to remain unsolved throughout the duration of the project. For conservation reasons, the usual lighting limitations were applied; i.e. exposure times and intensity of the lighting levels were kept respectively as short and as low as possible. The light levels were not to exceed 2,500 lux and the light sources had to have filters and emit very little heat. These two conditions were essentially easy to fulfil, but it soon became apparent that due to the relatively insensitive CCD-sensor of the MARC camera, the average light intensity had to be around 2,500 lux. This value, however, could only be reached through long exposure times. Other problems relating to this issue, particularly in the case of dark paintings, became evident during our work, however, we shall not go into detail here. One further potential source of anxiety for us was the fact that, even with such light levels, the aperture of the lens had to be opened to 5.6, an unacceptable value from a photographer's point of view since the depth of field is lost. Considering the advantages the MARC image offers, this is a relatively unimportant aspect which can be solved by technical compensation. Furthermore, in contrast to photography, the lighting has to be as even as possible in order to support the image-processing.

Both analogue photographs and digital images are equally affected by another difficulty. As a rule in the gallery, diffused light falls on the painting, whereas in the photo studio photographic lamps are used. These cause a disturbing reflection on the varnished surface of the painting which is filtered out with polarization filters. This gives rise to the unfortunate side effect that the colours of the painting, especially the dark areas, appear richer and therefore darker, a phenomenon which invariably results in an image which has a noticeably different appearance to that which we are used to in the gallery. In addition to this, the paintings were photographed without the protection of non-reflective glass. Behind glass, a painting appears richer in colour as well as somewhat more blue-green in hue. An additional difference is that the paintings are exhibited under a daylight colour temperature between 4,100 and 6,500 K, whereas for the MARC photograph HMI lamps with a colour temperature of about 5,600 K were used. Because of the high aims of the MARC project, this is not without consequence. Taken together, these factors mean that there is no way that one can expect the reproductions in this catalogue to convey perfectly the appearance of the original paintings in the gallery. A comparison of the reproductions in this catalogue with the original paintings in the gallery is, in effect, only possible to an extent. There are numerous preparatory steps before a MARC image acquisition can proceed, of which just a few will be mentioned. Firstly, the so called pre-view mode of the MARC acquisition software which we found to be most helpful when positioning and focusing the camera. The pre-view mode allows display of a quick although somewhat low resolution image of the chosen detail on the computer monitor. Secondly, the actual image acquisition is preceded by the acquisition of several colour control charts. In contrast to the analogue process, whereby grey and colour scales are photographed together with the painting, the colour charts used for MARC have considerably more grey and above all more colour tones. The charts are absolutely essential for the subsequent colour calibration since the exact colour value of each individual grey and colour hue on the chart are known quantities which thereby facilitate the correction of any "imported" colour deviations. In the traditional process, it is left up to the experience of the photographer to judge to which degree the grey and colour scales can be used after the wet-chemical development of the film. Corrections are, however, not possible and each new photographic session means an additional burden for the painting. With the MARC procedure, the corrections are purely numerical and are superior to the analogue judgement of the photographer. If the colour calibration has to be repeated, then one can return to the same digital raw data and a new image acquisition is rendered completely unnecessary. This is one of the most important advantages of the MARC process. After the colour

charts have been removed, the camera is once again carefully focused.

At this stage the actual digital acquisition can begin. While this is taking place, which process requires between 20 to 45 minutes, it is probably quite interesting to find out more about the MARC camera.

One of the motivations mentioned from the beginning was that MARC stands for an extremely accurate reproduction of the overall painting surface right down to the craquelure, a degree of resolution which is possible neither with 35 mm cameras nor with conventional CCD cameras. Whereas the photographer usually resorts to the medium and large-size box camera, a new digital solution had to be found for the MARC process. In the first 18 months of the project, a MARC camera was designed to allow digital images of up to 20,000 by 20,000 picture elements (pixels) to be recorded. This is of course a theoretical value which is on the borderline with what may be reproduced with the particular optical lens which was used. With such high resolution, any geometrical and colorimetrical distortion would be noticeably disturbing. In practical terms and for a number of other reasons, regardless of the format of the painting to be imaged for this catalogue, a format of 10,000 by 10,000 pixels seemed reasonable. One can, however, only get an impression of this scale by making a comparison with the average PC monitor which nowadays rarely has more than 1,024 by 768 pixels. A MARC picture would fill about 140 such PC monitors. To put it another way, 10,000 by 10,000 pixel resolution means that, with a one metre square painting, a resolution of one square centimetre of the painting surface yields 10,000 digital picture elements.

The full resolution of the MARC camera is achieved through two technical tricks. On the one hand, the CCD colour sensor is moved via stepper a fraction of the distance between two of its light sensitive areas. Through such tiny movements on two axes, an image size of 3,000 by 2,300 picture elements is achieved. This corresponds to the resolution of a 35 mm slide which is not of sufficient quality for a large art reproduction. In addition, the whole sensor is moved by motors within the camera in order to register the whole viewing area. Thus the sensor is moved little by little in the camera. Or to look at it another way: the complete image is made up of 63 parts – we call them tiles – which when "sewn" together give the complete digital image.

Since the intention behind the MARC project was to be able to produce a colorimetric high-resolution image, the decisive point was how many colour tones and nuances could be represented with the camera. Without going into too much detail, a 12 bit-representation per colour channel was chosen which is theoretically equivalent to 68 thousand million colour tones. In practice, however, the number lies far below this. It was recognized early on that the resultant data would be so enormous and that the rapid transmission of data from the camera to the computer would be essential. Because of these requirements, a special MARC interface was developed which allows a peak transmission speed of 15 MB per second.

One of the central tasks from the very beginning was that the acquisition software should be designed in such a way that once the development work had been completed, a photographer would be able to use it without having to have a thorough knowledge of the structure or programme language of the computer.

The Colour Calibration

In the meantime, the digital acquisition is complete. Whereas the photographer would now disappear into the darkroom to develop the conventional film, the subsequent step with MARC is the numerical processing of the raw data which essentially serves the purpose of a colour calibration. Before this important step can begin, the MARC image is built up from the raw data. Geometrical distortions are corrected, inhomogeneities of the sensor as well as systematic signal distortions and a vignetting of the lense are taken into account. The actual colour calibration begins with a transformation of the raw data (RGB) into a standardized colour space (XYZ). Such a colour space is nothing more than an aid with which to describe the complex phenomena of colour. A comparison of the values of the acquired colour charts with the standard colour charts allows the colour correction to be made, simultaneously taking into account the transformations caused by the lighting system selected for the acquisition. The final step is the transformation to the standard CIELAB colour space, which is close to the physiological conditions of the eye. Now the colorimetric high resolution image has only to be stored on either magnetic tape (Exabyte and DAT) or on an optical disk (CD/ROM).

As elegant and as straightforward as this might sound, there were numerous technical difficulties with the image acquisitions and the numerical processing which should not be swept under the carpet. In particular, the colour calibration proved to be inaccurate. After a troublesome removal of the inaccuracies, all of the images had to be recalibrated. Herein lies the crux of the matter. With photographic emulsion, the correct colour values cannot be recreated once the film has been developed and it therefore becomes necessary to take a new photograph, whereas further numerical calculations are possible with the MARC images. Thus, it was not at all problematic at the end of the day to make further corrections.

Printing

After the first two difficulties had been dealt with – the MARC camera and the colour calibration – additional problems followed. Doubts which arose as to how the digital images can be dealt with in the printing process were allayed at the start by pointing to the digital printing process of the future. However, as it turned out, the MARC images and technical development were obviously ahead of their time for the reproduction and printing industry. In the end, printing digital images with analogue technology proved to be a bottleneck for the MARC project.

In order to get an idea of the difficulties associated with the conventional printing process, it is necessary to consider this procedure step by step from the "original" photograph to the printed reproduction. Few people who hold an art catalogue in their hands could imagine how many steps are necessary to turn a photograph, a slide or transparency into a "beautiful" reproduction. How is the reproduction made and what innovations and advantages does the MARC process bring?

Described simply, the conventional method begins with any kind of photograph which, at the lithographer's, is put onto a drum scanner, then scanned to give a digital image. This produces a colour separation into cyan (c), magenta (m), yellow (y) and black (k) – the colours of the printing inks. These inks are not strictly standardized and therefore differ from one lithographer to the next. Additionally, colour corrections based on personal experience are carried out to compensate for any colours which are presumed to be incorrect. After this, the lightness of each individual pixel is translated into dots of different density. As already previously mentioned, not all colours can be printed in either the four or even seven-colour printing process. In these cases, the colours that cannot be printed are replaced by printable colours. This basically means that the colour space of the original picture is reduced to the colour space of the four or seven colour process, all of the colour tones being correspondingly affected by this reduction.

The picture is then exposed onto lithographic film. After this, in preparation for printing, the lithos together with the colour charts are exposed onto light-sensitive aluminium plates which are then developed. The lithographic print is produced from these four plates mounted onto a small printing proof press. Colour deviations are recognized and corrected from the colour charts which are printed with the image. The lithographic proof helps the customer of the catalogue to judge the quality of the colour reproduction. The desired changes are expressed with "less yellow" or "a little bit more blue". It is easy to understand that these "analogue" instructions do not always lead to adequate improvements. The customer may only know the original from brief observations, or from incorrect colour reproductions. A comparison in front of the original is in most cases not possible for the customer, let alone for the lithographer or the printer. New lithos have to be made if corrections are thought to be necessary. However, due to the additional expense, this rarely happens. When this time-consuming process from the photographic original to the lithograph has been completed, then the lithos are dispatched and the printing can begin. Since the printer does not know the original, he has to orientate himself using the lithographic proof.

All in all, this clearly demonstrates the uncontrollable nature of colour reproduction up to this time and, by extension, it explains the frequently inadequate quality of reproductions in art catalogues. The methods employed from the analogue photographic image to the printed reproduction have required numerous colour corrections. Unfortunately, however, with such a system, despite many checks and opportunities to make changes, the final print has only the remotest chance of being colorimetrically correct.

The lack of a digital printing technology meant that, through the MARC project, we were required to initiate improvements in the analogue printing process. This aspect of the project was underestimated by everyone. The main issue seemed to be to avoid using the drum scanner. Additionally, all the machines and materials used for printing needed to be physically characterized. This procedure involved the consideration of each individual part of the process: the image setter, image sharpening and shrinking, types of paper, the printing inks and the printing press, in order to establish precisely the degree and nature of colour bias for each component part so that it might then be compensated for. A syn-thetic colour chart which was used throughout the whole process proved to be extremely useful for the characterization. Once printed, its colour areas were colorimetrically measured and the deviations from the original data could be used as correction factors. This procedure gives information about the cmyk values – which we have discussed in relation to the printing inks – and how these are transposed into printable colour tones. All of this essentially applies for the synthetic colour chart which was chosen because it exclusively contains the printable colours. A painting with the corresponding printable colours could be printed satisfying everyone's standards. Of course, the artist's palette has many more hues, but unfortunately there are some that cannot be printed even with a combination of two or more inks. Here we come across a problem which had presented us with quite a puzzle in the context of the conventional analogue process. The MARC process deals with this situation by converting the unprintable colours into the next closest printable values. In contrast to the conventional procedure, most of the printable colours are left unchanged.

Following this final correction, further changes to the data should be unnecessary, particularly colour corrections with the eye. This is contrary to the normal printing tradition. At this stage, however, it may be necessary to make a compromise which, in some respects, goes against the basic principles of the MARC process. For practical reasons, the characterization of the printing press relative to the colour reproduction has to take place some time before the final printing. In practice, there can be some slight deviations whereby the printer can make an analogue correction by using the original colour control chart which is made available by the customer. At the same time, a digital image of this colour control chart is printed on each sheet thereby permitting a simple colour comparison.

The Prospects

While writing this contribution to the catalogue, we were in the middle of the first printing run of the reproductions. New errors and surprises did not leave much to be desired as far as drama was concerned. Technical difficulties and time pressure, let alone the previously mentioned considerations, left us in a position of not knowing how good or bad the printed MARC reproductions would eventually turn out. A concluding evaluation will therefore have to be omitted. We shall leave the success of the project open to conjecture, preferring on our part simply to list the following results:

1. The MARC camera stood the test extremely well considering the extraordinary time pressure for the first ever production of digital images for this catalogue. The only remaining problem, one which can, however, be dealt with, is the insensitive CCD sensor which results in photographic concessions. The software developed for the digital acquisition is easy to use even for someone with little experience of computers. The "tools" which were available for the colour calibration and separation on the printing press functioned satisfactorily, although there is still room for improvement.

2. At the end of the day, the result is the only thing that counts. The digital MARC images which were sent to the printers had surprisingly few colour deviations and were well above our expectations. In the comparison between the colours as they are and as they should be, the average colour deviations from the colour charts which were acquired with the 56 paintings was $\Delta E = 2.37$ with a minimum value of 1.72 and a maximum value of 3.56. ΔE is a useful and common measure in the CIELAB colour space: $\Delta E = 1$ means that a colour difference is just noticeable for the eye. For instance, a common transparent plastic file holder used every day in offices when laid over a white piece of paper already changes the colour by roughly $\Delta E = 5$ to 6. From these two values, the reader can see how close the MARC images are to the original paintings.

3. As soon as the first difficulties have been overcome, the subsequent printing process becomes considerably simpler, less susceptible to subjective interference, it is also faster than the conventional method. Above all, digital image acquisition saves having repeated photographic sessions. But in addition to this advantage: the wet-chemical development of the film, the drum scanner, the proofing and almost all of the "analogue" colour corrections are rendered unnecessary. An improved colour reproduction is only possible with a time-consuming colour calibration and a complete characterization of the machines used in the printing process. Once these requirements have been satisfied, the rest of the procedure poses, in our experience, no significant problems.

Everyone who has been involved in the production of this catalogue knows that we are facing one of the most revolutionary and exciting developments for the reproduction of art works in all our museum collections. With this move from traditional analogue technology to a digital process, it becomes clear that it will be necessary to consider changes and modifications in the technical, organizational and legal aspects of reproduction technology, not to mention possibly painful changes to some traditional professions. MARC is the beginning.

Translation by Michael D. Price and Nicholas Dorman

DIE FLÄMISCHE BAROCKMALEREI IN DER ALTEN PINAKOTHEK

Konrad Renger

Die flämische Malerei des Barock, also des 17. Jahrhunderts, ist neben der italienischen die wichtigste dieser Epoche. Es gab Malerschulen in verschiedenen Städten, in Brüssel, Gent oder in dem mehr nach Frankreich orientierten Lüttich, doch das Zentrum war Antwerpen, das nach seiner Eroberung durch die spanischen Truppen 1585 endgültig zu den südlichen, den katholischen Niederlanden gehörte. Während in den befreiten nördlichen, den protestantischen Niederlanden, hauptsächlich in der Provinz Holland unter Führung Amsterdams ein großer wirtschaftlicher Aufschwung einsetzte, stagnierte die Entwicklung im Süden und traf besonders die Handelsstadt Antwerpen, da die Schelde geschlossen und der Hafen praktisch stillgelegt war.

Im Gegensatz zur Wirtschaft blühte aber die Kunst dank der tiefverwurzelten Traditionen in der Stadt, dank vor allem der Künstlerpersönlichkeit Peter Paul Rubens, der hierher 1608 aus Italien zurückgekehrt war. Er prägte nachhaltig die Kunst Antwerpens, kaum ein Maler konnte sich seinem Einfluß entziehen, der noch über seinen Tod 1640 hinaus bis weit in die zweite Jahrhunderthälfte reichte. Rubens beherrschte alle Gattungen der Malerei – Historie, Porträt, Landschaft und gelegentlich auch Genre. In seinem Hauptgebiet, der Historienmalerei, fertigte er Altäre zur Neuausstattung der im Bildersturm entleerten Kirchen. Für die Höfe in Paris, London und Madrid schuf er Zyklen, die politische Allegorien, Mythologien und Jagdserien zum Thema hatten. Das Antwerpener Bürgertum verewigte er im Porträt und versorgte es mit religiösen und mythologischen Darstellungen. Es waren Rubens' Historienbilder, an denen der flämische Barock seine unverwechselbaren Formen entwickelte, die im Gegensatz zu der bürgerlichen holländischen Malerei standen.

Rubens' zehn Jahre älterer Freund Jan Brueghel d. Ä., zweiter Sohn von Pieter Bruegel d. Ä., war mit seinen Spezialthemen Landschaft und Blumen ein ebenso in ganz Europa geschätzter Maler. Er führte Gemein-schaftsarbeiten mit verschiedenen Antwerpener Malern, darunter auch Rubens, aus, wie damals überhaupt die Zusammenarbeit von Spezialisten an einem Gemälde häufig praktiziert wurde.

Die jüngeren Maler, Anthonis van Dyck und Jacob Jordaens, arbeiteten in ihren Anfängen in Rubens' Werkstatt, orientierten sich zunächst ganz an seinem Stil, um dann eine eigene Handschrift zu entwickeln. Das junge Talent Van Dyck arbeitete nach seiner Aufnahme als Meister in der Zunft im Jahre 1618 in Rubens' Werkstatt an großen Aufträgen mit, weilte von 1621–1627 in Italien und fand vor allem als Porträtist des Genueser Patriziats höchste Anerkennung. Nach einem vierjährigen Aufenthalt in seiner Vaterstadt Antwerpen ging er 1631 nach England, wo er Hofmaler bei Karl I. wurde. Sein Einfluß auf die englische Porträtmalerei reichte bis zum Ende des 18. Jahrhunderts. Ein Beispiel aus der englischen Zeit fehlt leider in dem sonst reichen Van Dyck-Bestand der Alten Pinakothek.

Jacob Jordaens war zu unbekanntem Zeitpunkt zum Protestantismus übergetreten und wählte in seinen zahlreichen Genredarstellungen Themen, die den protestantischen Moralvorstellungen der nördlichen Niederlande nahestanden, in ihren Formen aber unverkennbar flämisch blieben.

Von Adriaen Brouwer besitzt die Alte Pinakothek mit siebzehn Gemälden die bei weitem größte Sammlung seines nur ca. 60 Bilder umfassenden Œuvres. Der mit seinen Bauerndarstellungen in der Tradition Pieter Bruegels d. Ä. stehende Brouwer setzte thematisch wie künstlerisch neue Akzente, was seine frühzeitige Hochschätzung erklärt; Rembrandt besaß sieben und Rubens sogar siebzehn Bilder von seiner Hand.

Der Ruhm der flämischen Malerei war in ganz Europa verbreitet, und fürstliche Sammler allerorten wetteiferten im Erwerb der Meisterwerke von Rubens, Van Dyck oder Jan Brueghel d. Ä. Die Flamensammlung der Alten Pinakothek, eine der umfangreichsten überhaupt, verdankt ihren Reichtum verschiedenen Wittelsbacher Fürsten, deren Bestände um 1800 durch glückliche Erbschaftsfälle in München vereint wurden. Hier ragen besonders die Komplexe von Adriaen Brouwer, Jan Brueghel d. Ä. und vor allem Peter Paul Rubens heraus – nicht nur an Zahl, sondern auch hinsichtlich ihrer außerordentlichen Qualität.

Die Anfänge der Rubens-Sammlung gehen auf Bestellungen zweier Wittelsbacher Fürsten direkt bei Rubens zurück. Um 1616 hatte Herzog Maximilian I. von Bayern (reg. 1597–1651) vier Jagdbilder für Schloß Schleißheim bei München bestellt. Nur eines davon, die „Jagd auf Nilpferd und Krokodil" ist heute noch in München vorhanden. Ungefähr zur gleichen Zeit bestellte sein Vetter Herzog Wolfgang Wilhelm von Pfalz-Neuburg (reg. 1614–1653) für den Hochaltar seiner neuen Hofkirche das „Große Jüngste Gericht" (Nr. 20) und später noch drei weitere Bilder zur Ausstattung der Hof- und Pfarrkirche seiner Residenzstadt Neuburg.

Sein Enkel Johann Wilhelm (reg. 1690–1716) – inzwischen residierte diese Linie nicht mehr in Neuburg an der Donau, sondern in Düsseldorf – holte diese Bilder mit allerhöchster kirchlicher Erlaubnis in seine Galerie nach Düsseldorf. Der Kurfürst hatte gleich nach seinem Regierungsantritt begonnen, eine Gemäldesammlung mit hauptsächlich italienischer und niederländischer Kunst aufzubauen. Sein politischer Einfluß auf die südlichen Niederlande machte es ihm besonders leicht, aus Kirchen und Klöstern – oftmals mit dem nicht immer eingehaltenen Versprechen von Bezahlung und Lieferung von Kopien – wichtige Bilder nach Düsseldorf zu entführen.

Den Kern von Johann Wilhelms Sammlung flämischer Kunst bilden jedoch die 46 Rubens-Gemälde, die schon der 1719 erschienene Katalog vermeldete, von denen viele zu den wichtigsten Rubens-Bildern überhaupt gehören. Drei stammen aus dem Besitz des Herzogs von Richelieu, bei dem sie der französische Kunstkenner Roger de Piles gesehen und 1677 ausführlich beschrieben hat: „Amazonenschlacht" (Nr. 25), „Höllensturz der Verdammten" und „Trunkener Silen". In dem um 1710 errichteten Galeriegebäude war ein Saal ausschließlich Rubens gewidmet. Der 1778 erschienene Katalog hält in seinem Tafelteil noch die barocke, bis unter die Decke reichende dichte Hängung fest. Manches der dort erscheinenden Bilder ist inzwischen als nicht eigenhändig erkannt und in das Depot verbannt, aber dennoch können heute 25 Meisterwerke aus Johann Wilhelms Sammlung in der Alten Pinakothek oder der Barockgalerie Schleißheim gezeigt werden.

Die Düsseldorfer Galerie gehörte zu den bedeutendsten Gemälde-Sammlungen des 18. Jahrhunderts und wurde von vielen gebildeten Reisenden, darunter Joshua Reynolds, Johann Wolfgang von Goethe und Alexander von Humboldt besucht. Auch der deutsche Aufklärer Georg Forster und der Sturm-und-Drang-Dichter Wilhelm Heinse veröffentlichten Beschreibungen der Düsseldorfer Bilder, bleibende Zeugnisse für die Rubens-Rezeption des 18. Jahrhunderts.

Die Alte Pinakothek verdankt ihre reichen Schätze an flämischer Malerei neben der Düsseldorfer, vor allem der Münchner kurfürstlichen Galerie. Die Herkunft der meisten dieser Gemälde läßt sich nicht weiter als bis zum Inventar von 1748 zurückverfolgen. Der größte Teil dürfte von Kurfürst Max Emanuel (reg. 1679–1726) erworben worden sein, der seine Zeit als Statthalter in den spanischen Niederlanden von 1691 bis 1701 nutzte, um in großem Umfang hauptsächlich flämische Bilder zu kaufen. Nicht über alle seine Erwerbungen sind wir unterrichtet, nur zufällig wissen wir, daß der „Bethlehemitische Kindermord" und die „Löwenjagd", die ebenfalls Roger de Piles 1677 in der erwähnten Sammlung des Herzogs von Richelieu beschrieben hatte, von Max Emanuel erworben wurden.

Den beachtlichsten Ankauf machte Max Emanuel 1698 bei dem Antwerpener Kaufmann Gisbert van Colen mit 101 flämischen Bildern, darunter zwölf Rubens, fünfzehn Van Dycks und acht Brouwers. Van Colen war weitläufig verwandt mit der Familie von Rubens' zweiter Frau Helene Fourment. So erklärt sich, daß aus diesem Bestand besonders viele private Bildnisse stammen; hervorzuheben ist das prächtige Gemälde „Helene Fourment im Brautkleid" (Nr. 15).

Der Ruhm der Münchner Rubens-Sammlung beruht nicht allein auf der Anzahl, sondern genauso auf der Bedeutung, die einzelnen Bildern innerhalb seines Œuvres seit jeher beigemessen wird. Entsprechend stand die Münchner Sammlung stets im Interesse der Rubens-Forschung. Für die deutschen Autoren, in der ersten Hälfte des 20. Jahrhunderts auf diesem Gebiet federführend, war sie außerdem die nächstgelegene Galerie, und es ist kein Zufall, daß bereits Jakob Burckhardt für seine 1898 postum erschienenen „Erinnerungen aus Rubens" vornehmlich Beispiele aus der Alten Pinakothek wählte. Ebenso hat Hans Gerhard Evers 1942 seine Rubens-Monographie reich mit Abbildungen und Details von Münchner Bildern ausgestattet. Letztlich prägte dieses lange Zeit sehr einflußreiche Buch beim deutschen Publikum die Überzeugung, daß die Münchner Alte Pinakothek die Rubens-Sammlung schlechthin bewahrt.

FLEMISH BAROQUE PAINTING IN THE ALTE PINAKOTHEK

Konrad Renger

The most important painting of the 17th century, together with that of the Italian masters, is the work of the Flemish Baroque. Schools of painting existed in various cities – in Brussels and Ghent, and also in Liège, which was more closely oriented to France. The main centre, however, was in Antwerp, which, after its capture by Spanish forces in 1585, finally became part of the southern Catholic provinces of the Netherlands. While the liberated Protestant north, and in particular the province of Holland with its centre in Amsterdam, experienced a major economic boom, development stagnated in the south. The mercantile city of Antwerp was particularly affected by this, since access to the River Schelde was barred and the port was practically closed to trade.

In contrast to the economy, however, the arts flourished, thanks to certain deep-rooted traditions of that city, but above all to an outstanding artistic personality: Peter Paul Rubens, who had returned to Antwerp from Italy in 1608. Rubens made a deep and lasting impression on the art of the city. Virtually no painter was able to escape his influence, which continued to exert itself after his death in 1640 until well into the second half of the century. Rubens was a master of all kinds of painting, from historical subjects and portraiture to landscape and occasionally even genre depictions. His principal field of activity was history painting, and he executed a number of altar pictures with historical themes as part of the refurbishment of churches that had been stripped during the period of iconoclasm. He also painted cycles of works for the courts in Paris, London and Madrid, depicting political allegories, mythological subjects and series of hunting scenes. He immortalized the middle classes of Antwerp in his portraits and provided them with religious and mythological depictions. It was through Rubens' history paintings that the Flemish Baroque developed its own unmistakable forms, which are quite distinct from those exhibited by works painted for the Dutch middle classes.

Rubens' friend, Jan Brueghel the Elder, the second son of Pieter Bruegel the Elder, was ten years Rubens' senior. Brueghel was famous for his depictions of landscapes and flowers, for which he was greatly esteemed throughout Europe. It was not uncommon in those days for painters to work jointly on pictures, contributing those elements in which they specialized. Brueghel executed many such works in collaboration with other Antwerp painters, including Rubens himself.

Anthony van Dyck and Jacob Jordaens belonged to a younger generation of painters. In their early years, they worked in Rubens' workshop and took their artistic bearings wholly from their mentor, only later developing their own personal styles. After his adoption as a master into the guild in 1618, the talented young Van Dyck worked on major commissions in Rubens' workshop. Between 1621 and 1627 he stayed in Italy and met with great acclaim, particularly as a portraitist, among the patrician classes of Genoa. After returning to his home town, Antwerp, where he remained for four years, Van Dyck went to England in 1631 and became court painter to King Charles I. The artist's work continued to exert an influence on English portrait painting down to the end of the 18th century. The extensive collection of Van Dyck's pictures in the Alte Pinakothek unfortunately includes no examples of his work from the period of his stay in England.

At some unknown date, Jacob Jordaens converted to Protestantism, and in his numerous genre depictions, he selected subjects that were closely related to the Protestant moral values of the northern Netherlands. At the same time, his paintings remain undeniably Flemish in their forms.

The 17 paintings by Adriaen Brouwer in the possession of the Alte Pinakothek constitute by far the largest collection of his works, from an œuvre that comprises only about 60 pictures altogether. Brouwer, whose peasant scenes stand in the tradition of Pieter Bruegel the Elder, explored new thematic and artistic paths. This explains the high esteem in which he was held early in his career and the fact that Rembrandt owned seven and Rubens no less than 17 of his paintings.

Flemish painting was famed throughout Europe, and princely collectors everywhere vied with each other to acquire masterpieces by Rubens, Van Dyck and Jan Brueghel the Elder. The stock of Flemish paintings in the Alte Pinakothek is one of the largest in the world. It owes its depth and variety to a number of princes of the House of Wittelsbach whose collections were united in Munich around 1800 as the outcome of a series of fortunate dynastic circumstances. The paintings of Adriaen Brouwer, Jan Brueghel the Elder and above all Sir Peter Paul Rubens belong to the outstanding works of this collection, not only in terms of their numbers, but on account of their great historical significance.

The origins of the Rubens collection can be traced back to commissions that two Wittelsbach princes placed directly with that master. Around 1616, Duke Maximilian I of Bavaria (ruled 1597–1651) ordered four hunting pictures for his palace in Schleissheim outside Munich. Only one of these paintings, the "Hippopotamus and Crocodile Hunt", is still in the collection today. At roughly the same time, Maximilian's cousin, Duke Wolfgang Wilhelm of the Palatinate-Neuburg (ruled 1614–1653), commissioned "The Great Last Judgement" (No. 20) for the high altar of his new court church. Later, he ordered three further pictures for the court and parish church of his seat of residence in Neuburg.

By the time his grandson, Johann Wilhelm (ruled 1690–1716), succeeded to the electoral chair, this line of the family no longer resided in Neuburg. With the blessing of the highest instances of the Church, Johann Wilhelm proceeded to transfer the pictures his predecessors had commissioned to his new seat of residence in Düsseldorf. Immediately after his accession, the elector had begun to assemble a collection of paintings of his own, containing works mainly from Italy and the Netherlands. His political influence in the southern Netherlands made it relatively easy for him to remove important pictures from churches and monasteries to Düsseldorf – often with an unkept promise to reimburse the former owners and to replace the works with copies.

The nucleus of Johann Wilhelm's collection of Flemish art is formed by the 46 Rubens paintings that were already listed in the catalogue published in 1719. Many of these pictures are among the most important works Rubens painted. Three came from the collection of the Duke of Richelieu, where they were seen and described at length in 1677 by the French connoisseur of art Roger

de Piles: "The Battle of the Amazons" (No. 25), "The Fall of the Damned" and "Drunken Silenus". In the gallery erected in Düsseldorf around 1710, a whole hall was dedicated to the works of Rubens. The illustrated section of the catalogue published in 1778 shows the Baroque order of hanging, with pictures set out in close proximity to each other over the entire area of the walls and extending up to the ceiling. A number of the works included in that catalogue are no longer recognized as having been executed by Rubens himself and have been removed to store. Nevertheless, some 25 masterpieces from Johann Wilhelm's collection on display in the Alte Pinakothek or the Baroque gallery of Schleissheim Palace are still attributed to Rubens.

The Düsseldorf Gallery comprised one of the leading collections of paintings of the 18th century and was visited by many learned and distinguished travellers, including Joshua Reynolds, Johann Wolfgang von Goethe and Alexander von Humboldt. The German rationalist scholar Georg Forster, and the *Sturm und Drang* poet Wilhelm Heinse published descriptions of the pictures in the Düsseldorf collection, bearing lasting witness to the appreciation of Rubens' work in the 18th century.

The Alte Pinakothek owes its rich heritage of Flemish paintings not only to the Düsseldorf collection, but above all to the Electoral Gallery in Munich. The provenance of most of these works cannot be traced back further than the 1748 inventory. The majority of the pictures were probably acquired by Elector Max Emanuel (ruled 1679–1726), who took the opportunity during his term of office as governor of the Spanish Netherlands (1691–1701) to purchase large numbers of paintings – in particular the works of Flemish artists. Not all his acquisitions are documented, but it is recorded that "The Massacre of the Innocents" and the "Lion Hunt", which Roger de Piles also mentioned in 1677 as belonging to the collection of the Duke of Richelieu, were purchased by Max Emanuel.

The elector's most notable acquisition was the collection he bought from the Antwerp merchant Gisbert van Colen in 1698. It comprised 101 Flemish pictures, including 12 by Rubens, 15 by Van Dyck and 8 by Brouwer. Van Colen was distantly related to the family of Rubens' second wife, Helene Fourment, which explains why there were so many private portraits among these works, including the magnificent painting "Helene Fourment in Her Bridal Gown" (No. 15).

The reputation of the Rubens collection in Munich is not based solely on its size. At least as important is the eminence that has always been attached to the individual pictures within his œuvre. The Munich collection has, therefore, long been a focus of attention for research into Rubens and his work. For German scholars, who were dominant in this field in the first half of the 20th century, the Alte Pinakothek was also the most accessible gallery. It is thus no coincidence that Jakob Burckhardt based his "Erinnerungen aus Rubens" (Recollec-tions of Rubens), which appeared posthumously in 1898, mainly on works from the Alte Pinakothek. Hans Gerhard Evers' monograph on Rubens, published in 1942, is also full of illustrations and details of the paintings in the Munich collection. This influential book helped to create a conviction in Germany that the Alte Pinakothek in Munich houses the greatest collection of Rubens' paintings in the world.

KATALOG

CATALOGUE

Susanne Wagini (Text)
Lars Raffelt (Digitale Aufnahmen/Digital Acquisition)

1 Jan Brueghel der Ältere
(1568 Brüssel – 1625 Antwerpen)

Die Predigt Johannes des Täufers

Holz, 41 x 59 cm
Signiert und datiert unten rechts: BRVEGHEL 1598·
Inv. Nr. 834

1 Jan Brueghel the Elder
(1568 Brussels – 1625 Antwerp)

John the Baptist Preaching

Wood, 41 x 59 cm
Signed and dated bottom right: BRVEGHEL 1598·
Inv. No. 834

Das 1598 datierte Gemälde ist eine Kopie nach dem Bild seines Vaters Pieter Bruegel d. Ä. von 1566, das heute im Museum in Budapest hängt und bis ins 17. Jahrhundert, auch von anderen Malern, oft und gerne kopiert wurde. Gezeigt wird die Predigt Johannes des Täufers (Matthäus 3, 1–17), der zur Buße mahnt und auf das Kommen Christi hinweist. Auf einer Waldlichtung haben sich zahlreiche Personen um den Täufer geschart, die Gestalt des Johannes im Mittelgrund verliert sich fast in der Volksmenge, die zum eigentlichen Bildthema wird. Jan Brueghel d. Ä. zeigt hier die Vielfalt des Menschengeschlechts und die unterschiedlichen Reaktionen und Anteilnahmen am Geschehen: Männer, Frauen und Kinder, die verschiedenen Lebensaltern, Ständen und Nationalitäten zugehören. Auf die eindrucksvolle Schilderung der nahe an den Vordergrund gerückten Personen wird in der Detailfreude besondere Sorgfalt verwendet und auch die farbliche Gestaltung ist hier am prächtigsten.

Das Original des Vaters wurde in der Literatur unterschiedlich gedeutet. Vor allem sah man darin einen Gegenwartsbezug zu den seinerzeit häufig veranstalteten Waldpredigten unter freiem Himmel. Eine oft interpretierte Szene ist ein Zigeuner, der die Zukunft aus der Hand eines bärtigen Mannes in schwarzer spanischer Tracht liest – ein aus damaliger Sicht gotteslästerliches Unterfangen. Die Wertschätzung der Komposition beruhte jedoch höchstwahrscheinlich auf den künstlerischen Qualitäten und Fähigkeiten von Pieter Bruegel d. Ä., eine bunte Volksmenge darzustellen und weniger auf den eventuellen protestantischen, reformerischen Aussagen.

This picture, dated 1598, is a copy of a work painted in 1566 by Pieter Bruegel the Elder, the artist's father. The original, which now hangs in the Museum of Visual Arts in Budapest, was frequently copied by other painters until well into the 17th century.

The painting shows John the Baptist preaching (Matt. 3: 1–17), calling on the people to repent and telling of the coming of Christ. A large audience has gathered in a forest clearing around the Baptist. The figure of John in the middle distance is almost lost in the crowd, which becomes the real subject of the picture. In this work, Jan Brueghel the Elder depicts the sheer variety of mankind, the reactions and the degree of interest for these events shown by men, women and children of different ages, rank and nationality. Particular care for detail is devoted to the portrayal of the people in the foreground, where the coloration is also at its most splendid.

The original painting by Pieter Bruegel the Elder, on which this copy is based, has been subject to different interpretations. A contemporary reference was seen to the clandestine outdoor religious meetings that were common in Bruegel's time. One scene that has given rise to a great deal of speculation is that in which a gypsy predicts the future from the hand of a bearded man in black Spanish attire – a blasphemous undertaking in those days. However, the picture was probably appreciated more for its artistic qualities and the skills of Pieter Bruegel the Elder in depicting a motley crowd of people than for any Protestant reformist statement it might contain.

2 Jan Brueghel der Ältere
(1568 Brüssel – 1625 Antwerpen)

Seehafen mit der Predigt Christi

Holz, 78 x 119 cm
Signiert und datiert unten rechts: BRVEGHEL 1598·
Inv. Nr. 187

2 Jan Brueghel the Elder
(1568 Brussels – 1625 Antwerp)

Harbour Scene with Christ Preaching

Wood, 78 x 119 cm
Signed and dated bottom right: BRVEGHEL 1598·
Inv. No. 187

Dieses Hauptwerk unter Jan Brueghels d. Ä. „Weltland-schaften" zeigt die Berufung der Apostel Simon Petrus, Andreas, Jakobus und Johannes (Markus 1, 16–20): „Da er aber an dem Galiläischen Meer ging, sah er Simon und Andreas, seinen Bruder, daß sie ihre Netze ins Meer warfen; denn sie waren Fischer. Und Jesus sprach zu ihnen: Folget mir nach; ich will euch zu Menschen-fischern machen! Alsbald verließen sie ihre Netze und folgten ihm nach. Und als er von dannen ein wenig wei-terging, sah er Jakobus, den Sohn des Zebedäus, und Johannes, seinen Bruder, daß sie die Netze im Schiff flickten; und alsbald rief er sie."

Christus und die vier Jünger stehen im Mittelgrund an Bord eines Schiffes, von wo aus Christus dem im Hafen zusammengekommenen Volk predigt. Diese Szene ver-liert sich fast in der kleinfigurigen Menschenmenge. Davon abgetrennt ist der geschäftige Fischverkauf im Vordergrund, der die Aufmerksamkeit des Betrachters zuerst auf sich zieht. Menschen unterschiedlichster Nationalitäten und Stände sind hier versammelt. Unter ihnen fällt besonders eine vornehm gekleidete Gesell-schaft in der Mitte auf. Im Kontrast dazu steht links dane-ben eine Gruppe von armseligen, zerlumpten Gestalten, die Fische über dem Feuer braten und sich wärmen.

Brueghel ist einer jener Maler, die der Landschaft einen ganz wesentlichen Platz und Stellenwert in ihrem Schaf-fen eingeräumt haben. Seine sogenannten „Weltland-schaften" sind alle nach einem bestimmten Schema auf-gebaut. Der Betrachter blickt von einem erhöhten Standpunkt aus auf eine sich breit erstreckende Land-schaft mit sehr hohem Horizont. Durch eine farblich dif-ferenzierte Abfolge der einzelnen Bildgründe – Braun im Vordergrund, Grün im Mittelgrund und Blau im Hinter-grund – wird die Tiefenwirkung erzielt. Zusätzliches Gliederungselement sind die einzelnen Licht- und Schat-tenzonen.

Ein Charakteristikum der „Weltlandschaft" ist es, die Vielfalt der Welt widerzuspiegeln. Hier ist die biblische

This masterpiece among Jan Brueghel the Elder's pan-orama landscapes depicts the calling of the Apostles Simon Peter, Andrew, James and John (Mark 1: 16–20): "Now as he walked by the sea of Galilee, he saw Simon and Andrew his brother casting a net into the sea: for they were fishers. And Jesus said unto them, Come ye after me, and I will make you to become fishers of men. And straightway they forsook their nets, and followed him. And when he had gone a little further thence, he saw James the son of Zebedee, and John his brother, who also were in the ship mending their nets. And straightway he called them …"

Christ and the four Apostles are shown standing on a ship in the middle distance. Christ is preaching to the people gathered in the harbour. The event is almost lost in the mass of small-scale figures. The observer's atten-tion is first attracted to quite a different scene in the fore-ground, where a lively trade in fish is going on. Men and women of different nationalities and classes are gath-ered here. In the middle, a company of elegantly dressed people are boldly contrasted to a group of poor, shabbily dressed creatures to the left who are grilling fish and warming themselves over a fire.

Landscape painting plays a major role and enjoys a spe-cial status in Brueghel's work. His so-called "panorama landscapes" are all composed according to a similar pat-tern. From an elevated viewpoint, the observer has a broad view over the countryside to a horizon line set rel-atively high in the picture. A sequence of differently coloured grounds – brown in the foreground, green in the middle distance and blue in the distance – helps to create a sense of depth. Additional articulating elements are the individual zones of light and shade.

One function of the panorama landscape was to provide an image of the variety and multiplicity of the world. In this case, the biblical story that really took place on the Sea of Galilee is transposed to an imaginary landscape that becomes a setting for a vivid and colourful kaleido-

Geschichte, die eigentlich am Galiläischen Meer spielt, in eine Phantasielandschaft verlegt worden, die ein lebendiges, buntes Kaleidoskop darstellt. Zwar sind einzelne Bestandteile der Landschaft nach der Natur gemalt, aber frei zusammengestellt. So ist links auf dem Hügel das Scipionen-Grab von der Via Appia in Rom zu sehen. Die prägnante Felseninsel im Hintergrund stellt eine Ansicht vom neapolitanischen Castel dell'Ovo dar, wofür Brueghel seine Naturstudien aus Neapel in seitenverkehrter Abwandlung verwendete (vgl. Nr. 3). Durch die Kostüme der Figuren wird das Geschehen in die Gegenwart und in einen in aller Breite und mit erzählerischer Begeisterung geschilderten Alltag verlegt.

scope. Certain elements of the landscape are painted from life, but they are freely juxtaposed. Thus, the grave of the Scipios on the Appian Way in Rome can be recognized on the hill on the left of the picture, while the distinctive rocky island in the background is a view of the Castel dell'Ovo near Naples, for which Brueghel used sketch studies drawn from life in Italy in mirror image form (cf. No. 3). The dress of the figures sets the events in Brueghel's own times and in an everyday situation, which is depicted in great breadth and with abundant narrative enthusiasm.

3 Jan Brueghel der Ältere
(1568 Brüssel – 1625 Antwerpen)

Großer Fischmarkt

Holz, 58,5 x 91,5 cm
Signiert und datiert unten links: BRVEGHEL 1603
Inv. Nr. 1889

3 Jan Brueghel the Elder
(1568 Brussels – 1625 Antwerp)

Large Fish Market

Wood, 58.5 x 91.5 cm
Signed and dated bottom left: BRVEGHEL 1603
Inv. No. 1889

Das für Jan Brueghel d. Ä. ungewöhnlich große Gemälde, ein Hauptwerk unter seinen Weltlandschaften (vgl. dazu Nr. 2), weist weder eine untergeordnete christliche noch eine historische Szene auf. Gegenstand der detaillierten Schilderung ist ein Fischmarkt in einer weiten Hafenlandschaft vor einem Bergpanorama. Der Betrachter, der im Vordergrund auf einen erhöht liegenden Teil des Marktes blickt, kann seine Augen über das an Einzelszenen reiche Geschehen schweifen lassen: Fische werden angeliefert, in Holzbottichen und Körben feilgeboten, es wird beraten, gefeilscht, gekauft. Jede der Personen im Menschengewimmel ist liebevoll geschildert, kleine Geschichten werden erzählt. Mit dem vorne in der Mitte aus dem Bild herausschauenden, vornehm gekleideten Herrn hat sich Jan Brueghel wohl selbst in das Geschehen versetzt. Im durch eine Mauer abgesetzten, tiefergelegenen Hafenareal findet das geschäftige Markttreiben seine Fortsetzung.

Die Stadtansicht im Mittelgrund ist aus verschiedenen Bestandteilen unterschiedlicher Gegenden zusammengestellt. Die auf seinen Reisen skizzierten Gebäude und Landschaften kommen hier – wie auch in anderen Gemälden Jan Brueghels – in freier Kombination zur Darstellung. Am auffälligsten ist die felsige Insel in der Mitte mit einer imposanten Burg und einem flachen Ausläufer mit drei Windmühlen. Es handelt sich um das Castel dell'Ovo vor Neapel, ein von Brueghel häufig verwendetes Motiv, zu dem eine Zeichnung in Rotterdam existiert. Der große Kuppelbau in der Stadtansicht stellt sicher eine Erinnerung an St. Peter in Rom dar, während für die Hafengebäude Antwerpener Bauten vorbildlich waren. Für andere Szenen, wie den Pferdekarren, das ausgespannte Pferd und die beiden Männer, die auf der Begrenzungsmauer im Vordergrund sitzen, gibt es eine vorbereitende Zeichnung in London.

The dimensions of this panel are unusually large for a painting by Jan Brueghel the Elder. One of his major panorama landscapes (cf. No. 2), it contains neither a secondary Christian nor a historical scene. The subject of this detailed depiction is a fish market with an extensive view over a harbour to a backdrop of mountains. From an elevated vantage point, part of the market can be seen on an area of raised land in the foreground. From here, the view extends over a broad panorama filled with a variety of events. Fish are being brought in and offered for sale in baskets and wooden tubs. People are engaged in discussions, haggling over prices and buying wares. Each person in the crowd is depicted with loving detail, and little anecdotes are told. Brueghel probably portrayed himself in the figure of the elegantly attired man looking out of the picture in the middle foreground. The bustling activity of the market continues beyond the wall in the lower-lying area around the harbour.

The town seen in the middle distance is made up of a number of different elements from various places. As in other paintings by Brueghel, the sketches of buildings and landscapes he made in the course of his travels are freely combined here. The most striking example is the rocky island in the middle with its imposing castle and a flat spit of land with three windmills. This is based on the Castel dell'Ovo near Naples, a drawing of which exists in Rotterdam. It was a motif the painter used on many occasions. The large domed building in the town is certainly a reminiscence of St Peter's in Rome, while the buildings in the harbour are based on models seen in Antwerp. Other scenes, such as the horse and cart, the unbridled horse, and the two men sitting on the wall in the foreground, can be found in a preliminary sketch now in London.

4 Jan Brueghel der Ältere
(1568 Brüssel – 1625 Antwerpen)

Ansicht einer Hafenstadt
(Die Enthaltsamkeit des Scipio)

Kupfer, 72,5 x 107 cm
Signiert und datiert unten links: BRVEGHEL ·
160(0 oder 9) FEC. ANVERSA
Inv. Nr. 827

Das Gemälde zeigt im Vordergrund eine Illustration zur Römischen Geschichte des Livius (XXVI, 49–50), aus der zwei besonders gern dargestellte Szenen mit dem siegreichen Feldherrn Publius Cornelius Scipio Africanus entnommen sind. Nach der Schlacht und der Eroberung von Neu-Karthago gab es zwei Ereignisse, die Scipios Ideal von einer guten Regierung veranschaulichen. Er wollte das Volk durch Freundschaft in Freiwilligkeit an sich binden und nicht durch Angst und Knechtschaft. Sein Umgang mit den Geiseln war dafür beispielhaft.

Die bekannteste Szene wird am rechten Bildrand gezeigt. Scipio sitzt vor seinem Zelt, vor ihm eine Gefangene, ein Mädchen von ungewöhnlicher Schönheit, sowie ihr Verlobter und ihre Eltern. Er gab das Mädchen den Eltern und dem Verlobten Allucius unversehrt als Jungfrau zurück und knüpfte daran lediglich den Wunsch, daß Allucius ein Freund des römischen Volkes werde: „Deine Braut genoß bei mir die gleiche Achtung wie bei deinen Schwiegereltern, ihren eigenen Eltern. Sie wurde für dich so bewahrt, daß sie dir als unangetastetes, meiner und deiner würdiges Geschenk übergeben werden konnte. Diese einzige Belohnung mache ich für mich als Gegengabe zur Bedingung: Sei ein Freund des römischen Volkes!" Die dankbaren Eltern drängten Scipio, das für den Freikauf des Mädchens mitgebrachte Gold zumindest als Geschenk anzunehmen, was dieser großzügig dem jungen Paar als Brautgeschenk weitergab. Zurück in seiner Heimat pries Allucius Scipio als einen Mann, „der alles durch Waffen, dann aber durch Güte und Wohltaten besiege".

Livius führt ein weiteres „Exemplum virtutis" für die Großmut und Tugendhaftigkeit des Scipio an, das auch in dem Gemälde zu entdecken ist: Eine alte Frau hatte den Feldherrn angefleht, er möge die jungen und schönen Mädchen unter den Geiseln vor der Lüsternheit seiner Soldaten schützen. Scipio unterstellte sie daraufhin der Obhut eines vertrauenswürdigen Mannes. Diese Gruppe der Alten mit den Mädchen und ihrem zu-

4 Jan Brueghel the Elder
(1568 Brussels – 1625 Antwerp)

View of a Harbour Town
(The Temperance of Scipio)

Copper, 72.5 x 107 cm
Signed and dated bottom left: BRVEGHEL ·
160(0 or 9) FEC. ANVERSA
Inv. No. 827

In the foreground of the painting is an illustration of two particularly popular scenes from the history of Rome by Livy (XXVI, 49–50), showing the victorious general Publius Cornelius Scipio Africanus. After the conquest of Carthage, two events took place that demonstrate Scipio's ideal of good government. He wished to gain the support of the people voluntarily through friendship, not through fear and servitude. His treatment of the hostages was therefore exemplary.

The best-known scene is depicted on the right-hand edge of the picture. Scipio is sitting outside his tent. Before him are a female hostage, a girl of exceptional beauty, together with her fiancé, Allucius, and her parents. Scipio has restored the girl to her family and her betrothed untouched, her virginity intact. The only request he makes is that Allucius should be a friend of the Roman people. "Your betrothed enjoyed the same respect from me as she did from your parents-in-law, her own parents. She was kept from harm in such a way that she could be restored to you undefiled, a gift worthy both of me and of you. This one reward for myself I make a condition, as a gift in return: be a friend of the Roman people!" The grateful parents press Scipio to accept the gold they have brought with them to ransom their daughter; and he generously hands it to the young couple as a wedding present. Having returned home, Allucius extols Scipio as a man "who conquers everything by force of arms, but then triumphs through goodness and great deeds".

A further *exemplum virtutis* of Scipio's magnanimity and virtue quoted by Livy can be found in the painting. An old woman begs the general to protect the young and beautiful girls among the hostages from the lechery of his soldiers. Scipio thereupon places the young women in the care of a trustworthy man. This group, consisting of the old woman with the maidens and their staunch guardian, can be seen in the centre of the picture.

verlässigen Bewacher ist in der Mitte des Gemäldes zu erkennen.

Wie bei den übrigen Überschaulandschaften Jan Brueghels d. Ä. (vgl. Nr. 2) erschließen sich die einzelnen Szenen im personen- und detailreichen Gemälde erst bei näherer Betrachtung. Sie gehen fast unter in der Schilderung des Heerlagers und der Krieger im Vordergrund. In der sich weit erstreckenden Landschaft, ähnlich seinen anderen Weltlandschaften, erkennt man im Hintergrund der Hafen- und Stadtansicht das Castel dell'Ovo in Neapel, das er unter anderem auch in seinem „Großen Fischmarkt" (Nr. 3) zeigt.

As in Jan Brueghel the Elder's other panorama landscapes (cf. No. 2), the individual scenes in this richly detailed painting with its myriad figures become accessible only on closer scrutiny. The events are almost swamped by the depiction of the military camp and the warriors in the foreground. In the broad view presented here, Brueghel uses real topographical details, as in his other panorama landscapes. In the background, the harbour and town of Castel dell'Ovo near Naples can be recognized, a location that the artist also used in his "Large Fish Market" (No. 3).

5 Jan Brueghel der Ältere
(1568 Brüssel – 1625 Antwerpen)

Hendrick van Balen
(1575 Antwerpen – 1632 Antwerpen)

Die Weissagung des Propheten Jesaias

Kupfer, 40,2 x 50,5 cm
Inv. Nr. 1999

5 Jan Brueghel the Elder
(1568 Brussels – 1625 Antwerp)

Hendrick van Balen
(1575 Antwerp – 1632 Antwerp)

The Prophecy of Isaiah

Copper, 40.2 x 50.5 cm
Inv. No. 1999

Das Bildthema wird durch den Text der Weissagung des Jesaias (2, 4) im Alten Testament erläutert, der auf der Tafel in der Bildmitte zu lesen ist. Dort heißt es: „IUDICABIT GENTES, ET ARGUET POPULOS MULTOS, ET CONFLABUNT GLADIOS SUOS IN VOMERES ET LANCEAS SUAS IN FALCES. ISAIAE. II." (Und er wird richten unter Heiden und strafen viele Völker. Da werden sie ihre Schwerter zu Pflugscharen und ihre Spieße zu Sicheln machen).

So steht in der Bildmitte der Prophet Jesaias, mit der rechten Hand hält er die Texttafel, mit der anderen weist er auf eine Anhäufung von Rüstungen und Waffen. Zu seinen Füßen verbrennt ein Genius den Helm einer Prunkrüstung über einem Feuer. Die Beischrift weist ihn als PAX (Friede) aus, in seiner Linken hält er einen Ölzweig. Diese Waffenverbrennung als Friedensmotiv ist seit der Antike bekannt. Links im Hintergrund sind Männer in einer Schmiede damit beschäftigt, Waffen zu Sicheln und Pflugscharen umzuarbeiten. Als Versinnbildlichung der Früchte des Friedens haben sich rechts drei Frauengestalten als die Personifikationen von FOELICITAS (Glück), PIETAS (Frömmigkeit) und ABUNDANTIA (Überfluß) versammelt. Sie sind mit Attributen versehen und zusätzlich durch Beischriften kenntlich gemacht. Der Ort des Geschehens ist eine verzweigte, tonnengewölbte römische Ruine, die eine geheimnisvolle Atmosphäre umgibt und ähnlich in Brueghels Allegorien des Feuers und der „Schmiede des Vulkan" erscheint. Völlig unvermittelt hängen vom Gewölbe ein imposanter Messingleuchter und ein Waagebalken herab. Im Vordergrund entlang des Bildrandes finden sich neben Rüstungen und Waffen auch andere Produkte angehäuft, die mit Hilfe des Feuers gefertigt werden: grob geschmiedete oder gegossene Gegenstände aus unedlen Metallen sowie die Werkbank eines Goldschmieds und Münzprägers. Stillebenartig ausgebreitet und mit größter Sorgfalt geschildert, erinnern sie an gemalte Kunst- und Wunderkammern, in

The subject of this painting is the Old Testament prophecy of Isaiah (2: 4), the words of which can be read on the tablet in the middle of the picture: "IUDICABIT GENTES, ET ARGUET POPULOS MULTOS, ET CONFLABUNT GLADIOS SUOS IN VOMERES ET LANCEAS SUAS IN FALCES. ISAIAE. II." (And he shall judge among the nations, and shall rebuke many people: and they shall beat their swords into plowshares, and their spears into pruninghooks).

The prophet Isaiah stands in the centre of the picture holding the tablet in his right hand. With his other hand, he points to the piles of armour and weapons on the ground. At his feet, an allegorical figure identified as PAX (Peace) is burning the helmet of a magnificent suit of armour over a fire. In his left hand, he holds an olive branch. The burning of weapons was a familiar motif of peace since ancient times. In the background on the left, a number of men in a forge are reworking weapons into sickles and ploughshares. On the right, three female figures are gathered in an allegory of the fruits of peace. They are identified by attributes and inscriptions as personifications of FOELICITAS (Felicity), PIETAS (Piety) and ABUNDANTIA (Abundance). The scene is set in a labyrinthine barrel-vaulted Roman ruin that radiates a mysterious atmosphere and that reappears in similar form in Brueghel's allegorical depictions of fire and Vulcan's forge. Quite incongruously, an imposing brass chandelier and the beam of a pair of scales hang from the vaulted ceiling. In the foreground, along the edge of the picture, are depictions of armour, weapons and a number of other objects that are manufactured with the aid of fire: roughly forged or cast artefacts made of base metals, as well as the bench of a goldsmith and mintmaster. Arranged like a still life and painted with the utmost care for detail, they recall depictions of cabinets of art and curiosities *(Kunst- und Wunderkammern),* in the details of which the observer can immerse himself at length.

deren Details der Betrachter sich lange versenken kann. Das Gemälde ist eine Gemeinschaftsarbeit Jan Brueghels d. Ä. mit dem Figurenmaler Hendrick van Balen, der wohl auch für Entwurf und Komposition verantwortlich war. Er setzte seine Figuren in einem zweiten Arbeitsgang in das von Brueghel begonnene Werk.

Das Bild, das Christliches mit Mythologisch-Allegorischem verbindet, wird aufgrund der Friedensthematik mit dem 1609 geschlossenen zwölfjährigen Waffenstillstand zwischen Spanien und den Niederlanden in Zusammenhang gebracht.

The present work is the result of a collaboration between Jan Brueghel the Elder and the figure painter Hendrick van Balen, who was probably also responsible for the overall design and composition. In a second stage of the work, Van Balen painted his figures into the picture that Brueghel had begun.

The painting combines both Christian and mythological-allegorical motifs. Its treatment of the theme of peace has led historians to associate it with the 12-year truce that was concluded between the Netherlands and Spain in 1609.

6 Jan Brueghel der Ältere
(1568 Brüssel – 1625 Antwerpen)

Pieter van Avont (?)
(1600 Mecheln – 1652 Deurne b. Antwerpen)

Die Heilige Familie

Holz, 93,5 x 72 cm
Inv. Nr. 149

Durch üppige Blumen- und Fruchtgirlanden öffnet sich der Blick in eine Waldlandschaft mit der Heiligen Familie. Die Girlanden, von Engeln gehalten oder von Ästen gestützt, bilden den Rahmen für das Geschehen. In ihrer Führung in Form eines „M" wollte man den Hinweis auf das Monogramm von Maria sehen, doch handelt es sich wohl eher um die Idee eines Triumphbogens. Im Mittelgrund hat sich die Heilige Familie mit Maria, dem Jesuskind und Josef niedergelassen. Der Johannesknabe, der Jesus eine Traube reicht, und das Lamm mit einer Gruppe von drei Putten ergänzen die Szene, in deren Hintergrund Rehe äsen.

Zu diesem Gemälde schuf wahrscheinlich Pieter van Avont die Figurenstaffage, während die Landschaft und die Umrahmung von Jan Brueghel d. Ä. stammen. Hier zeigt sich eines seiner Spezialgebiete, die Blumenmalerei. Die Blumenkranz- und Girlandenbilder gelten sogar als seine spezielle Erfindung. Im Münchner Bild ist sie reich bestückt mit Blüten und Früchten, die Brueghel entweder nach der Natur oder nach wissenschaftlichen botanischen Werken malte. Seine Blumenstücke, bei denen es sich um regelrechte „Porträts" handelt, stellen Meisterwerke der Beobachtungsgabe dar. Neben einheimischen werden exotische und sehr wertvolle Pflanzen minutiös und feinmalerisch geschildert. Einzelne Bestandteile der Münchner Girlande, wie Rose, Lilie, Ähren, Trauben, können als Mariensymbole gedeutet werden, was aber die gleichzeitige Verwendung einer solchen Umkränzung bei mythologischen Themen – z. B. einer Demeter-Darstellung – nicht ausschloß. Dies bedeutet, daß es Brueghel auch hier vor allem um die Schönheit der dargestellten Pflanzen ging und nicht um eine strenge Mariensymbolik.

In die Girlande eingestreut sitzen die verschiedensten Vogelarten, u. a. Papageien, am Boden andere Tiere, wie Hasen, Meerschweinchen und Affen. Diese Tiere können die unterschiedlichste und zum Teil sogar gegenteilige Bedeutung haben. So gilt der Affe aufgrund seiner

6 Jan Brueghel the Elder
(1568 Brussels – 1625 Antwerp)

Pieter van Avont (?)
(1600 Malines – 1652 Deurne near Antwerp)

The Holy Family

Wood, 93.5 x 72 cm
Inv. No. 149

The eye is led through luxuriant garlands of flowers and fruit to a wooded landscape with the Holy Family. The garlands, supported by angels or the branches of trees, frame the scene and trace the form of the letter "M", which was thought to represent the monogram of "Mary". More likely, however, it was meant to suggest the idea of a triumphal arch. The Holy Family – the Virgin Mary, Jesus and Joseph – is depicted in the middle distance. The scene is complemented by the Infant John, who offers Jesus a bunch of grapes, and by a lamb with a group of three putti. Deer can be seen browsing in the background.

Pieter van Avont probably painted the figure staffage in this picture. The landscape and the frame of garlands are by Jan Brueghel the Elder. Flower painting was one of Brueghel's specialities. In fact, pictures with garlands and wreaths of flowers are regarded as his invention. This Munich work is replete with flowers and fruit, which Brueghel painted either from nature or from scientific botanical publications. His flower pieces, which are in the nature of "portraits", are masterpieces in the power of observation. Alongside native plants, a number of exotic, rare and valuable species are finely depicted in minute detail. Individual flowers and fruit in the garlands, such as the roses, lilies, ears of grain, or grapes, can be seen as Marian symbols; but this did not preclude their use elsewhere in the garlanding of mythological subjects, as in a Demeter depiction, for example. In other words, Brueghel was more concerned here with the beauty of the plants he painted than with any strict Marian symbolism.

Scattered about the garlands are all kinds of birds, including parrots; and on the ground are other animals such as rabbits, guinea-pigs and monkeys. The animals have quite different and, on occasion, contrary significances. For example, since the Middle Ages, the monkey was regarded as an image of the devil on account of its ugliness, and it was compared to the image of man in his

Häßlichkeit seit dem Mittelalter als ein Abbild des Teufels und wird mit dem in seine Sünden verstrickten Menschen gleichgesetzt. Der Papagei wurde ebenfalls mit einer komplexen Symbolik belegt. Vor allem brachte man ihn mit dem Lob Gottes in Verbindung, da er die besondere Fähigkeit besitzt, die menschliche Stimme nachzuahmen. So kann er „Ave" sprechen und auf Maria verweisen, andererseits ist er ein Symbol für Eva, da er umgekehrt „Eva" sagen kann. Von seinem Gefieder nahm man an, daß es vom Tau nicht naß werde und nahm dies als Hinweis auf die Reinheit und Keuschheit Marias. Dieses Spiel mit den Bedeutungen vertraut auf die Bildung des gelehrten Betrachters. Zudem trägt die Vielfalt der Tiere dem naturwissenschaftlichen Interesse Brueghels Rechnung. Die Meerschweinchen, die in Europa erst im 16. Jahrhundert eingeführt wurden, waren damals eine Rarität, ebenso wie Papageien, die als etwas Besonderes und Luxuriöses angesehen wurden.

Brueghels frühe Girlandenbilder rahmen ein Einsatzbild wie ein Medaillon, vergleichbar der in der Zusammenarbeit mit Peter Paul Rubens entstandenen Blumenkranzmadonna (Nr. 21). Als eine Weiterentwicklung ist die Verlegung der mittleren Szene in eine natürliche Landschaft zu bezeichnen. Das Münchner Gemälde, gleichzeitig Andachtsbild und Kunstkammerstück, ist ein gelungenes Beispiel für diese Verbindung einer Landschaft mit einer Girlande im Werk Jan Brueghels d. Ä. und wird um 1620 datiert.

state of sin. The parrot is also identified with a complex symbolism. In the first instance, it was associated with the praise of God, since it possesses the ability to imitate the human voice. It can articulate the word "Ave", for example, with its allusions to the Virgin Mary; but it is a symbol of Eve, too, for it can pronounce the reverse form of "Ave", namely "Eva". From the nature of its feathers, it was assumed that the parrot was not wetted by the dew, which was regarded as a reference to the purity and chastity of Mary. This game of significances relies on the education and knowledge of a learned observer, of course. In addition, the number and variety of the animals depicted is an expression of Brueghel's interest in natural science. Guinea-pigs, which were introduced to Europe only in the 16th century, were a rarity at that time, as were parrots, which were regarded as something exotic.

Brueghel's early garland works are in the form of a picture within a picture, with the floral details framing a medallion-like inset. The "Madonna in a Garland of Flowers", painted in collaboration with Rubens (No. 21), is an example of this. A further development of this theme saw the central scene placed in a natural landscape. The present work, painted c. 1620, served not only as a devotional picture, but would also have formed part of a cabinet of art (Kunstkammer). It is a most successful example of this linking of landscape painting with the garland form in Jan Brueghel the Elder's œuvre.

7 David Vinckboons
(1576 Mecheln – 1632 Amsterdam)

Der Gang nach Golgatha

Holz, 112 x 166 cm
Signiert und datiert unten rechts:
Dauid Vinck=Boons fes 1611
Inv. Nr. 838

Die signierte und 1611 datierte Kreuztragung Christi (Lukas 23, 26 – 31) gehört zu den bedeutendsten Werken von Vinckboons. In einer weiträumigen, in leichter Aufsicht angelegten Landschaft kommt ein vielfiguriger, fast endloser Prozessionszug von rechts aus der im Hintergrund gelegenen Stadt Jerusalem heran. Genau in der Mitte des Bildes ist der Wendepunkt der halbkreisförmigen Wegführung. Um einen baumbewachsenen Hügel herum zieht die Prozession nach links, wo im Hintergrund der Berg Golgatha, der Ort der Kreuzigung liegt. In die Mitte des Vordergrundes, nah an den Betrachter herangerückt, ist die wichtigste Szene gesetzt: Der zusammengebrochene Christus, dem Simon von Cyrene beim Tragen des Kreuzes hilft und dem die hl. Veronika das Schweißtuch reicht, umgeben von prügelnden Soldaten, klagenden heiligen Frauen, Maria und Johannes. Vor allem aber nutzt Vinckboons die Kreuztragung, um in der Darstellung der bunten Zuschauermenge zu schwelgen, in der sämtliche Lebensalter und Stände vertreten sind: Familien mit Kindern und Hunden, Bettler, Bauern und reich gekleidete Bürger. Als gliederndes Element der personenreichen Szenerie werden Licht- und Schattenzonen eingesetzt. Durch die genrehafte Schilderung erhält die Kreuztragung einen volkstümlichen Charakter und wird durch die Kleidung der Zuschauer zu einem zeitgenössischen Geschehen, wobei jedoch die Landschaft einen Idealtypus vertritt, und die Ansicht der Stadt Jerusalem mit Tempeln und Palästen vermutlich nach Stichen zusammengestellt wurde.
Die Kreuztragung ist ein in der niederländischen Malerei des 16. Jahrhunderts häufig verwendetes Thema, das in dieser Ausprägung als sogenannte „Volkreiche Kreuztragung" letztlich auf eine Erfindung der Brüder Van Eyck aus dem 15. Jahrhundert zurückgeht und unter anderem im Werk Pieter Bruegels d. Ä. tradiert wurde.

7 David Vinckboons
(1576 Malines – 1632 Amsterdam)

The Way to Golgotha

Wood, 112 x 166 cm
Signed and dated bottom right:
Dauid Vinck=Boons fes 1611
Inv. No. 838

This depiction of Christ bearing His Cross (Luke 23: 26 – 31), signed and dated 1611, is one of Vinckboons' most important works. In a broad landscape viewed from a slightly raised position, an almost endless procession of people can be seen approaching from the city of Jerusalem in the background on the right. Exactly in the centre of the picture is the turning point of the semicircular route. The procession turns to the left round a tree-lined mound and heads towards the hill of Golgotha, the place of Crucifixion, in the background. The most important scene of this depiction is set in the middle foreground, drawn up close to the observer. Christ has collapsed beneath His burden. Simon the Cyrenean helps Him bear the Cross, and Veronica hands Him her veil to dry His face. They are surrounded by flailing soldiers, by the lamenting women who belong to Christ's circle, and by Mary and John. Vinckboons, however, uses the scene of the bearing of the Cross to indulge in a depiction of the colourful crowds of onlookers, in which he portrays people of all ranks, walks of life and ages, including families with children and dogs, beggars, peasants and richly attired citizens. Light and shade are used as articulating elements in this densely populated scene. As a result of the genre-like depiction, "The Way to Golgotha" acquires a popular character, and the attire of the people turns it into a contemporary event. On the other hand, the landscape represents an ideal type, and the view of the city of Jerusalem with its temples and palaces was probably pieced together from engravings. Christ bearing the Cross had been a frequently depicted subject in 16th-century Netherlands painting. The present form with its throngs of people – sometimes known as the "multitudinous" type – is based on an invention of the Van Eyck brothers in the 15th century that was employed and handed down by Pieter Bruegel the Elder and others.

8 Sebastiaen Vrancx
(1573 Antwerpen – 1647 Antwerpen)

Wallfahrer bei einer Stadt
(Das Hagelkreuzfest von Ekeren)

Holz, 56,5 x 119,3 cm
Monogrammiert auf der Hinterhand des Pferdes links:
SV; datiert auf dem Sockel des Kreuzes: ad (?) 1622
Inv. Nr. 2058

Die vielfigurige Szene schildert ein konkretes Ereignis,
die alljährliche Feier um das Hagelkreuz von Ekeren.
Nach der Legende wurde der Ort Ekeren, wenige Kilo-
meter nördlich von Antwerpen gelegen, durch schwere
Hagelunwetter heimgesucht. Eines Tages blieben nach
solch einem schweren Unwetter Hagelkörner in Kreu-
zesform für längere Zeit liegen, was als Himmelszeichen
gedeutet wurde. Man veranstaltete Prozessionen und
Wallfahrten dorthin, und die Unwetter hörten auf. Aus
Dankbarkeit und um zukünftig den Hagel abzuwehren,
wurde an jener Stelle ein steinernes Kreuz errichtet. All-
jährlich fand am Jahrestag dieses legendären Ereignis-
ses eine Prozession statt, und zusätzlich wurden an die
Bedürftigen des Umlandes Speisen und Getränke ausge-
geben.
Das breitformatige Gemälde zeigt die Schar der Bedürftigen und Armen, die sich im weiten Kreis um die Kreuz-
säule niedergelassen haben, unter ihnen auch zwei Pil-
ger. Männer geben Brot aus und verteilen Speisen aus
einem großen Kessel, während rechts im Hintergrund
der Brei noch über dem Feuer kocht und Fässer ange-
zapft werden. Zu dieser alljährlichen Armenspeisung
sind die wohlhabenden Bürger herbeigekommen, um
das Ereignis zu beobachten. Eine Gruppe von reich
gekleideten Damen und einem Herrn, die in ein
Gespräch vertieft sind, fällt besonders auf. Andere wan-
dern zurück nach Ekeren, dessen Kirche St. Lambertus
den Ort überragt. Das viertürmige Gebäude am Horizont ist als das Lustschloß „Hof von Veltwijk" zu identifizieren und die Stadtsilhouette am rechten Bildrand
stellt Antwerpen dar.
Das auf der Hinterhand des Schimmels signierte und am
Sockel der Säule 1622 datierte Gemälde bot Sebastiaen
Vrancx reichlich Gelegenheit, das pittoreske Schauspiel
in aller Breite zu schildern und gleichzeitig als kulturge-
schichtliches Ereignis zu dokumentieren.

8 Sebastiaen Vrancx
(1573 Antwerp – 1647 Antwerp)

Pilgrims before a City
(The Hail-Cross Feast of Ekeren)

Wood, 56.5 x 119.3 cm
Monogram on the hindquarters of the horse on the left:
SV; dated on the plinth of the cross: ad (?) 1622
Inv. No. 2058

The painting, with its multitude of people, depicts a historical event: the annual celebrations around the "Hail
Cross" in Ekeren. According to legend, Ekeren, which
lies a few miles north of Antwerp, was struck by violent
hailstorms. After one such storm, huge hailstones lay on
the ground in the form of a cross for some time afterwards. This was interpreted as a sign of heaven. Proces-
sions and pilgrimages to Ekeren were organized, and
the storms abated. In gratitude for this relief and to ward
off future hailstorms, a stone column surmounted by a
cross was erected on the spot where the heavenly omen
had been found. Every year on the anniversary of this
legendary event, a procession was held, and paupers
from the whole area were given food and drink.
This broad panel in landscape format shows the crowd
of poor and needy gathered around the cross in a broad
circle. Among them are two pilgrims. Men are distributing bread, and warm food from a large pot. In the background on the right, gruel is being heated over a fire,
and barrels are being tapped. The wealthy burghers
have come to watch this annual feeding of the poor.
A group of richly attired ladies in conversation with a
gentleman stands out among the crowd. Other people
are already walking back to Ekeren, which can be identified by its landmark, the tall spire of St Lambert's
Church. The building on the horizon with four towers is
the palace of Veltwijk, and on the right-hand edge of
the picture the silhouette of the city of Antwerp can
be seen.
The painting, which is signed on the hindquarters of the
grey and dated 1622 on the plinth of the column, provided Sebastiaen Vrancx with an opportunity to depict
this picturesque pageant in great detail and at the same
time to document a significant event in the cultural history of the Flemish people.

9 Joos de Momper
(1565 Antwerpen – 1635 Antwerpen)

Der Hinterhalt (Berglandschaft)

Holz, 73 x 103,8 cm
Inv. Nr. 4963

Das Gemälde ist ein repräsentatives Beispiel für den von De Momper häufig variierten Typus der Berglandschaft. Von einem erhöhten Standpunkt aus blickt man auf eine eindrucksvolle Gebirgslandschaft. Der Blick geht über ein weites Tal, begrenzt von einem schroffen, baumbewachsenen Felsblock und einem hohen Bergmassiv, das sich bis an den Horizont erstreckt. Ein gewundener Weg führt von vorn zu einer Stadt mit mächtiger Kirche im Zentrum des Ausblicks. Belebt wird die Landschaft von kleinen Figuren: Jäger oder Soldaten, Wanderer und ein Hirte mit Schafen. Aus der Gruppe der vier diskutierenden Jäger im Vordergrund hat sich ein weiterer hinter die Felsen zurückgezogen, um seine Notdurft zu verrichten – ein drastisches Motiv, das im flämischen Bauerngenre nicht unüblich ist, aber bei Momper sonst nicht vorkommt und hier zu dem falschen Titel „Der Hinterhalt" führte. Die Schilderung der schroffen, zerklüfteten Felsformationen, die sicher von Mompers Alpenerlebnis auf seiner Italienreise inspiriert sind und dennoch frei komponierte, erfundene Hochgebirgslandschaften darstellen, waren bei den damaligen Kunstsammlern sehr beliebt.

Mompers Gemälde, eines von vielen ähnlichen, zeigt den Aufbau spätmanieristischer Landschaftsmalerei. Es ist noch immer dem Drei-Farben-Schema, der Abfolge von Braun, Grün, Blau verpflichtet, die die hintereinandergestaffelten einzelnen Gründe kennzeichnet und Tiefenwirkung erzielt. Der Wechsel von hellen und dunklen Zonen trägt zu diesem Effekt bei und belebt das Bild, wobei der braune Vordergrund die Folie für den Ausblick in das hell beleuchtete Tal bildet. Das mit schnellem, lockerem Pinselstrich und teilweise sehr dünnem Farbauftrag gemalte und ausgewogen aufgebaute Landschaftsbild stammt aus den späten Schaffensjahren des Künstlers und ist um 1620 zu datieren. Somit steht es am Übergang von der manieristischen Weltlandschaft zur naturalistischen Flachlandschaft des 17. Jahrhunderts.

9 Joos de Momper
(1565 Antwerp – 1635 Antwerp)

The Ambush (Mountainous Landscape)

Wood, 73 x 103.8 cm
Inv. No. 4963

The picture is an example of the mountain landscape type that De Momper painted in many different variations. From an elevated position, the observer has an impressive view across a broad valley to a high range of mountains that stretch to the distant horizon. On the left, the view is closed by a rugged, tree-lined outcrop of rocks. A winding path leads from the foreground to a town with a mighty church in the middle distance. The landscape is animated by small figures of hunters or soldiers, wayfarers and a herdsman with his sheep. A man who belongs to the group of four hunters engaged in conversation in the foreground has withdrawn behind the rocks to answer the call of nature. It is a rather extreme motif, but one that is not uncommon in Flemish peasant scenes. It does not occur, however, in any other works by Momper, and as a result, the painting was given the misleading title "The Ambush". Momper's depictions of steep, rugged mountains were very popular with art collectors at that time and were certainly inspired by his experience of the Alps during his journey to Italy. These landscapes are nevertheless freely invented compositions.

Momper's picture, one of many similar works by the artist, reveals the technique of late-Mannerist landscape painting. It is still indebted to the old three-colour sequence of grounds, brown, green and blue, used to create a sense of depth. The alternation of light and dark zones supports this effect and enlivens the picture. The brown tone of the foreground forms a foil for the view into the brightly lit valley. The landscape is distinguished by its balanced composition and is painted with swift, light brush strokes and a very thin application of paint in part. Dating from c. 1620, it belongs to the artist's late period and marks a transition from the Mannerist panoramic landscape to the naturalistic flat landscape of the 17th century.

10 Frans Francken der Jüngere
(1581 Antwerpen – 1642 Antwerpen)

Hexensabbat

Holz, 42 x 69 cm
Signiert an der Seitenwange der Holzkiste rechts:
D Jon FF INVENIT
Inv. Nr. 1987

10 Frans Francken the Younger
(1581 Antwerp – 1642 Antwerp)

Witches' Sabbath

Wood, 42 x 69 cm
Signed on the side of the wooden chest on the right:
D Jon FF INVENIT
Inv. No. 1987

Im Werk von Frans Francken d. J. gibt es mehrere der bereits im 16. Jahrhundert beliebten Hexenszenen. Die Darstellung des Münchner Gemäldes wurde nicht immer richtig gedeutet, noch im 19. Jahrhundert erscheint es in Inventaren als „Versuchung des hl. Antonius".

Das Bild zeigt einen düsteren Innenraum, der dicht gefüllt ist mit Hexen, seltsamen Gestalten und Mischwesen. Durch ein Fenster sieht man Hexen im Schnee oder Hagel bei ihrem schändlichen Treiben auf einer Richtstätte; eine hockt auf dem Balken des Galgens, andere fliegen durch die Luft. Im Raum selbst sind die Tätigkeiten der Hexen und phantastischen Wesen befremdlich und unerklärlich. Links wird ein kleiner, teufelartiger Gnom angebetet. Er steht auf einem dreibeinigen Schemel und hält eine funkensprühende Kerze in der Hand. Eine der Hexen kocht in einem riesigen Kessel ein Gebräu mit einem Widder als Zutat, weitere reiten auf ihren Besen durch den Kamin aus, auf dessen Sims eine Knochenhand als Kerzenleuchter steht. Sie stammt von einem Verbrecher und war wichtiges Utensil für bösen Zauber. Eine nackte Hexe wird von einem fledermausähnlichen Mischwesen im Flug emporgetragen, in ihrer Körperhaltung eine blasphemische Nachahmung des Gekreuzigten. Eine andere Nackte wird am Rücken mit Flugsalbe eingerieben und für den Ausritt vorbereitet. Überall verteilt finden sich die Requisiten der Zauber- und Hexerei sowie kabbalistische Zeichen und Beschwörungsformeln. Dem mystisch-dämonischen Thema ist die Farbgebung des Bildes angepaßt.

Der mitternächtliche Hexensabbat war eine Vorstellung, die die Menschen schon lange beschäftigte und in Schrecken versetzte. Geboren wurden diese Phantasien aus der Angst vor der Beherrschung der Welt durch den Teufel und der Umkehr der christlichen Ordnung. Franckens Gemälde beinhaltet eine Art Kompendium der schwarzen Magie und Hexerei, wobei er sich an der damals verbreiteten Hexenliteratur, den Unterlagen zu

Scenes with witches were very popular in the 16th century, and Frans Francken the Younger's œuvre contains a number of works belonging to this genre. The Munich painting has not always been correctly interpreted. As late as the 19th century, it was listed in inventories as "The Temptation of St Anthony".

The picture shows a sombre interior filled with witches, strange figures and hybrid creatures. Through a window, witches can be seen outside in the snow or hail conducting their terrible rites at a place of execution. One of them is squatting on the beam of the gallows; others are flying through the air. Within the room, the witches and the other fantastic creatures are indulging in all kinds of obnoxious and inexplicable activities. On the left of the picture, one group is worshipping a small, diabolic gnome who is standing on a three-legged stool holding a candle that gives off a fountain of sparks. In a huge cauldron, a witch is boiling some brew in which a ram forms one of the ingredients. Other witches are riding up the chimney on their brooms. On the mantlepiece is a skeleton hand that serves as a candelabra. It was the hand of a criminal and was an important implement of sorcery. A naked witch is borne aloft by a bat-like hybrid creature. The position she assumes is a blasphemous imitation of Christ on the Cross. Another naked figure is having her back rubbed with a flying ointment and is preparing to ride out. Scattered about everywhere are the tools of sorcery and witchcraft, and cabbalistic symbols and incantations. The mystic, demoniac mood is matched by the coloration of the picture.

The nocturnal witches' sabbath was a vision that had long fascinated people and at the same time filled them with horror. These fantasies were born of fear that the devil would come to rule the world and reverse the Christian order of things. Francken's painting is a compendium of black magic and witchcraft and seems to be based on the contemporary literature on witches, on records of witch trials and sermons against sorcery. All

Hexenprozessen und den Predigten gegen Hexerei orientiert zu haben scheint, deren abstruse Vorstellungen – eine Mischung aus volkstümlichem Aberglauben und Häresievorstellungen – er hier zur Darstellung bringt. Dabei ähneln einige seiner Spukgestalten Schöpfungen von Hieronymus Bosch oder Pieter Bruegel d. Ä.

Zur Themenwahl des um 1610 entstanenen Gemäldes könnte das 1606 vom Erzherzogspaar Albrecht und Isabella erlassene Edikt zur Hexenverfolgung Anlaß gegeben haben. Doch neben der abschreckenden, moralisierenden Aussage, gerichtet gegen sündiges, gotteslästerliches Verhalten, ist eine erotische Ausstrahlung der jungen und schönen nackten Frauen nicht zu leugnen. Überhaupt scheinen Teniers Hexengemälde, deren wohlkalkulierte Mischung von Schauder und Ergötzen regen Absatz fand, vorrangig der Unterhaltung gedient zu haben.

these abstruse ideas – a mixture of popular superstition and notions of heresy – reappear in his depiction. Some of the weird creatures he conjures resemble those of Hieronymus Bosch or Pieter Bruegel the Elder.

The choice of subject for this picture, painted c. 1610, was possibly influenced by the edict for the persecution of witches issued by Archduke Albrecht and his wife Isabella in 1606. As well as its deterrent, moralizing message, directed against sin and blasphemous behaviour, however, the painting also possesses an undeniably erotic aspect in the form of the young and beautiful naked women. It is known, for example, that Teniers' paintings of witches, with their calculated mixture of horror and delight, mainly served the purpose of entertainment and found a ready market.

11 Frans Francken der Jüngere
(1581 Antwerpen – 1642 Antwerpen)

Gastmahl im Hause des Bürgermeisters Rockox

Holz, 62,3 x 96,5 cm
Signiert unten Mitte: D ^{ov} ffranck · IN · et f
Inv. Nr. 858

Das signierte Gemälde zeigt den großen Empfangssalon im Hause des Nicolas Rockox (1560–1640), eines der wohlhabendsten und mächtigsten Bürger Antwerpens. Der gebildete Humanist und Freund von Peter Paul Rubens wurde neunmal zum Bürgermeister der Stadt gewählt. Sein großes Patrizierhaus „De gulden Rinck" schmückten viele Gemälde und Skulpturen, wie das nach seinem Tod abgefaßte Inventar bezeugt.

Frans Francken d. J. wählte den Blick auf die Kaminwand im Salon. In dem repräsentativen Raum mit Holzdecke und aufwendigen goldgeprägten Ledertapeten sind die Wände dicht mit Gemälden behängt. Den prominentesten Platz über dem Marmorkamin nimmt das sogenannte „schouwstuk", „Samson und Dalilah" von Peter Paul Rubens (heute London, National Gallery), ein. Das Gemälde rechts daneben zeigt die „Geldwechsler" von Marinus van Reymerswaele, darunter ein Diptychon von Quinten Massys mit Christus als Salvator Mundi und der betenden Maria, und links neben dem Durchgang der „Hl. Hieronymus" von Jan Sanders van Hemessen. Vom Türrahmen leicht überschnitten erkennt man im anschließenden Raum das Gemälde „Der ungläubige Thomas", das Rubens 1613–1615 als Epitaph der Familie Rockox für die Antwerpener Rekollektenkirche gemalt hatte, und das sicher nicht im Haus hing.

Die im Salon versammelten Gemälde, Kleinplastiken und antiken Büsten lassen sich anhand des Inventars identifizieren, das Raum für Raum den Besitz Rockox' aufführt. Doch der Eindruck der wahrhaftigen Wiedergabe einer Ausstattung im Hause Rockox täuscht, denn es handelt sich hier um eine idealisierte Ansicht. So ist nur das Kaminstück für den Empfangssaal bezeugt, die übrigen Gemälde befanden sich in anderen Räumen des Hauses. Mit der vornehmen Gesellschaft sind, anders als der Gemäldetitel vorgibt, nicht der Hausherr, seine Familie und Gäste gemeint, sondern Phantasiefiguren. Deren Tätigkeiten legen es nahe, in ihnen Allegorien der fünf Sinne zu sehen: das Gehör (Lautenspieler), das

11 Frans Francken the Younger
(1581 Antwerp – 1642 Antwerp)

Banquet in the House of Burgomaster Rockox

Wood, 62.3 x 96.5 cm
Signed bottom middle: D ^{ov} ffranck · IN · et f
Inv. No. 858

This signed painting shows the grand salon in the house of Nicolas Rockox (1560–1640), one of the wealthiest and most powerful citizens of Antwerp. An erudite humanist and friend of Rubens, Rockox was elected burgomaster of the city on nine occasions. His grand patrician house, "De gulden Rinck" (At the Golden Ring), contained a large collection of paintings and sculptures, as the inventory of his estate shows.

Frans Francken the Younger chose as his subject the fireplace wall of the reception room in Rockox's house. The room, which was used for formal occasions, is shown with a wooden ceiling and an elaborate, gold-embossed leather lining to the walls, which are covered with paintings. Pride of place over the marble fireplace is taken by the *schouwstuk* or showpiece, "Samson and Delilah" by Rubens (now in the National Gallery, London). The painting to the right of this is the "Tax Collector with His Wife" by Marinus van Reymerswaele, below which is a diptych by Quinten Massys showing Christ as Salvator Mundi and the Virgin praying. To the left of the doorway is Jan Sanders van Hemessen's "St Jerome"; and in the adjoining room, partly cut off by the door frame, Rubens' "Doubting Thomas" (1613–1615) can be seen. Rubens' picture was painted for the Rockox family as an epitaph in the "Recollecten" Church in Antwerp, and it is unlikely that the original hung in the house.

The paintings, small-scale sculptures and busts of the ancients that were gathered in the reception room can be identified on the basis of the inventory, which lists Rockox's possessions room by room. The impression of a true picture of the contents of the house is deceptive, however; for the painting represents an idealized view. The only work documented as hanging in this salon was the picture over the fireplace. The rest of the paintings hung in other rooms of the house. The distinguished society depicted here is not the owner and his family with guests, as the title of the painting would suggest,

Gesicht (Mann mit Brille, der ein Gemälde betrachtet), der Geruch (Frau, die an einer Blüte riecht), der Geschmack (Weintrinker und Muschelesser), das Gefühl (Mann am Kamin, der mit einem heißen Schürhaken verbrannt wird). Die Szene am Kamin wird amüsant erzählt, denn einer der beiden Knaben will das Opfer warnen, wird aber vom älteren mit an den Mund gelegtem Finger zum Schweigen ermahnt, um den Spaß nicht zu verderben.

Das von Frans Francken d.J. um 1630–1635 wohl für Nicolas Rockox gemalte Bild ist ein Paradebeispiel für die von ihm erfundene Gattung der Galeriebilder, die sich zu einer flämischen Spezialität entwickelte.

but imaginary figures who represent allegories of the five senses: hearing (the lutist), sight (the man with the spectacles studying a painting), smell (the woman smelling a flower), taste (the people drinking wine and eating shellfish) and touch (the man by the fire who is about to be burnt by a glowing poker). The scene by the fireplace is narrated as an amusing anecdote. One of the two boys is about to warn the victim, but the older boy places his finger over his lips, urging the other to keep silent, in order not to spoil the fun.

Painted c. 1630–1635 by Frans Francken the Younger, presumably for Nicolas Rockox, the picture is an outstanding example of the "picture gallery" genre, which Francken himself invented and which was to become a Flemish speciality.

12 Abraham Janssen van Nuyssen
(um 1575 Antwerpen – 1632 Antwerpen)

Der Olymp

Leinwand, 207 x 240 cm
Inv. Nr. 4884

Die Versammlung olympischer Götter ist ganz nah an den Betrachter herangerückt. Jupiter, den Adler zu seinen Füßen, sitzt mit in die Hand gestütztem Kopf und nachdenklichem Gesichtsausdruck in der Mitte. Vor ihm steht Venus, die energisch argumentierend den rechten Zeigefinger hebt. Zwischen die beiden hat sich der kleine Amor gedrängt, der seine Mutter zu beschwichtigen scheint. Juno, Jupiters Gemahlin, thront zu dessen Rechten, erkennbar an dem ihr beigegebenen Attribut, einem Pfau, und redet auf ihren Gatten ein. Auch Athena, die sich hinter dem Paar herabbeugt, scheint in den Disput verwickelt zu sein.

Mit ihren kräftigen, muskulösen Körpern füllen die Götter das Bild und sprengen fast den Rahmen. Die überlegte Komposition und die klar modellierten, skulpturalen Formen unterstreichen die Monumentalität des Gemäldes. Dramatische Akzente setzen die starken Schlagschatten im ansonsten ausgeleuchteten und in hellen Farben gemalten Bild, das charakteristisch für den Antwerpener „Klassizismus" zu Beginn des 17. Jahrhunderts ist, und um 1615 entstanden sein wird. Über die allgemeine Bezeichnung als Götterrat hinaus war das Thema des Gemäldes lange unklar. Nach neuesten Forschungen handelt es sich jedoch um eine Szene aus dem Epos Aeneis von Vergil (10. Buch). Jupiter ließ aus Mißbilligung der Zwietracht unter den Göttern und des damit zusammenhängenden Kampfes der Lateiner und Trojaner die Götter im Olymp zusammenkommen und mahnte sie zum Frieden. Venus jedoch klagte und trat entschieden für ihren Sohn, den Trojaner Aeneas ein, was den Zorn ihrer ewigen Gegenspielerin Juno erregte.

Formal bezieht sich Janssen jedoch auf ein inhaltlich anderes, berühmtes Vorbild: die Fresken Raffaels in der Villa Farnesina in Rom mit der Darstellung der Liebesgeschichte von Venus und Amor nach Lucius Apuleius. Aus Raffaels Götterrat übernahm Janssen einzelne Figuren, vor allem Jupiter sowie Venus und Amor.

12 Abraham Janssen van Nuyssen
(c. 1575 Antwerp – 1632 Antwerp)

Olympus

Canvas, 207 x 240 cm
Inv. No. 4884

The assembly of Olympian gods is pushed to the fore in close proximity to the observer. Jupiter, with an eagle at his feet, sits in the middle sunk in thought, his head propped on his hand. In front of him stands Venus, pleading her case vehemently and lending weight to her arguments with the raised forefinger of her right hand. Little Amor pushes himself between them, evidently trying to calm his mother. Seated to Jupiter's right, pleading insistently with him, is his wife Juno, who may be recognized by her attribute, a peacock. To the rear, bending forward over the couple, stands Pallas Athene, who also seems to be involved in the dispute.

The powerful, muscular bodies of the gods fill the entire picture, almost bursting its bounds. The well-considered composition and the clearly articulated, sculptural forms accentuate the monumentality of this painting. Dramatic accents are set by the bold areas of shadow in a work that is otherwise brightly lit and painted in light colours. The picture, dating from c. 1615, is a typical example of "Antwerp Classicism" at the beginning of the 17th century.

For a long time, little was known about the significance of the painting beyond the general theme of a council of the gods. According to recent research, it depicts a scene from Virgil's epic poem the "Aeneid" (book 10). In his displeasure at the discord between the gods and the resulting battle between the Latini and the Trojans, Jupiter has summoned the gods to Olympus and urges them to make peace. Venus, however, sues on behalf of her son, the Trojan Aeneas, which, in turn, arouses the scorn of her eternal opponent Juno.

Janssen based his figures on a famous model with a quite different content: Raphael's frescos in the Villa Farnesina in Rome, which depict the love of Venus and Amor as described by Lucius Apuleius. Janssen adopted individual figures from Raphael's council of gods, in particular, those of Jupiter, Venus and Amor.

13 Peter Paul Rubens
(1577 Siegen – 1640 Antwerpen)

Rubens und Isabella Brant in der Geißblattlaube

Leinwand, auf Holz aufgezogen, 178 x 136,5 cm
Inv. Nr. 334

13 Sir Peter Paul Rubens
(1577 Siegen – 1640 Antwerp)

Rubens and Isabella Brant in the Honeysuckle Bower

Canvas, mounted on wood, 178 x 136.5 cm
Inv. No. 334

Rubens porträtiert sich hier mit seiner ersten Frau Isabella Brant (1591–1626). Er hatte die achtzehnjährige Tochter des Antwerpener Stadtsekretärs Jan Brant 1609 geheiratet, ein Jahr nach seiner Rückkehr vom achtjährigen Italienaufenthalt. Wohl im Zusammenhang mit diesem Ereignis entstand das Gemälde, höchstwahrscheinlich als Geschenk für den Schwiegervater, in dessen Nachlaß ein entsprechendes Ehebildnis genannt wird.

Zuerst fällt auf, daß Rubens sich und seine junge Frau ganzfigurig und lebensgroß dargestellt hat. Dies war bis dahin ausschließlich dem höfischen Repräsentationsbildnis vorbehalten, auf dem die Ehepartner steif nebeneinander aufgereiht wurden. Doch entgegen dieser anspruchsvollen Form sitzen die Eheleute Rubens hier in ungezwungen lässiger Haltung nebeneinander vor einer Geißblattlaube, er auf der Lehne einer Gartenbank mit überschlagenem Bein, sie daneben auf dem Boden kauernd. Einander leicht zugeneigt legt Isabella ihre Rechte sanft auf die ihres Mannes, und beide blicken den Betrachter an. Ihre teure und modische Kleidung ist bis ins Detail genau wiedergegeben, um den gesellschaftlichen Rang zu bezeugen.

Neben der gegenseitigen Zuneigung der Ehepartner, die überzeugend zum Ausdruck kommt, enthält das Bild noch eine zweite, überpersönliche Bedeutungsebene. Offensichtlich waren die „Emblemata" des Andreas Alciatus (1522), eine damals weit verbreitete Sammlung von Sinnbildern, für Rubens inspirierend. Dort findet man die Begriffe „Ehe" und „eheliche Treue" durch ein auf einer Bank sitzendes Paar mit ineinander gelegten rechten Händen, der „dextrarum iunctio", versinnbildlicht. Weiterhin ist das die Laube umrankende Geißblatt – im Volksmund Jelängerjelieber genannt – ein Treuesymbol. So stellt Rubens hier gleichzeitig den abstrakten Begriff „Ehe" dar. Mit diesem in Form und Inhalt neuartigen Ehebildnis gelang ihm eines der schönsten und persönlichsten Gemälde dieser Gattung überhaupt.

This double portrait shows the artist with his first wife Isabella Brant (1591–1626). In 1609, a year after his return from his eight-year stay in Italy, Rubens married the 18-year-old daughter of Jan Brant, the town clerk of Antwerp. The painting was executed probably in connection with this event, and in all likelihood as a present to Rubens' father-in-law, in the inventory of whose estate a corresponding wedding picture is mentioned.

The first striking feature about this painting is the fact that Rubens portrays himself and his young wife fullheight and life-size, a tradition that had been reserved previously for formal court portraits, in which the couples usually stood stiffly next to each other. Here, in contrast, Rubens and his wife are seated beside each other in a relaxed, easy manner beneath a honeysuckle bush – he, perched on the arm of a garden bench with his legs casually crossed; she, squatting on the ground. Leaning slightly towards each other, the couple looks out towards the observer, Isabella resting her right hand lovingly on that of her husband. Their costly and fashionable attire is depicted in meticulous detail as a statement of their social rank.

In addition to the convincing expression of the couple's affection for each other, the picture contains a second, less personal level of significance. Rubens was evidently inspired by Andreas Alciatus' "Emblemata" (1522), a widely known collection of symbols, in which the terms "wedlock" and "marital fidelity" were represented by a couple sitting on a bench with their right hands entwined – the *dextrarum iunctio,* as it was termed. Furthermore, the honeysuckle winding about the bower was known in the vernacular as *Jelängerjelieber* (the longer the better) and was regarded as a symbol of marital love and constancy. Rubens' double portrait is, therefore, also a depiction of the abstract concept of "marriage". With this wedding picture, innovative in both its form and content, Rubens created one of the most beautiful and personal paintings of this genre.

14 Peter Paul Rubens
(1577 Siegen – 1640 Antwerpen)

Bildnis des Hendrick van Thulden
Holz, 123,6 x 105,1 cm
Inv. Nr. 316

Der Theologe Hendrick van Thulden (1580–1617) hatte in Löwen studiert, gehörte seit 1610 zum Kapitel der Antwerpener Kathedrale und wurde 1613 Pastor an der dortigen St. Georgskirche, wo er bis zu seinem Tode tätig war.

Das Kniestück zeigt Van Thulden im Dreiviertelprofil auf einem Stuhl sitzend. Mit kaum merklich zur Seite geneigtem Kopf blickt er aus dem Bild. Sein skeptischer, kritischer Gesichtsausdruck wird durch die untersichtige Perspektive, d. h. seinen Blick von oben herab, noch gesteigert. Die rechte Hand Van Thuldens umfaßt den Knauf der Armlehne, mit der linken hält er ein zugeklapptes Buch, wobei er eine Seite mit dem Finger als Lesezeichen markiert.

Das Gemälde wird von der Blockhaftigkeit des massigen, in Schwarz gekleideten Körpers dominiert. Der hohe, steife Mantelkragen umgibt den Kopf wie ein Schutzschild, wodurch das Gesicht als Zentrum für Farbe und Licht noch zusätzlich betont wird. Die Spannung, die sich aus dem Kontrast zwischen monumentaler Gestalt und lebhaftem, intensivem Gesichtsausdruck ergibt, wird durch die farbliche Gestaltung des Gemäldes unterstützt. Das helle, rosige Inkarnat leuchtet regelrecht aus der dunklen Umgebung heraus, wobei Rubens das Material der Stoffe, wie des changierenden Seidenkragens, in verschiedenen Schwarz- und Grauabstufungen meisterhaft wiedergibt. Der Hintergrund, der aus dünn aufgetragener brauner Farbe in schnellen Pinselstrichen angelegt ist, deutet die räumlichen Gegebenheiten nur an, rechts wird ein Fenster mit Himmelausblick von der Wand überschnitten.

Das so überzeugend charakterisierende, eindringliche Porträt Van Thuldens strahlt auch ohne das übliche Repertoire an barocken Würdeformeln, wie Säule, Vorhang oder Wappen, Kraft und Würde aus. Es ist ein hervorragendes Beispiel für die Porträtkunst von Rubens und dürfte um 1615, wenige Jahre vor dem Tod des Dargestellten, entstanden sein.

14 Sir Peter Paul Rubens
(1577 Siegen – 1640 Antwerp)

Portrait of Hendrick van Thulden
Wood, 123.6 x 105.1 cm
Inv. No. 316

The theologian Hendrick van Thulden (1580–1617) studied in Louvain and from 1610 belonged to the chapter of Antwerp Cathedral. In 1613, he became pastor of St George's Church in Antwerp, where he remained until his death.

This knee-length portrait shows Van Thulden three-quarter face seated on a chair. His head leans almost imperceptibly to one side and his eyes address the observer. The sceptical, critical expression of his face is intensified by the view from below. In other words, he appears to be looking down on the observer. Van Thulden's right hand is shown grasping the end of the chair's arm, and in his left hand he holds a closed book, his finger inserted to mark the page he is reading.

The picture is dominated by the massive, monolithic body attired in black. The high, stiff collar of the coat frames the head like a protective shield, accentuating the face as the focus of colour and light. The tension created by the contrast between the monumental figure and the alert, intense facial expression is heightened by the coloration of the painting. The light, rosy incarnadine shines out of the dark surrounding areas, although Rubens also captures in masterly manner the subtle gradations of tone in the grey and black materials, such as the shiny silk collar. The background, a thin layer of brown paint applied with rapid brush strokes, provides no more than an indication of the space. On the right-hand edge, a window affording a view of the sky, is cut off by a projecting wall.

This convincing portrayal of Van Thulden radiates a feeling of strength and dignity without the usual Baroque repertoire of columns, drapings or coats of arms that were used to denote rank. Painted c. 1615, only a few years before the pastor's death, this powerful depiction is an outstanding example of Rubens' portrait art.

15 Peter Paul Rubens
(1577 Siegen – 1640 Antwerpen)

Helene Fourment im Brautkleid

Holz, 163,5 x 136,9 cm
Inv. Nr. 340

15 Sir Peter Paul Rubens
(1577 Siegen – 1640 Antwerp)

Helene Fourment in Her Bridal Gown

Wood, 163.5 x 136.9 cm
Inv. No. 340

Der dreiundfünfzigjährige Rubens heiratete im Dezember 1630, vier Jahre nach dem Tode seiner ersten Frau Isabella Brant (vgl. Nr. 13), die erst 16 Jahre alte Helene Fourment (1614–1674), Tochter einer angesehenen Antwerpener Kaufmannsfamilie.

Stolz auf seine junge Frau, die von Erzherzog Ferdinand sogar als schönste Frau Flanderns gepriesen wurde, porträtiert Rubens sie auf einem Lehnstuhl sitzend. Das Porträt wurde von Rubens als Kniestück begonnen, das er dann aber zu einem ganzfigurigen Bildnis erweiterte. Helene, die den Betrachter freundlich anblickt, trägt ein weiß-goldenes Brokatkleid mit weiten, gepufften Ärmeln aus zartem, transparentem Stoff, darüber ein schwarzes Überkleid. Der weiße Spitzenkragen steht halbkreisförmig ab und rahmt ihr blondes Haupt, das ein Diadem und ein Orangenblütenzweig schmücken. Ketten, Ohrringe, eine große juwelenbesetzte Brosche am Ausschnitt und der Federfächer in ihrer Linken vervollständigen ihre aufwendige Aufmachung, der auch der repräsentative Rahmen entspricht. Ihr Sessel steht auf einer Terrasse zwischen zwei Säulen vor einem hoheitlichen, roten, opulenten Vorhang, den Boden bedeckt ein Orientteppich. Rubens verwendet das ganze Repertoire eines fürstlichen Repräsentationsbildnisses, um die gesellschaftliche Stellung seiner Frau zu unterstreichen, deren natürliche Unbefangenheit mit scheinbar kippelndem Stuhl dazu allerdings in reizvollem Gegensatz steht.

Da es sich bei dem weißen Brokatgewand von Helene wohl um ein Hochzeitskleid handelt und der Orangenblütenzweig zudem ein Symbol für Liebe und Keuschheit ist, wird das Porträt auf 1630/31 datiert.

In December 1630, four years after the death of his first wife, Isabella Brant (cf. No. 13), Rubens married Helene Fourment (1614–1674), the daughter of a respected Antwerp merchant's family. At the time of her marriage she was a mere 16 years of age. Rubens was 53. Proud of his young wife, whom Archduke Ferdinand extolled as the most beautiful woman in Flanders, Rubens portrayed her seated in an armchair. The portrait was begun as a knee-length study, but Rubens then extended it to a full-length picture. Helene, who looks out at the observer with a friendly expression, is wearing a black mantle over a white and gold brocade dress with wide puffed sleeves of a delicate, transparent material. The white lace collar stands out behind her head in a semicircle, framing her blond hair, which is adorned with a diadem and a sprig of orange blossom. A necklace, chains, earrings, a large jewelled brooch on her breast and a fan in her left hand complete these lavish trappings, which are in keeping with the grand setting. The chair is placed on a raised terrace between two columns with an opulent, regal red curtain. The floor is covered with an Oriental carpet. In this painting, Rubens employs the whole canon of stately formal portraiture to underline the social standing of his wife. Her natural, spontaneous manner and the apparent tilting of her chair stand in charming contrast to this.

In view of the fact that Helene's white brocade dress is probably a wedding dress and that the sprig of orange blossom was regarded as a symbol of love and chastity, the portrait has been dated to 1630/31.

16 Peter Paul Rubens
(1577 Siegen – 1640 Antwerpen)

Der hl. Christophorus

Holz, 76,9 x 68 cm
Inv. Nr. 72

Der hl. Christophorus war ein starker Riese. Auf der Suche nach dem mächtigsten König auf Erden erfuhr er von Christus und wollte ihm dienen. So begann er auf den Rat eines Eremiten, Reisende über einen großen Fluß zu tragen. Eines Nachts bat ein kleines Kind um seinen Dienst. Während des Weges durch das Wasser fühlte er das Kind immer schwerer werden, so daß Christophorus meinte, die ganze Welt auf seinen Schultern zu tragen. Am anderen Ufer angekommen offenbarte sich das Kind als Schöpfer der Welt, als Jesus Christus, und eröffnete Christophorus – das heißt übersetzt „Christusträger" –, er habe weit mehr als die Welt getragen.

Das Gemälde ist die Ölskizze für die Außenseite des Kreuzabnahmealtars der Antwerpener Kathedrale. Der Altar wurde 1611 von der Schützengilde bestellt, als deren Patron der Heilige fungierte. Rubens schuf den Entwurf um 1612/13 und arbeitete ihn sehr sorgsam aus – mehr als für eine Werkstattvorlage zur Übertragung in das große Format notwendig wäre. Die in der Skizze dargestellten Figuren des Christophorus und des Eremiten sind in der Ausführung je einem Flügel zugeordnet. Der Heilige erscheint als der legendäre Hüne, der das kleine Kind auf seiner Schulter balanciert. Tief gebeugt unter der Last Christi, auf einen Stab gestützt und mit verkrampften Gesichtszügen, die seine Anstrengung offenbaren, bahnt sich Christophorus seinen Weg durch das Wasser. Rubens verwendete als Vorlage für den muskulösen Körper und die Haltung des Heiligen die antike Skulptur des Herkules Farnese, die er während seiner Italienreise gezeichnet hatte. Auf der rechten Seite steht der Eremit am Ufer, in der Hand eine Laterne, mit der er das Kind anleuchtet. Geblendet vom grellen Licht versucht es den Umhang vor das Gesicht zu ziehen. In der dunklen Nachtstimmung – nur ein schmaler Lichtstreifen erhellt den Horizont – hebt sich der fast weiße Hautton des Kindes deutlich ab. Einen farbigen Akzent im hauptsächlich in Braun- und Grautönen gemalten Bild setzt lediglich der rote Umhang Christi.

16 Sir Peter Paul Rubens
(1577 Siegen – 1640 Antwerp)

St Christopher

Wood, 76.9 x 68 cm
Inv. No. 72

St Christopher was a giant of a man who was known for his great strength. In his search for the mightiest king on earth, he heard about Christ and resolved to serve Him. Following the advice of a hermit, he began to carry travellers across a great river. One night, a small child requested his services, but during the crossing the child became heavier and heavier. On reaching the opposite bank, Christopher was exhausted and said he felt as if he had been carrying the entire world on his shoulders. The child revealed himself to be Jesus Christ, the Creator of the world. Christopher, whose name means "the bearer of Christ", had, therefore, borne much more than the world.

This painting was a modello for the outer face of the wings of the Deposition Altarpiece in Antwerp Cathedral. The altar was commissioned in 1611 by the guild of riflemen, whose patron saint was St Christopher. Rubens made the preliminary design c. 1612/13 and elaborated it in greater detail than was normal for a workshop sketch that was to be transferred to a large panel. The figures of Christopher and the hermit depicted in the modello were executed on separate wings of the altarpiece.

The saint is portrayed as the legendary giant, balancing the little child on his shoulders. Bent beneath the enormous burden of Christ, supporting himself on his staff, and with his face screwed up in evident exertion, Christopher wades through the waters. Rubens modelled the muscular body and the bearing of the saint on the Classical sculpture of the Farnese Hercules, which he had drawn during his stay in Italy. On the right-hand side of the picture, the hermit can be seen standing on the bank of the river holding a lantern, which he shines on the child. Dazzled by the bright light, Christ attempts to draw His robe over His face. The almost pure white tone of the child's skin stands out strikingly in the dark, nocturnal mood of this picture, in which the only other illumination is a narrow strip of light on the horizon. In a painting restricted largely to brown and grey tones, the only colourful accent is Christ's red cloak.

17 Peter Paul Rubens
(1577 Siegen – 1640 Antwerpen)

Grablegung Christi

Holz, 83,7 x 66,2 cm
Inv. Nr. 59

17 Sir Peter Paul Rubens
(1577 Siegen – 1640 Antwerp)

The Entombment

Wood, 83.7 x 66.2 cm
Inv. No. 59

Bei diesem Gemälde handelt es sich um die Skizze für das wohl 1616 vom Domherrn Sebastian Briquet gestiftete Hochaltarbild der Kapuzinerkirche in Cambrai, welches sich heute in der dortigen Kirche St.-Géry befindet. Thematisch handelt es sich um ein der Grablegung zeitlich vorangehendes Ereignis, die Salbung Christi, die lediglich im Johannesevangelium beschrieben wird (Joh. 19, 39 f.).

Der Leichnam Christi liegt diagonal im Bild vor dem Eingang zum Felsengrab auf einem Salbstein. In seiner blockhaften Form spielt dieser Salbstein gleichzeitig auf einen Sarkophag an. Mehrere Personen umstellen im Halbkreis den toten Leib Christi: Johannes hält den Oberkörper und stützt ihn mit seinem Knie, Maria steht klagend daneben, Nikodemus und Joseph von Arimathaia breiten das Leichentuch aus, zwei Frauen im Vordergrund waschen den Körper Christi, und über eine steinerne Treppe nahen zwei Frauen mit Salbkrug und Korb, die wohl die im Evangelium genannten „Spezereien" wie Myrrhe und Aloe für die Salbung enthalten. Schemenhaft sind zwei weitere trauernde Frauen im Hintergrund erkennbar.

Johannes hält den Oberkörper Christi derart, daß er ihn dem Betrachter präsentieren kann. Die seltsam verdrehten Beine Christi, sein fahles, leichengraues Inkarnat und die Wundmale, die in der Mitte am Boden demonstrativ plazierten Nägel, Dornenkrone und Kreuzestitulus machen aus dem Gemälde ein Andachtsbild, das das Mitleiden des Betrachters anregen will.

Farblich ist die Ölskizze sehr differenziert angelegt. Im Kontrast zum hellen Leichnam auf dem weißen Leintuch sind die Gewänder der umstehenden Personen in kräftigem Gelb, Rot und Blau wiedergegeben.

This was the modello for the painting for the high altar in the church of the Capucin monks in Cambrai (now in the church of St Géry, Cambrai), donated probably in 1616 by the canon, Sebastian Briquet. The subject depicted is not the actual Entombment of Christ, but the anointment preceding this, an act that is mentioned only in St John's Gospel (19: 39 f.).

The body of Christ rests diagonally on an anointing stone before the entrance to the sepulchre. The block-like shape of this stone suggests the form of a sarcophagus. A number of persons are grouped in a semicircle about the corpse. John supports Christ with his arms and knee. Mary stands next to him lamenting. Nicodemus and Joseph of Arimathaea spread out the winding sheet. In the foreground, two women are washing the body of Christ. Two other women, bearing a jug and a basket, can be seen approaching down a flight of stone steps to the rear, presumably bringing the myrrh and aloes mentioned in the Bible for the anointment. The outlines of two further mourning women are recognizable in the background.

John holds the upper part of Christ's body as if to present it to the observer. The curious twisting of Christ's legs, the pale, ash grey incarnadine of the body, and the stigmata, the nails, the crown of thorns and the inscription from the Cross, all demonstratively placed in the middle foreground, make this a devotional picture that is meant to move the observer to compassion.

The coloration of this oil sketch is richly varied. In contrast to the pale corpse on the white shroud, the robes of the persons in attendance are painted in bright yellow, red and blue.

18 Peter Paul Rubens
(1577 Siegen – 1640 Antwerpen)

Christus am Kreuz

Holz, 145,3 x 91,8 cm
Inv. Nr. 339

18 Sir Peter Paul Rubens
(1577 Siegen – 1640 Antwerp)

The Crucifixion

Wood, 145.3 x 91.8 cm
Inv. No. 339

Der Gekreuzigte wird von Rubens im Typus des sogenannten „Einsamen Kruzifixus" dargestellt, unter Aus-
lassung des erzählerischen Geschehens auf Golgatha.
Unvermittelt ragt das Kreuz am vorderen Bildrand auf
und füllt das schmale Hochformat des Gemäldes fast
ganz aus. Im Hintergrund ist die Silhouette der Stadt
Jerusalem in Nachtstimmung schemenhaft erkennbar.
Durch diese Verdunkelung wird der hell beleuchtete,
muskulöse Körper Christi um so mehr hervorgehoben.
Christus ist mit weit nach oben gezogenen Armen an
das Kreuz geheftet, das Haupt ist zur Seite gefallen und
das Kinn auf die Brust gesunken. Es entsteht eine selt-
same Ambivalenz zwischen dem einerseits toten,
schwer hängenden Körper und der dennoch dynamischen, spannungsvollen Drehung des Oberkörpers nach
links. Christus soll über den Tod hinaus als Sieger
gezeigt werden.

Der Typus des „Einsamen Kruzifixus" mit seiner lebens-
echten Schilderung und seinem starken Empfindungs-
gehalt hatte sich bereits im 16. Jahrhundert herausge-
bildet und entwickelte sich zu einem Andachtsbild,
an dem die gegenreformatorischen Forderungen nach
historischer Richtigkeit programmatisch umgesetzt
wurden. Dieses Bemühen um Authentizität ist auch hier
offenkundig: Der Kreuzesstamm wird als runder, unbe-
hauener Baumstamm wiedergegeben, ganz realistisch
mit zwei Keilen im Boden verankert. In Anlehnung an
die altertümliche, als richtig erachtete Darstellung ist
Christus mit vier Nägeln statt mit dreien an das Kreuz
genagelt, wobei die Nägel nicht durch die Handflächen,
sondern durch die das Körpergewicht besser haltenden
Handwurzelknochen geschlagen sind. Die hebräische
Inschrift auf dem Kreuzestitulus ist philologisch richtig
in Aramäisch wiedergegeben.

Rubens beschäftigte sich mehrfach mit dem Bildthema,
aber die eindringliche Münchner Formulierung aus der
Zeit um 1615 wurde für viele nachfolgenden Künstler
vorbildlich und fand weite Verbreitung.

Rubens portrays this scene in the "solitary Crucifix"
form, in which many of the narrative details of Golgotha,
as described in the Gospels, are omitted. The Cross rises
abruptly in the foreground from the bottom edge of the
painting, almost entirely filling the narrow vertical
panel. In the background, the shadowy silhouette of the
city of Jerusalem can be seen in the darkness. The
brightly lit, muscular body of Christ on the Cross is
accentuated even further by this darkening of the scene.
His arms are drawn up; His head lolls to one side, His
chin sunk on His chest. The dead, heavily hanging body
on the one hand and the dynamic twisting of the trunk
on the other evoke a strange sense of ambivalence.
Christ was to be shown as triumphant over death.

The "solitary Crucifix" type, with its realistic depiction
and strong emotional content, was intended to arouse
the compassion of the observer. It had its origins in the
16th century and developed into a devotional picture
form in which the demands of the Counter-Reformation
for historical correctness were realized in programmatic
fashion. This striving for authenticity is also evident in
Rubens' painting. The main stem of the Cross is depicted
as an unsquared tree trunk, realistically fixed in the
ground with two wedges. In accordance with ancient
depictions of the Crucifixion, which were regarded as
more accurate, Christ is fixed to the Cross with four nails
instead of three; and the nails are not driven through the
palms of the hands, but through the carpal bone at the
base of the hand, where the weight of the body would be
borne more effectively. In philological terms, the
Hebrew superscription affixed to the Cross is also correctly given in Aramaic.

Rubens painted the "solitary Crucifix" form on a number
of occasions, but the urgent formulation of this theme in
the Munich painting, dating from c. 1615, provided a
model for subsequent generations of artists and the
inspiration for many later works.

19 Peter Paul Rubens
(1577 Siegen – 1640 Antwerpen)

Die Niederlage Sanheribs

Holz, 97,7 x 122,7 cm
Inv. Nr. 326

19 Sir Peter Paul Rubens
(1577 Siegen – 1640 Antwerp)

The Defeat of Sennacherib

Wood, 97.7 x 122.7 cm
Inv. No 326

Das Gemälde zeigt die alttestamentarische Geschichte der Rettung Jerusalems vor der Bedrohung durch die Assyrer (2. Könige 19, 34 – 36): „Und ich will diese Stadt beschirmen, daß ich sie errette um meinetwillen und um meines Knechtes David willen. Und in dieser Nacht fuhr aus der Engel des Herrn und schlug im Lager von Assyrien hundertfünfundachtzigtausend Mann. Und als man sich früh am Morgen aufmachte, siehe, da lag alles voller Leichen. So brach Sanherib, der König von Assyrien, auf und zog ab, kehrte um und blieb zu Ninive."

Die Schilderung der nächtlichen Szene mit dem Eingriff der himmlischen Macht ist äußerst dramatisch. In der Mitte öffnet sich der dunkle Himmel, und eine Gruppe von vier Engeln mit Blitz- oder Flammenbündeln fährt strafend auf das Heer der Assyrer nieder. Der starke Lichtschein, der aus der Wolkenöffnung gemeinsam mit den Engeln hervorbricht, beleuchtet die Szene gewitterartig. Im Zentrum steht König Sanherib, der mit angstverzerrtem Gesicht von seinem sich aufbäumenden Pferd nach hinten stürzt. Krampfhaft versucht er, sich in der Mähne festzuhalten. Seine Begleiter flüchten entsetzt nach allen Richtungen auseinander – zu Pferde und zu Fuß – oder sind bereits getötet worden, wie die am vorderen Bildrand hingestreckten Männer, von denen einer durch die helle Beleuchtung seines Körpers besonders hervorgehoben wird.

Rubens hat die biblische Beschreibung, in der Sanherib am nächsten Morgen offensichtlich unerwartet mit seinen toten Soldaten konfrontiert wird, umgeändert und den König der Assyrer in den Brennpunkt der nächtlichen Ereignisse gestellt.

Einzelne Motive des Gemäldes, vor allem der von dem sich aufbäumenden Pferd stürzende Sanherib, beziehen sich auf Vorbilder wie die Anghiarischlacht Leonardo da Vincis und werden in anderen Kampf- und Jagdszenen von Rubens dieser Zeit um 1617 wiederverwendet. Das Gemälde mit der „Bekehrung Pauli" in London (Courtauld Institute; ehem. München, Alte Pinakothek) wird in

The subject of this painting is the deliverance of Jerusalem from the Assyrians, as described in the Old Testament (2 Kings 19: 34 – 36): "For I will defend this city, to save it, for mine own sake, and for my servant David's sake. And it came to pass that night, that the angel of the Lord went out, and smote in the camp of the Assyrians an hundred fourscore and five thousand: and when they arose early in the morning, behold, they were all dead corpses. So Sennacherib King of Assyria departed, and went and returned, and dwelt at Nineveh."

The nocturnal scene with the attack of the heavenly host is depicted in a most dramatic form. In the middle of the picture, the dark heavens open and a group of four angels bearing sheaves of lightning or flames descends to smite the Assyrian army. The intense light that bursts through the clouds with the angels illuminates the scene as in a thunderstorm. Sennacherib is portrayed in the centre, falling from his rearing horse, his face distorted with fear. Desperately he seeks to cling to the mane of his horse. His companions flee in panic in all directions, mounted and on foot. Others have already been killed, as the bodies of the soldiers stretched out in the foreground at the bottom of the picture show. One of them in particular is picked out by the bright light that falls on his body.

Rubens modifies the biblical story – in which Sennacherib wakes the following morning and, to his apparent surprise, is confronted with his dead soldiers – and makes the Assyrian king the focus of the nocturnal events.

Elements of the painting were inspired by other models. In particular, the figure of Sennacherib falling from his rearing horse is a reworking of motifs from Leonardo's "Battle of Anghiari", the influence of which is also evident in other hunting and battle scenes painted by Rubens at that time (c. 1617). "The Conversion of Paul" in the Courtauld Institute, London (formerly, Alte Pinakothek, Munich), is regarded by art historians as a pendant

der Literatur als Pendant zur „Niederlage Sanheribs" betrachtet. Thematisch ist die Darstellung eines durch himmlische Gewalt vom Pferd Stürzenden dem Sanherib vergleichbar, zudem stimmen die Maße beider Gemälde überein. Während die Bekehrung des Paulus ausgesprochen häufig in der flämischen Malerei seit Mitte des 16. Jahrhunderts gezeigt wird, findet man die Sanherib-Szene kaum dargestellt.

Besonders gut sichtbar ist in den hellen Partien des Gemäldes die streifig aufgetragene Imprimitur, die durch die dünne, lasierende Malschicht durchscheint und über die Maltechnik von Rubens Auskunft gibt. Er setzte die einfarbig getönte Imprimitur in breiten Pinselstrichen über den Kreidegrund, um den Bildgrund zu beleben, die darüberliegenden Farbtöne zusammenzubinden und nicht zuletzt um eine räumliche Tiefenwirkung zu erzielen.

to "The Defeat of Sennacherib". Thematically, the depiction is certainly comparable to that of Sennacherib being thrown from his horse by heavenly powers; and the two paintings have similar dimensions. Whereas the conversion of Paul was a common theme in Flemish painting from the mid-16th century onwards, the story of Sennacherib was rarely depicted.

Clearly visible in the lighter areas of the painting is the imprimatura. Applied in banded manner and shining through the thin glaze of paint, it provides an insight into Rubens' technique. He applied the monochrome imprimatura with broad brush strokes over the gesso to enliven the ground, to unify the colour tones on top, and not least to achieve a sense of spatial depth.

20 Peter Paul Rubens
(1577 Siegen – 1640 Antwerpen)

Das Große Jüngste Gericht

Leinwand, 606 x 460 cm
Inv. Nr. 890

20 Sir Peter Paul Rubens
(1577 Siegen – 1640 Antwerp)

The Great Last Judgement

Canvas, 606 x 460 cm
Inv. No. 890

Das „Große Jüngste Gericht" – so benannt zur Unterscheidung vom „Kleinen Jüngsten Gericht" (Nr. 22) – ist das größte Leinwandbild im Besitz der Alten Pinakothek. Nach ihm wurden die Proportionen des zentralen Saales beim Bau durch Leo von Klenze bestimmt. Das von Herzog Wolfgang Wilhelm von Pfalz-Neuburg als Hochaltarbild für die Hofkirche in Neuburg a. D. bestellte Gemälde war 1617 vollendet.

Das Jüngste Gericht wird im wesentlichen im Matthäusevangelium geschildert (vgl. Nr. 22). Die Abfolge von Auferstehung der Toten und Scheidung in Erlöste oder Verdammte fügt Rubens einer ovalen Komposition ein. Unten sieht man Skelette aus ihren Gräbern steigen sowie Menschen, deren Auferstehungsleib bereits ein fortgeschritteneres Stadium erreicht hat. Dann trennen sich zwei gegenläufige Bewegungsströme aus eng verflochtenen Menschenleibern. Entsprechend Christi Urteilsspruch, der auf einer Wolkenbank als Weltenrichter thront, dürfen sie entweder zu seiner Rechten als Auserwählte in den Himmel aufsteigen, oder werden zu seiner Linken als Verdammte in die Hölle gestürzt. Die Ausführung seines Schiedsspruches obliegt Engeln, die einerseits die Seligen fürsorglich in den Himmel geleiten oder aber unter Anführung vom Erzengel Michael die Verdammten zur Hölle zurückstoßen, wo sie von Teufeln und Monstern gepackt und gequält werden. Im Gegensatz zu Michelangelos „Jüngstem Gericht" in der Sixtinischen Kapelle in Rom, das Rubens inspirierte, steht bei seinem „Großen Jüngsten Gericht" nicht die Verdammnis im Vordergrund, sondern dem Betrachter wird gleichzeitig die Hoffnung auf Auferstehung und Erlösung tröstend und verheißend vor Augen geführt.

Die Wirkung des Gemäldes beruht auf den großartig angelegten Figuren sowie der Farb- und Lichtwirkung. Dieser Reiz führte schließlich dazu, daß das Hochaltarbild in Neuburg zumeist durch ein anderes Gemälde verdeckt war, da die „Nuditäten" heftige Kritik erregten, und daß es 1692 aus der Kirche entfernt wurde.

"The Great Last Judgement", so named to distinguish it from "The Small Last Judgement" (No. 22), is the largest canvas in the possession of the Alte Pinakothek. The dimensions of the central hall of this gallery, designed by Leo von Klenze, were determined by the size of this painting. Commissioned by Duke Wolfgang Wilhelm of the Palatinate-Neuburg for the high altar of the court church in Neuburg on the Danube, the picture was completed in 1617.

The Last Judgement is described largely in the Gospel according to St Matthew (cf. No. 22). In an oval composition, Rubens depicts the sequence of events surrounding the resurrection of the dead and their division into the blessed and the damned. Visible at the bottom of the picture are skeletons and human beings who have already gained corporeal form in readiness for resurrection and who are rising from their graves. Two streams of entwined bodies can be seen moving in different directions. Christ sits on high on a bank of clouds, as judge over all the world. According to His judgement, the blessed to His right have been chosen to ascend to heaven, while those to His left are damned and are plunged into hell. His commands are executed by angels, who conduct the blessed with solicitude into heaven or, led by the Archangel Michael, cast down the damned to hell, where they are seized and tormented by devils and monsters. In contrast to Michelangelo's "Last Judgement" in the Sistine Chapel in Rome, which was a source of inspiration for Rubens, damnation is not the central theme of "The Great Last Judgement". The observer is also presented with the comforting prospect of resurrection and redemption.

The impact of this painting is based on the superb arrangement of writhing figures and the coloration and lighting of the naked bodies. It was these that led to the altarpiece being covered by another painting for many years, since its display of nudity provoked fierce criticism. The work was removed from the church in 1692.

90

21 Peter Paul Rubens
(1577 Siegen – 1640 Antwerpen)
Jan Brueghel der Ältere
(1568 Brüssel – 1625 Antwerpen)

Madonna im Blumenkranz

Holz, 185 x 209,8 cm
Inv. Nr. 331

Die Madonna in Dreiviertelfigur hält ganz sanft das stehende nackte Kind auf ihrem Knie. Sie präsentiert dem Betrachter ihren Sohn, der lächelnd aus dem Bild schaut. Seine Pose und die frontale Ausrichtung erinnern an Salvator Mundi-Darstellungen. Der Blick der Mutter ist dagegen nachdenklich – vielleicht in Vorahnung der Passion – auf die leere Wiege gerichtet.

In augentäuscherischer Weise wird die Darstellung von Mutter und Kind als eigenständiges Bild im Bild mit schwarzem Rahmen gezeigt, das von einem Reigen aus elf Putten umgeben ist, die eine Blumengirlande umspielen. Verwirrend ist jedoch, daß sich die Realitätsebenen verwischen: Der Kopf der Madonna blickt durch den sie umgebenden Rahmen wie durch ein Fenster hindurch, ihr Kopf liegt in einer Ebene mit dem Blumenkranz. Die Putten halten entweder die Enden des roten Bandes, mit dem das Marienbild an einer muschelförmigen Kartusche aus Stein befestigt zu sein scheint, oder sie fassen spielerisch in die üppige Blumengirlande, ohne sie jedoch wirklich zu halten. Durch den so täuschend plastisch gemalten Blumenkranz wird der Charakter eines Gnadenbildes gesteigert, denn in gleicher Weise schmückte man damals tatsächlich hochverehrte Bilder an heiligen Festtagen. Einzelne Blüten – wie Rosen, Lilien, Malven, Himmelsschlüssel – in der nach unten voluminöser werdenden Girlande können symbolisch mit Maria verbunden werden.

Die sehr naturgetreu, in leuchtenden Farben wiedergegebenen Blumen wurden von Jan Brueghel d. Ä., dem „Blumen-Brueghel", gemalt. Auf ihn, den damals führenden Blumenmaler Antwerpens, geht wohl überhaupt die Erfindung eines blumenumkränzten Bildes zurück (vgl. auch Nr. 6). Er gab den Auftakt für zahlreiche Blumenkranzmadonnen, die zu einer flämischen Besonderheit wurden. Der Gönner Brueghels, Kardinal Federigo Borromeo, war ein ausgesprochener Liebhaber der Blumengirlanden, die ihm fast wichtiger als das umrahmte Motiv waren. Allgemein wurden damals die

21 Sir Peter Paul Rubens
(1577 Siegen – 1640 Antwerp)
Jan Brueghel the Elder
(1568 Brussels – 1625 Antwerp)

Madonna in a Garland of Flowers

Wood, 185 x 209.8 cm
Inv. No. 331

The Madonna is shown seated in three-quarter length, gently holding the naked child in a standing position on her knee, presenting Him to the observer. The pose of the smiling child, looking out of the picture, and the frontal view are reminiscent of Salvator Mundi depictions. The expression on Mary's face, in contrast, is pensive – perhaps in premonition of the Passion – and her eyes are turned to the empty crib.

In the manner of an optical illusion, mother and child are presented as an independent picture within a picture – within a black frame that is in turn surrounded by a round of 11 putti playing about a garland of flowers. One confusing aspect is the blurring of the various planes. The head of the Madonna peering through the frame as through a window, for example, is in the same plane as the wreath of flowers. The putti are either holding the ends of the red ribbon with which the Marian image seems to be attached to a shell-shaped stone cartouche at the top, or they are grasping playfully at the splendid garland of flowers without really holding it. The strikingly three-dimensional execution of the wreath of flowers strengthens the character of the painting as a miraculous image; for in Rubens' times, greatly revered pictures were often decorated in the same way on feast days. Some of the flowers in the garland, which increases in volume towards the bottom, were well-known Marian symbols. These include the rose, the lily, the mallow and the primrose.

The flowers, painted true to life in luminous colours, are the work of Jan Brueghel the Elder, who was also known as "Flower Brueghel". At that time he was the leading flower painter in Antwerp, and the invention of garlands of this kind as a framing device to pictures is probably attributable to him (cf. No. 6). He inspired numerous depictions of Madonnas surrounded by wreaths of flowers, which became a speciality of Flemish painting. Cardinal Federigo Borromeo, Brueghel's patron, was a great lover of these garlands. They were almost more

Blumengemälde – seien es Buketts in Vasen oder Girlanden – außerordentlich hoch eingeschätzt und bewertet. Sie gehörten mit zu den teuersten Kunstwerken. Dennoch war der Zweck der kostbaren Girlanden eine christliche Darstellung zu schmücken und deren Bedeutung als Objekt der Verehrung hervorzuheben.

Einen besonderen Reiz des für dieses Thema ungewöhnlich großformatigen Gemäldes bewirkt das Zusammentreffen der unterschiedlichen künstlerischen Auffassungen: die großzügig angelegten Figuren von Rubens neben den detailliert und fein gemalten Blüten von Brueghel, die die Illusion eines frischen Blumenschmuckes erwecken.

Für die Gesichtszüge von Maria und Christus dienten Rubens offensichtlich seine Frau Isabella und das Söhnchen Albert als Modell. Für den Christusknaben mit den Gesichtszügen Alberts gibt es eine Entwurfszeichnung (St. Petersburg, Eremitage). Auch der Putto mit Korallenkette in der oberen rechten Bildecke ähnelt einer Ölskizze vom zweijährigen Albert von 1616 (Berlin, Gemäldegalerie).

Die „Blumenkranzmadonna" ist das bekannteste Beispiel für die oft praktizierte Zusammenarbeit der beiden miteinander befreundeten Künstler. Weder Bestimmungsort noch Auftraggeber des um 1616/17 entstandenen Gemäldes sind bekannt.

important to him than the motif they framed. Flower paintings, whether in the form of garlands or bouquets in vases, enjoyed enormous popularity and prestige in those days and were among the most expensive works of art on the market. The purpose of these precious flower arrangements was nevertheless to adorn a Christian motif and to underline its significance as an object of veneration.

One fascinating aspect of this picture, which is unusually large for the subject, is the collaboration between two men of different artistic temperament: Rubens with his bold, generously proportioned figures, and Brueghel with his fine, exquisitely detailed flowers that evoke the illusion of fresh floral decorations.

Rubens evidently took the facial features of his wife Isabella as a model for those of Mary, and of his little son Albert for the Infant Jesus. A preliminary sketch exists for the portrayal of Jesus with Albert's physiognomy (Hermitage, St Petersburg). The putto with the coral necklace in the top right-hand corner of the picture also bears a certain resemblance to an oil sketch of Albert at the age of two, made in 1616 (Gemäldegalerie, Berlin).

The "Madonna in a Garland of Flowers" is the best-known example of a repeated collaboration between the two artists, who were good friends. The picture dates from c. 1616/17, but neither the location for which it was intended nor the patron are known.

22 Peter Paul Rubens
(1577 Siegen – 1640 Antwerpen)

Das Kleine Jüngste Gericht

Holz, 183 x 120 cm
Inv. Nr. 611

Das Matthäusevangelium (25, 41–46) beschreibt das Jüngste Gericht: „Dann wird er auch sagen zu denen zur Linken: Gehet hin von mir, ihr Verfluchten, in das ewige Feuer, das bereitet ist dem Teufel und seinen Engeln!... Und sie werden in die ewige Pein gehen; aber die Gerechten in das ewige Leben."

Der Sturz der Verdammten, deren Körper in ihrer dynamischen Verschlingung wie in einem Wirbel niedergehen, ist bildbeherrschend. Der Erzengel Michael, bewaffnet mit Blitzbündel und Schild, hindert die verdammten Seelen am Aufstieg in den Himmel und stößt sie mit Unterstützung seiner Engelschar zur Hölle zurück. Im Zentrum des Geschehens hebt er sich trotz Aureole kaum von den wirbelnden Körpern ab. Links zeigt der Landschaftsausblick kleinfigurig zahllose ihren Gräbern entsteigende Tote, in der rechten Bildecke ist der Eingang zur Hölle dargestellt, zu dem die Verdammten von Teufeln und anderen Höllenwesen unter Anwendung von brutaler Gewalt gezerrt werden.

Gegenüber dem „Großen Jüngsten Gericht" (Nr. 20) hat sich der Akzent hier stark verlagert, denn der gleichzeitige Aufstieg der Seligen in den Himmel ist in der Bildtiefe nur angedeutet, wie auch der thronende Christus als Weltenrichter mit Maria und Fürbitte leistenden Heiligen in den Hintergrund zurücktreten. Anfänglich wurde das Gemälde als Höllensturz gemalt, dem Rubens dann bald darauf den rundbogigen Abschluß hinzufügte. Erst mit dieser oberen Erweiterung wurde dem ausschließlich die Verdammnis darstellenden Höllensturz der hoffnungsvolle Aspekt der Auferstehung zum Ewigen Leben beigegeben und somit das Bildthema zu einem Jüngsten Gericht abgeändert.

Bei den stürzenden Körpern in ihren vielfältigen Drehungen und Wendungen, die hier so offensichtlich im Zentrum seines Interesses stehen, erweist sich die Virtuosität von Rubens Malkunst. Für wen das um 1620 entstandene Bild gemalt wurde, ist heute nicht mehr bekannt.

22 Sir Peter Paul Rubens
(1577 Siegen – 1640 Antwerp)

The Small Last Judgement

Wood, 183 x 120 cm
Inv. No. 611

In the Gospel according to St Matthew (25: 41–46), the Last Judgement is described in the following words: "Then shall he say also unto them on the left hand, Depart from me, ye cursed, into everlasting fire, prepared for the devil and his angels... And these shall go away into everlasting punishment: but the righteous into life eternal."

The dominant theme of this picture is the fall of the damned in a dynamic, tangled whirl of bodies. Together with a host of angels, and armed with bolts of lightning and a shield, the Archangel Michael repulses the damned in their bid to ascend to heaven and hurls them back to hell. At the centre of this struggle, he is scarcely distinguishable from the mass of entwined bodies, despite his aureole. On the left of the picture, in a view of a distant landscape, the dead can be seen: a host of tiny figures, rising from their graves. In the bottom right-hand corner is the entrance to hell, into which devils and other creatures are dragging the damned by brute force. Compared with "The Great Last Judgement" (No. 20) there is a fundamental shift of view in the present work. The ascent of the blessed into heaven is intimated only in the depths of the picture; and Christ, enthroned on high as judge over all the world, with Mary and the saints as intercessors, recedes into the background. Initially, the painting was a depiction of "The Fall of the Damned", but shortly afterwards, Rubens enlarged the panel, adding the lunette at the top. With this extension, the exclusive theme of damnation and the descent into hell was complemented by the idea of hope for resurrection and eternal life. The subject of the picture was thus changed to a study of the Last Judgement.

Rubens' virtuosity as a painter is revealed in his handling of the mass of twisting, rotating, plunging bodies, which were evidently his main interest here. Today, it is no longer known for whom this work, dating from c. 1620, was painted.

23 Peter Paul Rubens
(1577 Siegen – 1640 Antwerpen)

Amor schnitzt den Bogen

Leinwand, 142 x 108 cm
Signiert und datiert am unteren Ende des Bogens:
P · P · RVBENS · F · 16 · 14
Inv. Nr. 1304

Das Gemälde ist eine freie Wiederholung nach einem Bild von Parmigianino, das sich heute im Kunsthistorischen Museum in Wien befindet. Das Vorbild, 1531/34 für einen Kunstsammler in Parma gemalt, wurde 1585 nach Spanien verbracht und 1603 für die Sammlung Kaiser Rudolfs II. in Prag erworben. Rubens könnte das Gemälde Parmigianinos während seines Spanienaufenthaltes 1603 gesehen haben, oder er arbeitete nach einer der vielen Kopien des hochgeschätzten Bildes. Dabei hielt er sich nicht getreu an die Vorlage, sondern nahm deutliche Veränderungen vor: Das Format ist vergrößert, die Figuren haben mehr Volumen erhalten. Amor steht nun in einer Landschaft, seinen linken Fuß nicht mehr auf zwei Bücher, sondern auf eine grasbewachsene Erhebung gesetzt. Auch die beiden geflügelten Putten zu Füßen des Amor werden nun in ganzer Figur gezeigt, ihre Pose ist verändert. Der dunkelhaarige Junge liegt auf dem Bauch und liebkost das sich sträubende Mädchen. Mit seinem linken Zeigefinger deutet Amor auf diese Szene, während Parmigianinos Amor alle Finger zum Führen seines Schnitzmessers benötigt. Eine wichtige Veränderung betrifft auch die Haut, die bei Parmigianino in einem gelblich-rosa Ton mit grauen Schatten wiedergegeben wird. Rubens dagegen setzt kalte blau-graue Schatten, die durch leuchtendes Gelb und Rot akzentuiert werden. Er verwendet die unvermischten Grundfarben Gelb, Blau und Rot so, wie es der Antwerpener Mathematiker Franciscus Aguilonius in seinem Buch über die Optik beschrieben hat. Da Rubens dieses 1613 erschienene Werk illustrierte, dürfen wir annehmen, daß ihm der Inhalt gut bekannt war. Damit stehen auch die vergrößerten Flügel und der Mantel des Amor in Verbindung, weil sie ihm Gelegenheit boten, große Flächen mit kräftigen Farben (Rot, Blau, Weiß) zu bemalen.

Der „Amor" gehört zu einer kleinen Gruppe von nur acht Gemälden, die Rubens signierte und datierte, fünf davon tragen die Jahreszahl 1614.

23 Sir Peter Paul Rubens
(1577 Siegen – 1640 Antwerp)

Cupid Cutting His Bow

Canvas, 142 x 108 cm
Signed and dated on the lower end of the bow:
P · P · RVBENS · F · 16 · 14
Inv. No. 1304

"Cupid Cutting His Bow" is a freely adapted copy of a work by Parmigianino that today belongs to the collection of the Kunsthistorisches Museum, Vienna. The original was painted in 1531/34 for a connoisseur in Parma and was removed to Spain in 1585. In 1603, it was acquired for the collection of Emperor Rudolf II in Prague. Rubens possibly saw Parmigianino's painting in 1603 during his stay in Spain, or he may have modelled his own work on one of the many copies of the original, which was greatly admired. Rubens did not adhere to the model, however, but made evident modifications to it. He enlarged the dimensions and increased the volume of the figures. Cupid now stands in a landscape. His left foot no longer rests on two books, but on a grassy mound. The two winged putti at his feet are here shown full length, and their pose has been changed. The dark-haired male putto lies on his belly caressing the reluctant little girl. Cupid points to this scene with the forefinger of his left hand, whereas Parmigianino's Cupid needed his whole hand to hold the knife. An important change was made to the coloration of the skin, which in Parmigianino's work has a yellowish pink tone with grey shading. In contrast, Rubens creates cool, blue-grey shadows accentuated by bright yellows and reds. He also uses unmixed primary colours – yellow, blue and red – in the manner described by the Antwerp mathematician Franciscus Aguilonius in his book on optics. Since Rubens had provided the illustrations to this work, which appeared in 1613, it may be assumed that he was familiar with the contents. Cupid's coat and his enlarged wings should be seen in this context, for they gave Rubens the opportunity to paint greater areas in bold colours (red, blue and white).

"Cupid Cutting His Bow" is one of only eight paintings Rubens signed and dated, five of which bear the date 1614.

24 Peter Paul Rubens
(1577 Siegen – 1640 Antwerpen)

Zwei Satyrn

Holz, 75,3 x 61 cm
Inv. Nr. 873

24 Sir Peter Paul Rubens
(1577 Siegen – 1640 Antwerp)

Two Satyrs

Wood, 75.3 x 61 cm
Inv. No. 873

Während seiner gesamten Schaffenszeit stellte Rubens Historien aus der griechisch/römischen Mythologie dar, darunter bevorzugt Themen aus dem bacchantischen Bereich. Zum Gefolge des Weingottes Bacchus gehören Satyrn, Naturdämonen als Mischgestalten aus Mensch und Ziege. Die wilden, rohen Naturwesen sind lüsterne Verfolger von Nymphen und erschrecken mit Vorliebe die Menschen.

Rubens' „Zwei Satyrn" nehmen eine Sonderstellung ein, da sie nicht in eine personenreiche Szene integriert werden, sondern auf zwei Köpfe mit Porträtcharakter reduziert sind. Einer der Satyrn wird frontal als Brustbild gezeigt, mit Bockshörnern auf der Stirn, efeubekränzt und ein Löwenfell um die nackte Schulter geschlungen. Mit der Rechten zerdrückt er eine Weintraube und schaut dabei den Betrachter mit gesenktem Kopf an. Der sprechende Ausdruck, Efeukranz und um die Brust geschlungenes Fell erinnern an eine Giulio Romano-Zeichnung, vermutlich ein Entwurf für eine Gartenherme. Hinter diesem Satyr erscheint ein zweiter, im Profil nach links gewendet, den Kopf mit einem Löwenfell bedeckt, trinkt er mit geschlossenen Augen genüßlich Wein aus einer Schale. Für die ungewöhnliche Zusammenstellung der beiden Satyrköpfe – einer frontal, der andere im Profil – könnte Rubens von antiken Gemmen inspiriert worden sein. Der weintrinkende Satyr taucht auch in Rubens' Münchner Gemälde „Der trunkene Silen" (um 1617/18) auf, dort jedoch eingebunden in eine Erzählung.

Throughout his creative life, Rubens painted historical scenes based on Greek and Roman mythology and was attracted in particular to Bacchanalian themes. The satyrs, who were often depicted in the train of the wine god Bacchus, were natural demons in hybrid form, part man, part goat. These wild, uncouth creatures of nature were lecherous pursuers of nymphs and delighted in frightening humans.

Rubens' "Two Satyrs" occupies a special place in this genre. It is not a depiction of a scene crowded with figures, but a study of two heads in the nature of a portrait. One of the satyrs is seen full-face in a half-length portrayal, with buck horns growing from his brow, a garland of ivy about his head, and a lion's skin slung over his bare shoulder. In his right hand he is squeezing a bunch of grapes. With lowered head, he fixes the observer with his gaze. The telling look, the ivy wreath and the fur draped over his breast are reminiscent of a Giulio Romano drawing, which was probably a design for a herm in a garden. Behind this satyr is a second figure, seen in profile facing left, his head covered with a lion's skin. With closed eyes and with evident pleasure, he is drinking wine from a shallow bowl. Rubens was possibly inspired to this unusual constellation of the two satyrs' heads – one seen frontally, the other in profile – by Classical intaglios. Another satyr drinking wine appears in his "Drunken Silenus" (c. 1617/18), also in Munich; but there the figure forms part of a narrative scene.

25 Peter Paul Rubens
(1577 Siegen – 1640 Antwerpen)

Die Amazonenschlacht

Holz, 121 x 165 cm
Inv. Nr. 324

In Mythen werden die kriegerischen Auseinanderset-zungen zwischen griechischen Helden und den Amazo-nen, einem in Kleinasien am Fluß Thermodon angesie-delten kämpferischen Frauenvolk, geschildert. Die Darstellung der Amazonenkämpfe als Geschlechter-kampf war seit der Antike sehr beliebt. Rubens, der sich mit diesem Thema mehrfach auseinandersetzte, fand die eindrucksvollste Umsetzung mit dem Münchner Gemälde, das den Inbegriff einer Schlacht bildet. Das geschilderte Ereignis ist jedoch ebensowenig bestimm-bar wie die einzelnen Figuren benennbar sind, und ent-gegen bisheriger Traditionen verlegte er das Kampfge-schehen auf eine Brücke. In wilder Jagd verfolgen die Griechen die fliehenden Amazonen. Als Höhepunkt im allgemeinen Schlachtengewimmel findet mitten auf der Brücke ein Kampf von zwei Griechen mit einer Amazone statt, der sie die Fahne zu entreißen versuchen. Das Pferd des einen Griechen hat sich mit dem einer weite-ren Amazone im Aufbäumen ineinander verbissen, wie die Pferde überhaupt eine wichtige Rolle in der Drama-tik des Kampfes spielen. Genau im Scheitel der Brücke liegt ein Enthaupteter, der Kopf wird von einer weg-sprengenden Amazone als Trophäe emporgehalten. Zu beiden Uferseiten stürzen Verwundete und Gefallene derart, daß ihre Bewegungen im aufspritzenden Wasser zusammentreffen. Beim Blick durch den Brückenbogen erkennt man ein Boot mit Flüchtenden und im Hinter-grund eine brennende Stadt.

Neben antiken Sarkophagreliefs bezog Rubens seine Anregungen von Leonardos Anghiarischlacht, Raffaels Fresko der Schlacht an der Milvischen Brücke im Vati-kan und vor allem Tizians Schlacht von Cadore, ehemals Dogenpalast in Venedig.

Das um 1615 entstandene Gemälde von verhältnismäßig kleinem Format gehörte dem Antwerpener Kaufmann Cornelis van der Geest. Die Ansicht seiner Sammlung, 1628 durch Willem van Haecht gemalt (heute Antwer-pen, Rubenshuis), dokumentiert dies.

25 Sir Peter Paul Rubens
(1577 Siegen – 1640 Antwerp)

The Battle of the Amazons

Wood, 121 x 165 cm
Inv. No. 324

The legend of the Amazons tells of a warlike race of women who dwelt on the River Thermodon in Asia Minor. Their battles with Greek heroes form the subject of many myths and had been popularly portrayed since Classical times as a struggle between the sexes. Rubens depicted the theme on a number of occasions. This Munich picture, which can be seen as the epitome of bat-tle, is his most impressive treatment of the subject. It is as difficult to determine the actual event, however, as it is to identify the individual figures. Contrary to tradition, Rubens also transferred the scene of battle to a bridge. Caught up in a furious chase, the Greeks can be seen pursuing the fleeing Amazons. The climax of the general turmoil is the battle in the middle of the bridge between an Amazon and two Greeks who are trying to wrest a banner from her. The horse of the mounted Greek and that of another Amazon rear up and bite each other. Indeed, the horses as a whole play an important role in the drama of this battle. On the crown of the bridge lies the body of a decapitated warrior. An Amazon gallops off, holding the head aloft as a trophy. Dead and wounded on both sides can be seen falling from the bridge, so that the general sense of movement spills into the agitated waters. The view through the arch of the bridge reveals a boat full of fleeing warriors and a burn-ing city in the distance.

As models, Rubens used reliefs from ancient sarcophagi, as well as Leonardo's "Battle of Anghiari", Raphael's fresco of the "Battle of Constantine" in the Vatican and, in particular, Titian's "Battle of Cadore", formerly in the Ducal Palace in Venice.

Painted c. 1615, the work depicts these dramatic events on a relatively small panel. It was owned by Cornelis van der Geest, an Antwerp wholesale merchant, as is docu-mented by the depiction of his chamber of art, painted in 1628 by Willem van Haecht (now in the Rubenshuis, Antwerp).

26 Peter Paul Rubens
(1577 Siegen – 1640 Antwerpen)

Medici-Zyklus:
Die Landung in Marseille

Holz, 64 x 50 cm
Inv. Nr. 95

26 Sir Peter Paul Rubens
(1577 Siegen – 1640 Antwerp)

The Medici Cycle:
The Landing in Marseilles

Wood, 64 x 50 cm
Inv. No. 95

Die französische Königin Maria Medici (1573–1642), Witwe Heinrichs IV. (1553–1610), bestellte 1622 bei Peter Paul Rubens einen 24 großformatige Gemälde umfassenden Zyklus. Er war für eine Galerie im Westflügel ihres Palais du Luxembourg zu Paris bestimmt und wird heute im Louvre ausgestellt. Zusätzlich war für den Ostflügel ein entsprechender Zyklus mit ebenfalls 24 Gemälden zum Nachruhm ihres verstorbenen Gatten geplant, der jedoch nie vollendet wurde.

Der Auftrag zur Verherrlichung des Lebens und der Taten der Königin wurde für Rubens zu einem der anspruchsvollsten, denn der historisch-politische Hintergrund war sehr heikel. Maria Medici, die seit der Ermordung ihres Gatten 1610 als Regentin fungierte, war von ihrem 1617 mündig gewordenen Sohn Ludwig XIII. aus Paris vertrieben worden und nach einer vorläufigen Aussöhnung 1621 zurückgekehrt. Mit dem Gemäldezyklus wollte sie ihre erneute politische Präsenz demonstrieren. Die schwierige Aufgabe – unter Rücksichtnahme auf die verschiedensten Interessen und der taktvollen Entschärfung der für Maria weniger ruhmreichen Situationen – meisterte Rubens durch eine allegorische Überhöhung der Ereignisse.

Die farblich differenziert angelegten, eigenhändigen Ölskizzen, von denen sich 16 in der Alten Pinakothek befinden, dienten Rubens' Mitarbeitern als Vorlagen für die auszuführenden Gemälde. Mit Ausnahme der „Glücklichen Regierung" (Nr. 30) entstanden alle Münchner Skizzen im Jahre 1622. In der Eremitage in St. Petersburg gibt es weitere Entwürfe für den Zyklus, die jedoch eine frühere Planungsphase dokumentieren, weniger detailliert sind und auch kaum Farbangaben machen.

Bereits zu Rubens' Zeiten wurden die Ölskizzen, mit denen der Meister seine Ideen locker, unmittelbar und frisch auf einer Holztafel festhielt, als Sammlungsobjekte geschätzt. Mittels der Skizze klärte der Künstler seine Bildkonzeption und gab dem Auftraggeber eine

In 1622, Maria de' Medici (1573–1642), Queen of France and the widow of King Henri IV (1553–1610), commissioned Rubens to paint a cycle of 24 large-scale pictures to grace a gallery in the west wing of her newly-built Palais du Luxembourg in Paris. Today, the paintings can be seen in the Louvre. A pendant cycle of 24 works to the glory of her deceased husband was planned for the east wing of the palace, but was never completed.

The commission to celebrate the deeds and events of Maria de' Medici's life was one of the most demanding assignments of Rubens' career, for the politico-historical background was extremely delicate. Maria de' Medici, who had acted as regent on behalf of her son, the future King Louis XIII, since the assassination of her husband in 1610, was driven out of Paris by Louis when he came of age in 1617. In 1621, after a provisional settlement had been reached, she returned to Paris. With this cycle of paintings, she wished to demonstrate her renewed political presence. Rubens accomplished the difficult task of reconciling the many different interests involved and tactfully playing down the less glorious situations in Maria's life by elevating the events to an allegorical plane.

The oil sketches made by Rubens himself in a broad range of colours served as models for the large-scale paintings that were executed with the assistance of his workshop. Sixteen of these sketches are in the Alte Pinakothek. With the exception of "The Happy Reign" (No. 30), all the Munich sketches were made in 1622. A number of other sketches for the cycle are in the Hermitage in St Petersburg. These represent an earlier phase in the planning of the programme, however, and are less detailed and contain fewer indications of coloration.

The oil sketches, in which Rubens recorded his ideas on wood panels in an easy, spontaneous and immediate manner, were already prized as collectors' pieces during the master's lifetime. They served to clarify the artist's visual concepts and to give the client an idea of the pro-

Vorstellung vom auszuführenden Gemälde. An den Münchner Skizzen lassen sich die Veränderungen und Modifikationen der Themen gut ablesen.

Das Programm beginnt mit Szenen aus Kindheit und Erziehung Marias, der Tochter des Großherzogs von Toskana und der Johanna von Österreich. Anschließend folgen die mit ihrer Hochzeit mit Heinrich IV. am 5. Oktober 1600 in Zusammenhang stehenden Darstellungen.

Die erste der hier abgebildeten Ölskizzen schildert Marias Ankunft in Marseille am 3. November 1600. Sie und ihr Gefolge – ihre Begleiterinnen sind ihre Schwester Eleanora von Mantua und ihre Tante Christina, Großherzogin von Toskana – werden von zwei allegorischen Gestalten, der Francia (Frankreich) mit Helm und blauem Umhang und der Massilia, Verkörperung der Stadt Marseille, begrüßt. Das Verdeck der goldenen Prunkgaleere, ein Rundbogen mit bekrönender Laterne und dem Wappen der Medici, bildet den würdigen Rahmen für Maria, darüber schwebt die geflügelte Fama, die mit ihren Trompeten den Ruhm und die Größe des Hauses Medici verkündet. Das Schiff schmückt eine Galionsfigur, die ein Ruder trägt als vorausweisendes Detail auf die Regentschaft Marias. In der unteren Hälfte des Gemäldes sind Neptun und sein Gefolge damit beschäftigt, das Schiff sicher im Hafen anzulegen. Drei Nereiden haben sich untergehakt, bilden eine Kette und befestigen das Tau an einem Pfahl.

posed painting. Comparisons between the Munich sketches and the final versions provide a clear idea of the changes and modifications made to the contents in the course of realizing these works.

The cycle begins with scenes from the childhood and education of Maria de' Medici, who was the daughter of Grand Duke Francesco I of Tuscany and Johanna of Austria. These are followed by depictions related to her wedding to Henri IV on 5 October 1600.

The first of the oil sketches illustrated here shows Maria's arrival in Marseilles on 3 November 1600. She and her companions – her sister, Eleanora of Mantua, and her aunt, Christina, Grand Duchess of Tuscany – are greeted by two allegorical figures: Francia (France), wearing a helmet and blue robe, and Massilia, the personification of the city of Marseilles. The magnificent golden galley, with its round, arched canopy, crowned by a lantern and the crest of the Medicis, forms a fitting setting for Maria. Above her head hovers the winged goddess Fama, who proclaims with her trumpets the fame and glory of the House of Medici. The ship is adorned by a figurehead holding a tiller as an augury of Maria's future regency. In the lower half of the painting, Neptune and his attendants can be seen helping the ship to moor safely in the harbour. Three nereids have linked arms to form a chain and are fixing the rope to a stake.

27 Peter Paul Rubens
(1577 Siegen – 1640 Antwerpen)

Medici-Zyklus:
Die Krönung der Königin

Holz, 54 x 88,4 cm
Inv. Nr. 97

Der Medici-Zyklus besteht hauptsächlich aus hochformatigen Gemälden; eine Ausnahme bilden drei außerordentlich große Breitformate, die im Palais du Luxembourg an der dem Eingang gegenüberliegenden Stirnwand der Galerie und seitlich – diese rahmend – hingen und den inhaltlichen Höhepunkt des Zyklus bilden.

Thematischer Auftakt der drei querformatigen Gemälde war das erste politisch hoch bedeutsame Ereignis für Maria, ihre Krönung am 13. Mai 1610 in St. Denis, womit ihre Regentschaft legitimiert wurde. Bereits am 20. März 1610, vor seinem Aufbruch zur Belagerung Jülichs, hatte Heinrich IV., dem mehrfach der Tod vorhergesagt worden war, die Regentschaft an Maria übertragen, was im vorausgehenden Gemälde geschildert wird.

Die Skizze mit der Krönung zeigt den Augenblick, als Kardinal Joyeuse der knienden Maria die Krone auf das Haupt setzt. Der neben seiner Mutter stehende Dauphin Ludwig wird in die Zeremonie eingebunden, indem er die Krone berührt. Prinzessinnen tragen die lange Schleppe, und hinter dieser Hauptgruppe steht die erste Gemahlin des Königs, Margarethe von Valois, mit ihrem Hofstaat. Da die Ehe mit ihr kinderlos blieb, konnte Heinrich IV. sich scheiden lassen und seine zweite Ehe mit Maria eingehen. Bei der malerischen Rückenfigur handelt es sich um den Herzog von Vendôme, den ältesten Sohn von Heinrich IV. und seiner Mätresse Gabrielle d'Estrées. Maria hatte diesen Mann lange Zeit gefürchtet, und seine hier so auffällige Präsenz ist sicher von politischer Bedeutung. König Heinrich IV. wohnt der Zeremonie auf einer Tribüne im Hintergrund bei. Die allegorische Ausschmückung der Szene ist auf die beiden über Maria schwebenden Genien beschränkt, die „Reichtum" und „Wachstum" versinnbildlichen, während die beiden Hunde im Vordergrund wohl auf die Tugenden Treue und Ergebenheit anspielen.

27 Sir Peter Paul Rubens
(1577 Siegen – 1640 Antwerp)

The Medici Cycle:
The Coronation of the Queen

Wood, 54 x 88.4 cm
Inv. No. 97

The Medici Cycle consists largely of pictures of vertical format. The exceptions are three unusually large horizontal canvases, one of which hung on the end wall of the gallery in the Palais du Luxembourg opposite the entrance. It was flanked on each side by the other two. In terms of their content, these three works form the climax of the series.

Thematically, this trio of paintings begins with a depiction of the first event of major political significance in Maria's life: her coronation on 13 May 1610 in St Denis, at which her powers of regency were legitimized. Henri IV, whose death had been prophesied on many occasions, had conferred these powers on Maria as early as 20 March 1610, prior to his departure to besiege Jülich. This event forms the subject of the previous picture in the series.

The sketch of the coronation shows the moment when Cardinal Joyeuse places the crown on the head of Maria, who is kneeling before him. The Dauphin Louis, standing at his mother's side, is tied into the ceremony by having him touch the crown. Maria's long train is borne by a row of princesses. Standing behind this central group are the king's first wife, Margaret of Valois, and members of the court. Since his marriage to Margaret had remained without offspring, Henri was able to obtain a divorce and marry Maria. The figure seen in a pictorially effective rear view is the Duke of Vendôme, Henri's eldest son by his mistress Gabrielle d'Estrées. For a long time, Maria had feared the duke, and his conspicuous presence on this occasion is certainly of political significance. King Henri IV watches the ceremony from a gallery in the background. The allegorical embellishments to this scene are confined to two genius spirits hovering over Maria, symbolizing "prosperity" and "growth". The two dogs in the foreground are probably an allusion to the virtues of loyalty and devotion.

28 Peter Paul Rubens
(1577 Siegen – 1640 Antwerpen)

Medici-Zyklus:
Apotheose Heinrichs IV.
und Proklamation der Regentschaft

Holz, 54 x 92 cm
Inv. Nr. 102

Gleich im Anschluß an die Krönungsszene werden die dramatischen Ereignisse des darauffolgenden Tages (14. Mai 1610) verbildlicht, die Ermordung Heinrichs IV. und die Übernahme der Staatsgeschäfte durch Maria in Stellvertretung für ihren Sohn Ludwig XIII. Das für die Stirnwand im Zentrum der Galerie im Palais du Luxembourg vorgesehene Gemälde stellt in der Vereinigung beider Ereignisse den Höhe- und gleichzeitig Wendepunkt im Leben der Königin in symbolischer Umdeutung dar: Die Ermordung Heinrichs IV. wird mit seiner Apotheose gleichgesetzt, die Proklamation ihrer Regentschaft als Huldigung vor Maria veranschaulicht.

Bei seiner Apotheose, der Vergöttlichung, auf der linken Bildhälfte der Skizze wird Heinrich IV. von Saturn, dem Gott der Zeit, und Jupiter zum Himmel emporgetragen und von Herkules, Minerva, Merkur und Venus in Empfang genommen. Dieser Aufnahme in den Olymp angemessen erscheinen Lorbeerkranz und seine antike Rüstung, die ihn wie einen römischen Kaiser aussehen lassen. Den Himmel überfängt ein weiter Bogen mit den Sternkreiszeichen Löwe, Jungfrau und Waage. Den Tod Heinrichs betrauern ausdrucksvoll zwei Victorien, eine ringt die Hände, die andere rauft sich die Haare. Am Bildrand entflieht eine dämonische Gestalt mit Fackel und Dolch, die Personifikation der Zwietracht. Diese Figur wurde nicht im Galeriegemälde ausgeführt, da man die damals umlaufenden Gerüchte fürchtete, Maria sei in die Ermordung ihres Mannes verwickelt gewesen. Statt dessen malte Rubens im Gemälde für das Palais du Luxembourg an dieser Stelle eine unverfänglichere feuerspeiende Schlange, die von einem Pfeil durchbohrt wird.

Die rechte Bildhälfte zeigt Maria in schwarzer Witwentracht und mit Schleier, majestätisch thronend unter einem opulenten Baldachin mit gedrehten Säulen, die als Verweis auf den Thron Salomons auf die Weisheit der Königin anspielen. Umgeben ist sie von Minerva, der Göttin der klugen Kriegsführung und von Prudentia, der

28 Sir Peter Paul Rubens
(1577 Siegen – 1640 Antwerp)

The Medici Cycle:
The Apotheosis of Henri IV
and the Proclamation of the Regency

Wood, 54 x 92 cm
Inv. No. 102

Immediately after the coronation scene, the dramatic events of the following day (14 May 1610) are portrayed: the assassination of Henri IV and the assumption of the affairs of state by Maria in her role as regent for her son Louis XIII. The painting, which was foreseen for the end wall in the centre of the gallery in the Palais du Luxembourg, unites these two events and thus represents in symbolic form the apogee and the turning point in the life of the queen. The assassination of Henri IV is equated with his apotheosis; and the proclamation of Maria's regency is depicted as a homage to the queen.

In the apotheosis or deification of the king, shown in the left-hand half of the sketch, Henri is borne up to heaven by Jupiter and Saturn, the god of time, where he is welcomed by Hercules, Minerva, Mercury and Venus. In keeping with this reception on Olympus are the laurel wreath and the king's classical armour, which lend him the appearance of a Roman emperor. Spanned over the heavens is a broad arch in which three signs of the zodiac can be seen: Leo, Virgo and Libra. Two personifications of victory bewail Henri's death, one wringing her hands in anguish, the other tearing her hair. On the left-hand edge of the picture, a demonic figure with a torch and a dagger can be seen slinking off – the personification of discord. This was omitted from the final version of the painting, for fear of rumours that Maria herself might be involved in the murder of her husband. In the painting that hung in the Palais du Luxembourg, Rubens replaced this figure with a less equivocal depiction of a fire-breathing serpent pierced by an arrow.

The right-hand half of the picture portrays Maria de' Medici, wearing the black mourning robes and veil of a widow, seated majestically on her throne beneath an opulent baldachin with twisted columns – a reference to the throne of Solomon and thus to the wisdom of the queen. She is flanked by Minerva, the goddess of the wise conduct of war, and by Prudentia, the personifica-

Personifikation der Klugheit. Francia überreicht Maria einen Globus und Providentia (Vorsehung) übergibt ihr das Staatsruder, beides Zeichen der Regierungsgewalt. Die Königin, die Hände bescheiden vor die Brust gelegt, greift nicht selbst danach, sondern Prudentia nimmt sie für sie in Empfang. Stellvertretend für den Staat huldigt eine Gruppe von knienden Höflingen der Königin.

tion of wisdom. Francia hands Maria the orb, and Providentia (providence) hands her the helm of state, both tokens of governmental power. The queen, her hands folded modestly on her breast, does not reach out to take these emblems of authority herself. Prudentia accepts them on her behalf. Representing the state, a group of kneeling courtiers pays homage to the queen.

29 Peter Paul Rubens
(1577 Siegen – 1640 Antwerpen)

Medici-Zyklus: Der Götterrat

Holz, 55 x 92 cm
Inv. Nr. 103

29 Sir Peter Paul Rubens
(1577 Siegen – 1640 Antwerp)

The Medici Cycle: The Council of Gods

Wood, 55 x 92 cm
Inv. No. 103

Das dritte und letzte der großen querformatigen Wandbilder an prominenter Stelle der Medici-Galerie hat den „Götterrat" zum Thema, der auf einen politischen Schachzug Marias Bezug nimmt. Kurz nach Übernahme der Regentschaft plante Maria eine Allianz der beiden großen katholischen Monarchien Spanien und Frankreich, die durch eine Doppelhochzeit – ihres Sohnes Ludwig XIII. mit der spanischen Infantin Anna von Österreich sowie des spanischen Thronfolgers Philipp mit Marias Tochter Elisabeth – 1615 besiegelt werden sollte.

Die Skizze zum Götterrat zeigt die im Olymp versammelten Götter, die unter Jupiters Vorsitz über die Hochzeiten beraten. Der Friede als weibliche Gestalt mit Schlangenstab tritt zusammen mit der Eintracht, die mit einem Pfeilbündel in den Armen kniet, vor den Götterrat, um die Zustimmung zur friedenssichernden Doppelhochzeit einzuholen. Mit der Gestalt des Friedens ist gleichzeitig Maria gemeint, was im ausgeführten Gemälde durch die Gesichtszüge deutlicher wird. Juno als Beschützerin der Ehe und Amor spannen in Anspielung auf die Doppelhochzeit zwei Taubenpaare unter ein goldenes Joch vor einen zweigeteilten Globus, der die beiden zu vereinigenden Länder symbolisiert. Einige der Götter lagern in der linken Bildhälfte auf einer Art „Bank", womit Rubens auf einfallsreiche Weise eine am Bestimmungsort vorhandene Türöffnung einbezieht. Unter ihnen ist lediglich Pan mit seinen Bocksfüßen zu identifizieren.

In der rechten Bildhälfte vertreiben Apoll, bewaffnet mit Bogen und Pfeilköcher, und Minerva mit Lanze und Schild die Verkörperungen der Laster sowie andere mißgünstige Dämonen: Die Frau ganz rechts mit Fackel stellt wohl Discordia (Zwietracht) dar, die kniende mit Maske Fraus (Betrug), der Mann in Rückenansicht mit Schlange Furor (Raserei). Mars, in Rüstung und mit gezücktem Schwert, wird von Venus sanft aber bestimmt daran gehindert, den Dämonen zu Hilfe zu eilen. Über dieser dramatischen und dunklen Szene

The third and last of the large, horizontal-format paintings given pride of place in the Medici Gallery has as its subject "The Council of the Gods". The picture makes reference to a political gambit of Maria's. Soon after assuming power as regent, she planned an alliance between the two great Catholic monarchies, Spain and France, which was to be sealed in 1615 by a double marriage: between her son Louis XIII and the Spanish Infanta, Anna of Austria, and between Philip, the heir to the Spanish throne, and Maria's daughter Elisabeth.

The sketch for "The Council of Gods" shows the immortals assembled on Olympus under the leadership of Jupiter, deliberating on the weddings. The female figures of Peace, holding the caduceus, and Concord, kneeling with a sheaf of arrows in her arms, petition the gods to consent to the marriage plans, which would guarantee peace. Peace is also a portrayal of Maria, a detail that is brought out more clearly in the facial features in the final version of the painting. Juno, the protectress of marriage, and Amor harness two pairs of doves in a golden yoke on a globe divided into two parts – an evident reference to the double marriage and the two countries to be united. In the left-hand half of the picture, some of the gods can be seen reclining on what looks like a bench or ledge. This was an imaginative device used by Rubens to accommodate an existing door opening in the wall where the picture was to be hung. The only identifiable figure among this group is Pan with his goat's feet.

In the right-hand half of the painting, Apollo, armed with a bow and a quiver of arrows, and Minerva, with lance and shield, drive out the personifications of vice and other malevolent demons. The female figure with a torch on the extreme right is probably Discordia. The kneeling figure with a mask is Deceit, and the man with his back turned to the observer, holding a snake, is Fury. Mars, seen in his armour with a drawn sword, is being restrained, gently yet firmly, by Venus from dashing to the aid of the demons. Over this dark and dramatic scene

fährt Luna mit ihrem Himmelsgespann. Durch die Lichtführung werden die beiden Bereiche – links der himmlische, als Ort von Harmonie und Eintracht, und rechts unten der dämonische – voneinander getrennt.

Für die Figuren hat Rubens in dieser Skizze Anleihen bei antiken Skulpturen gemacht, vor allem der Apoll als Zitat des Apoll von Belvedere fällt in diesem Zusammenhang auf.

rides Luna in her heavenly chariot. The two parts of this picture – on the left, the heavenly realm of harmony and concord, and at the bottom right, the demonic depths – are clearly separated and contrasted in their lighting.

Rubens drew on a number of models from Classical sculpture for the portrayal of the figures of this work. Apollo, for example, is clearly based on the Apollo Belvedere.

30 Peter Paul Rubens
(1577 Siegen – 1640 Antwerpen)

Medici-Zyklus: Die glückliche Regierung

Holz, 64,8 x 50,8 cm
Inv. Nr. 100

30 Sir Peter Paul Rubens
(1577 Siegen – 1640 Antwerp)

The Medici Cycle: The Happy Reign

Wood, 64.8 x 50.8 cm
Inv. No. 100

Die Bildfolge der zweiten Längswand in der Galerie im Palais du Luxembourg war Maria Medicis Regentschaft gewidmet, wobei auch ihre Auseinandersetzungen mit dem Sohn – allerdings entschärft – thematisiert werden. Bezeichnend dafür ist, daß das Gemälde mit ihrer „Flucht aus Paris" 1625 nachträglich auf ihren Wunsch wieder entfernt wurde. Ihr 1617 mündig gewordener Sohn Ludwig XIII. hatte sie aus Paris vertrieben. Heute existiert zu diesem wenig ruhmreichen Ereignis nur noch die Ölskizze in München. Als Ersatz malte Rubens „Die glückliche Regierung", ein Bild das wegen seiner brillanten Farbigkeit und des flüssigen Malstils einer der prächtigsten des Zyklus ist. Er vollendete dieses Gemälde 1625 vor Ort in Paris, kurz vor der feierlichen Eröffnung der Galerie.

Das Thema hält Rubens in einem Brief als „Glück der Regierung der Königin und Blüte des Königreichs von Frankreich" fest, wobei er die Darstellung selbst folgendermaßen beschreibt: „... zusammen mit dem Wiederaufleben der Wissenschaft und Künste durch die Freigiebigkeit und den Glanz ihrer Majestät, welche, auf einem Thron sitzend, in ihrer Hand eine Waage faßt und durch ihre Weisheit und ihren Gerechtigkeitssinn die Welt im Gleichgewicht hält".

Die Skizze zeigt Maria thronend unter einem üppig mit Fruchtgirlande und Kranz geschmückten Baldachin. In der Rechten hält sie als Sinnbild der gerechten Herrschaft eine Waage. Minerva steht neben ihr, die Personifikationen von Großmut und Überfluß überbringen Blumen, Früchte und Schmuck, die von vier Putten als Verkörperungen von Kunst und Wissenschaft – Pinsel, Panflöte, Buch, Winkel und Zirkel verweisen darauf – in Empfang genommen werden, während Unwissenheit, Verleumdung und Neid gefesselt und besiegt zu Füßen Marias liegen. Einer der Putten zieht Ignorantia am Eselsohr. Links führt Saturn, der Gott der Zeit und Repräsentant des Goldenen Zeitalters, Francia vor die Königin. Zwei Genien verkünden mit ihren Posaunen

The sequence of pictures along the second long wall of the gallery in the Palais du Luxembourg was dedicated to themes from Maria de' Medici's regency. These also included her dispute with her son, although this was toned down in form. Of significance in this context is the fact that the painting of "The Queen's Departure from Paris" was subsequently removed in 1625 at her request. Her son, Louis XIII, who came of age in 1617, had forced her to flee the capital. Today, the only work commemorating this inglorious episode is the oil sketch in Munich. As a substitute for this picture in Maria's gallery, Rubens painted "The Happy Reign", the brilliant coloration and fluent brushwork of which make it one of the most magnificent paintings in the cycle. Rubens executed this work in 1625 in Paris, completing it shortly before the festive opening of the gallery.

In a letter, he describes the subject of this painting as "the happy rule of the queen and the flowering of the Kingdom of France", and goes on to refer to the actual depiction in the following terms: "... with the revival of the sciences and the arts through the liberality and the splendour of Her Majesty, who sits upon a shining throne and holds a pair of scales in her hands, keeping the world in equilibrium by her prudence and equity".

The sketch shows Maria enthroned on high beneath a canopy richly decorated with a garland of fruit and a wreath. In her right hand, she holds a pair of scales as a symbol of just rule. Beside her stands Minerva, and the personifications of generosity and abundance hand her flowers, fruit and jewels. These are accepted on behalf of the queen by four putti who represent the arts and sciences, as the paintbrushes, pan-pipes, the book, set square and compasses indicate. Ignorance, calumny and envy have been overcome and lie in fetters at Maria's feet. One of the putti can be seen pulling Ignorantia's donkey's ear. On the left of the picture, Saturn, the god of time and representative of the Golden Age, leads Francia before the queen. Two genius spirits proclaim

den Ruhm der französischen Königin. Maria ist auf diese Weise selbst zum Sinnbild für Gerechtigkeit und zur Verheißung eines neuen Goldenen Zeitalters geworden. Als wiedergekehrte Göttin der Gerechtigkeit kann sie auch mit entblößter Brust dargestellt werden, was ansonsten dem Porträt einer Königin ohne allegorischer Überhöhung nicht angemessen wäre.

Das Programm zum gesamten Zyklus entwarf Rubens in Absprache und Zusammenarbeit mit Maria, ihrem geistlichen Ratgeber Claude de Maugis, Abbé von Saint-Ambroise, dem Humanisten Nicolas-Claude Fabri de Peiresc und dem Kardinal Richelieu. Obwohl zeitgenössische Beschreibungen, Kommentare und Deutungen vorhanden sind und dabei helfen die Szenen zu entschlüsseln, bleiben manche Fragen offen.

the glory of the French queen with their trumpets. Maria herself thus becomes a symbol of justice and of the promise of a new Golden Age. As the goddess of justice returned to earth, she may be portrayed with a bared breast, something that without allegorical sublimation, would not have been appropriate in a portrait of a queen.

The programme for the entire cycle was drawn up by Rubens in consultation and collaboration with Maria de' Medici, with her spiritual adviser Claude de Maugis, the Abbé of Saint-Ambroise, with the humanist and connoisseur of Classical antiquity Nicolas-Claude Fabri de Peiresc and with Cardinal Richelieu. Although contemporary descriptions, commentaries and interpretations still exist to help decipher the scenes, a number of questions remain unanswered.

31 Peter Paul Rubens
(1577 Siegen – 1640 Antwerpen)

Polderlandschaft mit einer Kuhherde

Holz, 81 x 106 cm
Inv. Nr. 322

31 Sir Peter Paul Rubens
(1577 Siegen – 1640 Antwerp)

Polder Landscape with Herd of Cows

Wood, 81 x 106 cm
Inv. No. 322

Auf einer Weide, von einem Gewässer und Bäumen gesäumt, sieht man eine Herde von elf Kühen sowie zwei Mägde und einen Knecht beim Melken. Der aus dem Anfang unseres Jahrhunderts stammende Titel „Polderlandschaft" trifft eigentlich nicht zu, denn es handelt sich nicht um dem Meer abgerungenes, künstlich geschaffenes Land, sondern offensichtlich um eine sanft geformte, natürliche Landschaft. Die Weide im Vordergrund scheint wie eine „Insel" von links in das Bild geschoben, ein Eindruck, der durch den Zufälligkeit suggerierenden Bildausschnitt verstärkt wird: Rechts fungieren zwei abgestorbene, bildeinwärts gerichtete Baumstämme als rahmendes Motiv, während am linken Bildrand eine Kuh unvermittelt abgeschnitten wird. Den Abschluß nach hinten bildet eine Baumreihe, die lediglich links den Blick bis zum hohen Horizont freigibt.

Die Kühe, die in den unterschiedlichsten Körperdrehungen und -wendungen und bei verschiedenen Tätigkeiten gezeigt werden – liegend, stehend, wiederkäuend, grasend, trinkend, pissend, sich an einer anderen Kuh reibend – sind versatzstückartig ins Bild gesetzt und kehren in anderen Landschaften von Rubens wieder.

Die ruhige Stimmung des Gemäldes ist Ergebnis von Farbe und Lichtführung. Der sanfte Schein der untergehenden Sonne bricht von hinten durch die Baumreihen, so daß sich die Stämme konturiert abheben und die Wipfel in silbriges Licht getaucht werden. Auf der ruhigen Wasseroberfläche spiegeln sich die Bäume, am Himmel ziehen dunkle Regenwolken ab. Die sehr differenziert eingesetzten Grün- und Brauntöne ergeben eine verhaltene Farbigkeit, aus der als einziger Farbfleck das rote Hemd des Knechts heraussticht.

Rubens begann Mitte des zweiten Jahrzehnts sich mit der Landschaft als eigenständiger Gattung zu beschäftigen. In der Münchner „Polderlandschaft", die um 1618/20 enstanden ist, wird im additiven Vorgehen seine Suche nach Formulierungen noch deutlich erkennbar.

Two maids and a farm labourer can be seen milking a herd of 11 cows in a pasture bordered by a pond and trees. The title, "Polder Landscape", which dates from the beginning of the 20th century, is not strictly accurate. The land is not an area that has been claimed from the sea, but evidently a gently moulded natural landscape. The pasture in the foreground seems almost like an "island" pushed into the picture from the left, an impression that is reinforced by the seemingly random segment of the landscape shown. On the right, the view is framed by the leaning stumps of two dead trees, whilst on the left-hand edge a cow is simply cut off in the middle. To the rear, the scene is closed by a screen of trees. Only on the left is there an open view to a distant, high horizon line. The cows are shown in all kinds of positions, twisting and turning this way and that and engaged in a variety of activities: standing, lying on the ground, grazing, chewing the cud, drinking, urinating and rubbing themselves against other cows. They are inserted into the picture as standard figures and reoccur in other landscapes by Rubens.

The painting owes its peaceful mood to the coloration and lighting. The soft rays of the setting sun shine from the rear through the rows of trees, bringing out the contours of their trunks and bathing their tips in a silvery light. The forms of the trees are reflected on the calm surface of the water. The dark rain clouds in the sky recede. The subtly varied use of green and brown tones creates a subdued coloration, against which the sole spot of colour, the red smock of the farm labourer, stands out vividly.

Rubens began painting landscapes as an independent genre in the middle of the second decade of the 17th century. In the Munich "Polder Landscape", dating from c. 1618/20, he uses an additive system of composition, in which his search for a satisfactory means of formulation is still clearly recognizable.

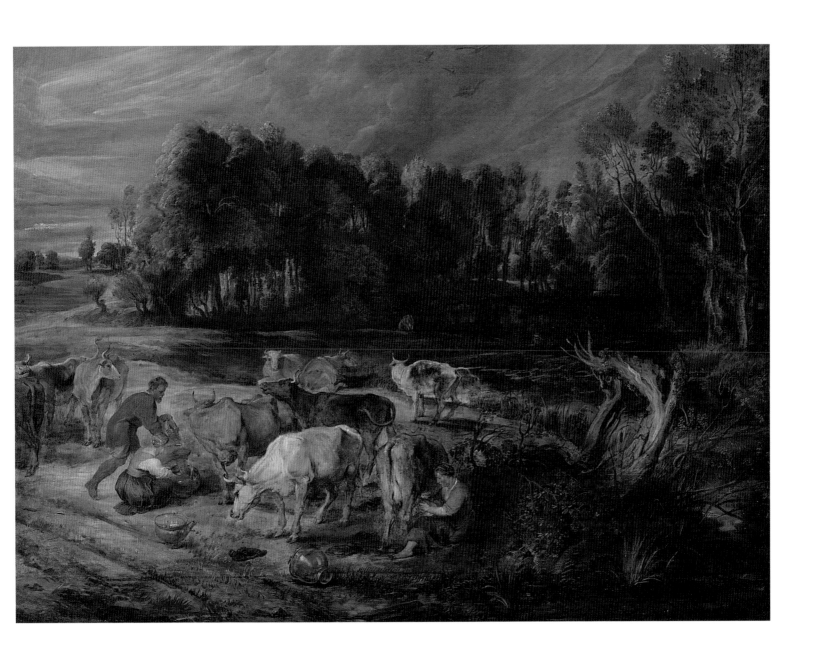

32 Anthonis van Dyck
(1599 Antwerpen – 1641 London)

Selbstbildnis

Leinwand, 82,5 x 70,2 cm
Inv. Nr. 405

32 Sir Anthony van Dyck
(1599 Antwerp – 1641 London)

Self-Portrait

Canvas, 82.5 x 70.2 cm
Inv. No. 405

Das Aussehen Van Dycks, der sich in diesem Brustbildnis als eleganten jungen Mann darstellt, stimmt in großen Zügen mit einer überlieferten Beschreibung des italienischen Kunstschriftstellers Giovanni Pietro Bellori (1672) überein: „Er war noch ein Jüngling, dem kaum der Bart sproß. Neben seiner Jugend zeichneten ihn Ernst und Bescheidenheit sowie der Adel seiner Erscheinung aus, obwohl er klein von Gestalt war. Sein Auftreten glich mehr dem eines Adeligen als eines Bürgerlichen; auch fiel er durch seine erlesene Kleidung auf. Im Atelier von Rubens im Umgang mit Edelleuten vertraut geworden und auch auf Grund seiner natürlichen Vorzüge wollte er die Aufmerksamkeit auf sich lenken. So kleidete er sich nicht nur in Seide, sondern schmückte seinen Hut mit Federn und trug quer über die Brust eine goldene Kette ...“

Sehr aufmerksam, geradezu eindringlich schaut Van Dyck den Betrachter an, den Kopf unmerklich gesenkt. Der intensive Blick verrät das Selbstbewußtsein des jugendlichen Künstlers, dessen Begabung frühe Bewunderung fand. Die elegante schwarze Kleidung unterstreicht seinen gesellschaftlichen Anspruch ebenso wie die goldene Kette, die über der linken Schulter sichtbar wird. Es scheint jene zu sein, die ihm Herzog Ferdinando Gonzaga 1622 in Mantua als Zeichen seiner Anerkennung schenkte. Die Kette wurde erst später im Zuge einer allseitigen Anstückung und Überarbeitung des um 1621 begonnenen Gemäldes eingefügt, wobei Van Dyck auch die Haltung von Arm und Hand, die ursprünglich an den Kragen faßte, veränderte.

Zwei weitere Porträts des jugendlichen Malers in New York und St. Petersburg, allerdings als Kniestücke konzipiert, hängen engstens mit dem Münchner Gemälde zusammen, das wohl als Vorlage gedient hat.

Van Dyck's appearance in this half-length portrait, in which he depicts himself as an elegant young man, corresponds broadly to the description of him by the Italian art historian and theoretician Giovanni Pietro Bellori (1672): "He was still a young man, whose beard had scarcely started to grow. In addition to his youth, he was remarkable for his seriousness and modesty and for the nobility of his appearance, even though he was slight of stature. His bearing resembled that of an aristocrat rather than a commoner; and he was conspicuous for his exquisite clothing. Accustomed to dealings with the nobility from Rubens' workshop, and by virtue of his natural superiority, he was determined to attract attention to himself. He therefore attired himself not merely in silk, but adorned his hat with feathers and wore a gold chain upon his breast ..."

In this self-portrait, Van Dyck regards the observer attentively, with a note of insistence, his head lowered imperceptibly. The intense gaze reveals the self-assurance of a young artist whose gifts had been recognized at an early age. The elegant black attire lends weight to his social aspirations, as does the gold chain visible over his left shoulder. It is probably the chain that had been presented to him in Mantua in 1622 by Duke Ferdinando Gonzaga as a token of his recognition. The chain was added at a later date when the picture was reworked and extended on all four edges. In the course of these alterations, Van Dyck also changed the position of the arm and hand, which in the original version of the portrait, begun c. 1621, was shown grasping the collar.

Two other self-portraits by the young painter – knee-length studies, now in New York and St Petersburg – are closely related to the Munich work, which probably served as a model.

33 Anthonis van Dyck
(1599 Antwerpen – 1641 London)

Bildnis des Bildhauers Georg Petel

Leinwand, 73,3 x 57,2 cm
Signiert Mitte links: V. Dyck. f.
Inv. Nr. 406

33 Sir Anthony van Dyck
(1599 Antwerp – 1641 London)

Portrait of the Sculptor Georg Petel

Canvas, 73.3 x 57.2 cm
Signed middle left: V. Dyck. f.
Inv. No. 406

Das Gemälde zeigt den Bildhauer Georg Petel in Halbfigur. Den Kopf ins Dreiviertelprofil gewendet, blickt er weit nach links, was dem Bildnis Lebendigkeit und Spontaneität verleiht. Wie bei anderen Porträts von Van Dyck ist Georg Petel in leichter Untersicht gezeigt. Den um den Oberkörper und Arme geschlungenen dunklen Umhang hält er vor der Brust mit der aus dem Stoff auftauchenden linken Hand zusammen. Im bildfüllenden Porträt werden weder Angaben zum Raum noch Hinweise auf die künstlerische Tätigkeit des Dargestellten gegeben. Das gesamte Interesse Van Dycks ist auf das ausdrucksstarke, lebhafte Gesicht Petels konzentriert.

Der 1601/02 im oberbayerischen Weilheim geborene Georg Petel war einer der bedeutendsten deutschen Bildhauer zu Anfang des 17. Jahrhunderts. Nach seiner Ausbildung bereiste der Künstler, der sich auf Elfenbeinfiguren spezialisiert hatte, die Niederlande, Frankreich und Italien. Bei diesen Reisen dürfte er sowohl Anthonis van Dyck als auch Peter Paul Rubens kennengelernt haben, denen er freundschaftlich verbunden blieb. Petel starb 1634 im Alter von nur 33 Jahren in Augsburg, wo er seit 1625 als Meister tätig war.

Das von Van Dyck signierte Gemälde ist vermutlich 1628 während eines Antwerpenaufenthalts von Petel entstanden. Die Identifizierung des Dargestellten ermöglicht ein seitenverkehrter Stich in Joachim von Sandrarts 1675 erschienener „Teutschen Academie der Edlen Bau-, Bild- und Mahlerey-Künste". Sandrart verwendete als Vorlage das Münchner Gemälde, das sich seinerzeit in seinem Besitz befand. Noch 1698 wird es im Nachlaß seines Großneffen aufgezählt, aus dem es wahrscheinlich Kurfürst Johann Wilhelm für die Düsseldorfer Galerie erwarb, und von dort gelangte es später nach München.

The painting is a half-length portrait of the sculptor Georg Petel. The head is turned three-quarter face towards the observer, which gives the work its liveliness and spontaneity. As in other portraits by Van Dyck, the subject is viewed from slightly below. With his left hand peeping out of the dark material and clasped before his breast, Petel holds together the edges of the robe draped about his arms and the upper part of his body. The portrait fills the whole canvas, and there are neither details of the surrounding space nor any references to Petel's artistic work. Van Dyck's entire interest is concentrated on the lively, expressive physiognomy.

Georg Petel, born in Weilheim, Upper Bavaria, in 1601/02, was one of the most important German sculptors of the early 17th century. After completing his apprenticeship, the artist, who had specialized in ivory figure carving, travelled about the Low Countries, France and Italy. It was presumably in the course of these journeys that he made the acquaintance of Van Dyck and Rubens, with both of whom he maintained a close friendship. In 1634, at the early age of 33, Petel died in Augsburg, where he had worked as a master since 1625.

Van Dyck's signed portrait was probably painted in 1628 when Petel was staying in Antwerp. The identification of the subject was made on the basis of a reverse-image engraving in Joachim von Sandrart's "Teutsche Academie der Edlen Bau-, Bild- und Mahlerey-Künste", which appeared in 1675. Sandrart, who was then the owner of the Petel portrait, took it as a model for his engraving. As late as 1698, it was listed as belonging to the estate of his grand-nephew, from which Elector Johann Wilhelm of the Palatinate evidently acquired it for the Düsseldorf Gallery. From there it was later removed to Munich.

34 Anthonis van Dyck
(1599 Antwerpen – 1641 London)

Bildnis des Malers
Theodor Rombouts

Holz, 122,9 x 90,8 cm
Inv. Nr. 603

34 Sir Anthony van Dyck
(1599 Antwerp – 1641 London)

Portrait of the Painter
Theodor Rombouts

Wood, 122.9 x 90.8 cm
Inv. No. 603

Das halbfigurige Porträt zeigt den Antwerpener Historien- und Genremaler Theodor Rombouts (1597–1637). Auf einem fast bildparallel gestellten Stuhl sitzend, ruht sein rechter Unterarm auf der Lehne, den linken Arm hat er raumgreifend in die Hüfte gestützt, und so wendet Rombouts sich mit einer leichten Drehung dem Betrachter zu. Gekleidet ist er in vornehme spanische Tracht. Vom einfarbigen braunen Hintergrund und der schwarzen Kleidung heben sich nur der Kopf, gerahmt von der hellen Halskrause, und die Hände mit den weißen Manschetten ab. Links im Hintergrund ist eine Säule angedeutet, und auf einem kleinen Tischchen neben dem Stuhl liegen eine antike Büste und eine Zeichnung. Selbstbewußt blickt der Maler den Betrachter an, seine Körperwendung verleiht dem Porträt eine gewisse Unmittelbarkeit.

In der selbstsicheren Pose, kostbaren Kleidung, der nobilitierenden Säule und den Attributen manifestiert sich der vom Dargestellten beanspruchte gesellschaftliche Rang. So stammen die Attribute nicht mehr aus dem handwerklichen Bereich des Malers, sondern zeigen ihn als Kenner und Besitzer von Kunstwerken. Der Künstler, der sich aus dem Stand des gewöhnlichen Handwerkers erhoben hatte, sah sich als Mitglied einer gebildeten, gesellschaftlichen Elite von nahezu aristokratischem Rang. Dieses Selbstverständnis und der entsprechende Bildnistypus, der hier zur Anwendung kommt, fand vor allem durch Van Dycks Porträtstichsammlung der „Iconographie" Verbreitung (vgl. unter Nr. 35).

Das Rombouts-Porträt und sein Gegenstück – Ehefrau mit Tochter (Nr. 35) – wurden erst in der zweiten Hälfte des 19. Jahrhunderts aufgrund älterer Inventareinträge als zusammengehörig erkannt und richtig identifiziert. Nach Malstil und Alter der Dargestellten entstanden beide Gemälde um 1632.

Theodor Rombouts (1597–1637) was an Antwerp painter of history and genre scenes. This half-length portrait shows him seated on a chair set almost at right-angles to the picture plane, his right lower arm resting on the arm of the chair. His left arm, supported on his hip, extends into space. With a slight rotation of his body, Rombouts turns to address the observer. He wears the Spanish attire of a distinguished person. Only his head and his hands, framed by the light lace collar and the white cuffs, stand out against the monochrome brown ground and the black clothing. In the background on the left is the outline of a column, and on a small table next to the chair are a Classical bust and a drawing. Rombouts looks at the observer with a confident expression. The turning of the body also gives this portrait a certain immediacy and directness.

The self-assured pose, the rich attire, the column, which lends a note of nobility, and the other attributes all testify to the subject's claims to social standing. Hence the attributes are not taken from the artist's workshop, but show him to be a connoisseur of the arts and a collector. The artist, who has raised himself above the level of a common craftsman, regarded himself as a member of an educated, social élite of almost aristocratic rank. This expression of self-assurance, combined with the type of portrait used here, had been made familiar through the collection of portrait engravings in Van Dyck's "Iconography" (cf. No. 35).

The Rombouts portrait and its pendant, the portrait of his wife and their daughter (No. 35), were correctly identified and seen in relationship to each other only in the second half of the 19th century on the strength of references in older inventories. Judging by the style of painting and the age of the subjects, the two portraits date from c. 1632.

35 Anthonis van Dyck
(1599 Antwerpen – 1641 London)

Bildnis der Gemahlin des Theodor Rombouts und ihrer Tochter

Holz, 122,8 x 90,7 cm
Inv. Nr. 599

Anna van Thielen, Gemahlin des Theodor Rombouts (Nr. 34), wird zusammen mit ihrer Tochter Anna Maria (geb. 1628) porträtiert. Das kleine Mädchen steht links neben der Mutter, hat deren Arm umfaßt und schmiegt sich an sie. Den Kopf wendet es aus dem Bild schauend weit nach links. Die Mutter, ungerührt von dieser liebevollen Geste, sitzt sehr aufrecht und blickt den Betrachter mit erhobenem und kaum merklich zur Seite geneigten Kopf an. Die leichte Untersicht vermittelt von der Dargestellten einen kühlen, fast arroganten Eindruck. Das Porträt ist als Pendant zu Theodor Rombouts gestaltet. Seine Gemahlin sitzt ebenfalls auf einem schräg in den Raum gestellten Stuhl, der aber nach links ausgerichtet ist, so daß sich die Ehepartner gegenübersitzen. Wie ihr Mann ist Anna van Thielen aufwendig gekleidet. Sie trägt ein weißes Hemd und Brusttuch, darüber ein Kleid mit goldbesticktem Mieder, gepufften Ärmeln, weißen Spitzenmanschetten und einem breiten Kragen mit Spitzenbordüre. Im Goldschmuck und der reichen Kleidung drückt sich ihr gesellschaftlicher Status und Selbstbewußtsein aus. Auch die Säule als Würdeformel im neutral gehaltenen Hintergrund fehlt nicht.

Die beiden Rombouts-Bildnisse sind farblich einander angeglichen, bei der Frau sorgt das rote Kleid der Tochter für einen frischen Akzent im insgesamt zurückhaltenden, dunklen Farbton des Gemäldes. Die Malweise des bräunlichen Hintergrunds mit seinen flüchtigen, transparenten Strichen kontrastiert zur sorgfältigen Malweise von Gesichtern, Gewändern und Händen, auf die durch dieses Mittel die Aufmerksamkeit des Betrachters gelenkt wird.

Mit dem Bildnispaar der Rombouts' gelang Van Dyck die Verbindung eines Künstlerbildnisses mit einem Familienporträt, das er auf zwei Einzeltafeln verteilte. Die Figur der kleinen Tochter verschleift die Grenze zwischen dem Ehepaarbild in Gegenstücken und dem Familienbild als Gesamtdarstellung. Aus dem Alter des Mädchens von etwa drei bis vier Jahren läßt sich auf

35 Sir Anthony van Dyck
(1599 Antwerp – 1641 London)

Portrait of the Wife of the Painter Theodor Rombouts and Their Daughter

Wood, 122.8 x 90.7 cm
Inv. No. 599

Anna van Thielen, the wife of Theodor Rombouts (No. 34), is portrayed with their daughter Anna Maria (born 1628). The young girl stands on the left of the picture, pressing herself against her mother's side and holding her arm. The child's gaze is turned to the far left. Her mother, unmoved by this display of affection, sits upright on her chair looking directly at the observer, her head held erect and bent almost imperceptibly to one side. The view of the subject, slightly from below, creates a cool, almost arrogant impression. This portrait was conceived as a pendant to that of the painter Theodor Rombouts. Like him, Rombouts' wife is also portrayed seated on a chair, set at an angle to the picture plane, but turned to the left in this case, so that the couple face each other.

Like her husband, Anna van Thielen is elaborately dressed. She wears a white chemise and tucker beneath a dress with a gold embroidered bodice, puffed sleeves, white lace cuffs and a broad collar with lace edging. Her gold jewellery and rich attire are expressions of her social standing and self-assurance. Even the column behind her is a cipher of dignity in an otherwise neutral background.

The two Rombouts portraits are matched in their coloration. In that of the wife, the red dress of the daughter provides a brighter accent in a picture of generally subdued, dark tones. The brushwork of the brownish background, painted transparently with swift strokes, is contrasted with the meticulous manner in which the faces, the clothes and the hands are depicted; and it is to these that the viewer's attention is directed.

With his pendant paintings of the Rombouts, Van Dyck succeeded in uniting the individual portrait of an artist with family portraiture, divided between two panels. The little daughter serves to blur the borders between pendant pictures of a married couple on the one hand and a group depiction of a family on the other. The young girl is about three or four years old, which helps

eine Datierung um 1632 schließen, was auch mit der spontanen Malweise übereinstimmt.

Van Dycks Ruhm gründet vor allem auf seinen vornehmen, eleganten und zurückhaltenden Porträts, die offensichtlich den Vorstellungen und Repräsentationsansprüchen sowohl der höfischen als auch der bürgerlichen Auftraggeber entsprachen. In dem Kupferstichwerk „Icones principum virorum", der sogenannten „Iconographie", stellte er die Bildnisse berühmter Persönlichkeiten seiner Zeit zusammen. Die Herrscher, Feldherrn, Künstler und Gelehrten, die nach seinen Vorlagen gestochen wurden, zeigen jene distanzierte und überlegene Haltung, die seine gemalten Porträts kennzeichnet.

to date the work to c. 1632. This is corroborated by the spontaneous brushwork of the painting.

Van Dyck's fame is based largely on his distinguished, elegant, restrained portraiture, which evidently met the expectations and representational needs of both his aristocratic and middle-class patrons. In the copperplate engravings contained in his "Icones principum virorum", known as the "Iconography", he made a collection of the portraits of famous people of his age. The engravings of rulers, generals, artists and scholars made from his drafts reveal the same detached, superior bearing as is found in his painted portraits.

36 Anthonis van Dyck
(1599 Antwerpen – 1641 London)

Beweinung Christi

Leinwand, 203,5 x 156,3 cm
Inv. Nr. 404

36 Sir Anthony van Dyck
(1599 Antwerp – 1641 London)

Lamentation of Christ

Canvas, 203.5 x 156.3 cm
Inv. No. 404

Die Beweinung Christi ist ein Ereignis, das nicht in der Bibel überliefert wird. Ein tradierter Bildtypus dafür ist die „Pietà", der hier Verwendung findet. Der tote Christus wird von seiner trauernden Mutter, die mit tränengefüllten Augen klagend zum Himmel aufblickt, dem Betrachter zur Andacht präsentiert. Aufrecht lehnt der erschlaffte Körper an ihrem Bein und wird von Johannes unter dem Arm gestützt. Der Kopf Christi ist auf das Knie seiner Mutter gesunken. Eine weitere Frau, wohl Maria Magdalena, steht hinter der Gruppe und ringt verzweifelt die Hände. Die Personen, die eng um Christus herum angeordnet sind, werden vom Eingang zur Grabeshöhle umfangen. Im Vordergrund sind Leidenswerkzeuge – Nägel, Hammer, Dornenkrone – und der Kreuzestitulus auf dem Boden verteilt.

Van Dyck schildert den Leichnam ungeschönt und sehr eindringlich: der muskulöse Körper, Hände und Füße durch die Wundmale verfärbt, das leichengraue Gesicht mit verdrehten Augen, Blutspuren in Bart und Haar, der geöffnete, verschobene Mund. Durch die Drastik in der Schilderung des Leichnams Christi sowie von Trauer und Schmerz der begleitenden Personen erhöht Van Dyck die Intensität des Gemäldes, die zusätzlich durch die etwas derben, ungelenken Figuren und den groben Farbauftrag verstärkt wird. Mit dieser durch Mitleiden zur Andacht bewegenden Darstellung schuf Van Dyck ein für die Gegenreformation geradezu programmatisches Andachtsbild, das trotz der geforderten realitätsnahen Schilderung die Würde Christi nicht verletzt.

Das Bild, das in Van Dycks frühester Schaffensphase um 1616/17, noch vor seiner Aufnahme in der Antwerpener Malergilde (1618), entstand, belegt die offensichtliche Kenntnis der Werke von Peter Paul Rubens, besonders dessen 1616 für die Kapuzinerkirche in Brüssel geschaffenen Altarwerks mit gleicher Thematik. Die zum Münchner Bild gehörende vorbereitende Ölskizze befindet sich ebenfalls in der Alten Pinakothek.

The Lamentation of Christ is an event that is not recorded in the Bible. It is nevertheless commonly depicted in painting and sculpture in the traditional form of the pietà, in which the body of Christ is presented to the observer in the arms of His mourning mother. In this picture, the limp body rests in an upright position against Mary's leg and is supported under the arm by John. Christ's head leans on His mother's knee. A second female figure, probably Mary Magdalene, stands behind this group wringing her hands in despair. The figures, grouped closely about the body of Christ, are framed by the entrance to the Holy Sepulchre to the rear. On the ground at the front of the picture, the instruments of torture can be seen – the nails, hammer and crown of thorns – as well as the inscription from the Cross.

Van Dyck paints an unflattering yet extremely powerful picture of the corpse, with a muscular body, the hands and feet wan and marked by the stigmata, the face ashen grey, and with rolling eyes. There are traces of blood in the hair and beard, and the mouth sags open and is distorted. With this uncompromising portrayal of the body of Christ and of the sorrow and anguish of those in attendance, Van Dyck heightens the emotional expression of the painting; and this is reinforced by the somewhat rough and awkward execution of the figures and the coarse brushwork. The depiction evokes a sense of reverence by arousing the compassion of the observer. Here, Van Dyck paints an almost programmatic devotional picture for the Counter-Reformation, a picture that, despite the realism of its portrayal, does not offend the dignity of Christ.

The painting, dating from c. 1616/17, belongs to Van Dyck's earliest period of work before he was admitted to the Guild of St Luke in Antwerp in 1618. It reveals an evident knowledge of the works of Rubens, and in particular his altarpiece with the same subject matter, painted in 1616 for the church of the Capucin monks in Brussels. The preliminary oil sketch for the Munich picture is also in the Alte Pinakothek.

37 Anthonis van Dyck
(1599 Antwerpen – 1641 London)

Ruhe auf der Flucht nach Ägypten

Leinwand, 134,7 x 114,8 cm
Inv. Nr. 555

37 Sir Anthony van Dyck
(1599 Antwerp – 1641 London)

Rest on the Flight into Egypt

Canvas, 134.7 x 114.8 cm
Inv. No. 555

Die Ruhe auf der Flucht nach Ägypten wird in den Evangelien nicht erwähnt, sondern geht auf apokryphe Texte zurück. Seit dem Beginn des 16. Jahrhunderts wurde sie ein beliebtes Thema, wobei die Heilige Familie genrehaft in der Landschaft plaziert werden konnte.

In der Mitte des Bildes, ganz nah an den Betrachter herangerückt, sitzt Maria und hält das nackte Kind auf dem Schoß. Es ist beim Trinken eingeschlafen und umfaßt noch mit beiden Händen die Brust seiner Mutter. Maria umarmt es zärtlich und legt schützend ihren Schleier um das Köpfchen. Links neben Maria steht Joseph, beugt sich zu dem Kind und weist gleichzeitig mit seiner Rechten nach links. Marias Blick folgt der Richtung dieser Geste, die wohl als Aufforderung zur Fortsetzung ihrer Flucht zu verstehen ist. Der Wald im Hintergrund der Figurengruppe gibt rechts den Blick auf einen abendlich rot gefärbten Himmel frei.

Die Ausgewogenheit des Bildes beruht auf der Dreiecksfiguration von Mutter und Kind. Auch farblich ist diese Mitte hervorgehoben. So sind Mariens Kleid, Mantel und Tuch auf den Dreiklang von Rot, Blau und Weiß angelegt, während Joseph und der Hintergrund in zurückhaltenden braunen Tönen wiedergegeben werden.

Das Gemälde, das in Komposition und Farbgebung stark von Tizian beeinflußt ist, wird nach Van Dycks Italienaufenthalt, zwischen 1627 und 1632 in Antwerpen entstanden sein. Er malte es höchstwahrscheinlich für seinen Bruder Theodor (1605–1668), damals Kanoniker an der dortigen St. Michaelskirche, in dessen Nachlaß eine „Vlucht naer Egypten" verzeichnet ist; zudem ist dem Bruder ein zeitgenössischer Nachstich gewidmet. Bei der Stichunterschrift handelt es sich um einen aus der mariologischen Literatur entnommenen Text, der die zärtliche und beschützende Liebe Mariens hervorhebt. Das läßt den Schluß zu, daß das Gemälde als Andachtsbild aufzufassen ist.

Depictions of the Rest on the Flight into Egypt are not based on the Gospels, but on apocryphal texts. The subject provided an opportunity to portray the Holy Family in a genre-like manner set in a landscape. It was a popular theme in painting from the early 16th century onwards. In Van Dyck's depiction, Mary, holding the naked child on her lap, is seated in the middle foreground of the picture in close proximity to the observer. Jesus has fallen asleep while suckling and still clasps His mother's breast with both hands. Mary tenderly embraces the child and pulls her veil protectively over His head. On the left, next to Mary, stands Joseph, bending over Jesus and at the same time pointing with his right hand out of the picture to the left. Mary's eyes are turned in this direction, and the gesture is probably meant as an exhortation to resume their flight. The forest behind the group of figures opens on the right to allow a glimpse of the red-tinged evening sky.

The composition owes its balance to the triangular configuration of mother and child. This central area is also accentuated in its coloration. Mary's attire – dress, robe and veil – forms a triad of red, blue and white. Joseph and the background, in contrast, are depicted in subdued brown tones.

In its composition and coloration, the picture is strongly influenced by Titian. It was probably painted between 1627 and 1632 in Antwerp after Van Dyck's stay in Italy. In all likelihood, he painted it for his brother Theodor (1605–1668), who at that time was canon to St Michael's Church in Antwerp. There is mention of a "Vlucht naer Egypten" in the inventory of Theodor's estate, and a contemporary engraving of the Munich picture, with a dedication to Van Dyck's brother, also exists. The inscription to the engraving contains a text taken from Mariological literature that describes the gentle, protective love of the Virgin. This suggests that the painting was intended as a devotional picture.

38 Anthonis van Dyck
(1599 Antwerpen – 1641 London)

Beweinung Christi

Holz, 108,7 x 149,3 cm
Monogrammiert und datiert auf der Rückseite:
AVDF (Antonis van Dyck fecit) 1634
Inv. Nr. 606

Die breitformatige Tafel zeigt Maria mit ihrem toten Sohn. Beide Figuren sind dem Winkel eines gestürzten Kreuzes einbeschrieben. Durch die begleitenden trauernden und verehrenden Engel und Putten entsteht eine Kombination der Bildtypen „Marienklage" und „Engelspietà". Maria stützt den Oberkörper ihres toten Sohnes mit ihren Beinen und schaut zum Himmel auf. Ihr Blick und die Gebärde – sie umfaßt ein Handgelenk Christi und präsentiert das Wundmal sowohl Gottvater als auch dem Betrachter, ihre andere Hand ist weit geöffnet und weist mit der Handfläche nach oben – beinhalten sowohl ihren Schmerz als auch das Wissen um die heilbringende Wirkung des Opfertodes ihres Sohnes.

Die Aufmerksamkeit des Betrachters wird durch die Farb- und Lichtregie geweckt: Der helle Körper Christi auf dem weißen Leichentuch hebt sich stark vom dunklen, intensiv blauen Gewand Mariens ab. Auf dem Boden liegen Nägel und Dornenkrone, in den Wolken erscheinen Engelsköpfe, und auf der rechten Seite nähern sich zwei Engel und ein kleiner weinender Putto. Auch bei diesem Bild, das zu Van Dycks Gemälde gleichen Inhalts von ca. 1616/17 (Nr. 36) motivische und formale Unterschiede aufweist, zeigt sich Van Dycks Begabung, die Gefühle des Betrachters durch ein gewisses Pathos zu rühren.

Das 1634 datierte Gemälde entstand in einer Zeit, als Van Dyck, der seit 1632 Hofmaler in Diensten König Charles' I. in London war, 1634/35 zu einem Zwischenaufenthalt in den Niederlanden weilte. Damals fertigte er auch die in Stil und Konzept ähnliche Beweinung für die Antwerpener Rekollektenkirche (heute Museum Antwerpen). Das Münchner Bild zeigt mit dem lockeren Pinselstrich und der von Blau dominierten Farbigkeit deutlich den Einfluß Tizians.

38 Sir Anthony van Dyck
(1599 Antwerp – 1641 London)

Lamentation of Christ

Wood, 108.7 x 149.3 cm
With monogram AVDF (Antonis van Dyck fecit)
and the date 1634 on the back
Inv. No. 606

This horizontal panel shows Mary holding the body of her dead son. The two figures are inscribed within the angle of a fallen cross. The presence of the mourning company of angels and putti makes this work a combination of picture types: a lamentation of the Virgin, and a pietà with angels. Supporting the upper part of Christ's body with her legs, Mary looks up to heaven. She grasps the wrist of Jesus as if to show the wound to God and the observer, while motioning upwards with the open palm of her other hand. The expression on her face and her gestures convey a sense of anguish as well as an awareness of the promise of salvation that the sacrificial death of her son implies.

The attention of the viewer is aroused by the handling of light and colour. The brightness of the body of Christ on the white shroud is boldly contrasted with the deep blue of Mary's robe. On the ground lie nails and the crown of thorns. The heads of angels appear in the clouds; and on the right-hand side of the picture, two angels and a weeping putto look on. In this painting, which differs in form and content from Van Dyck's depiction of the same subject dating from c. 1616/17 (No. 36), the artist again demonstrates his ability to stir the emotions with his sense of pathos.

Van Dyck remained in London as court painter in the service of King Charles I from 1632 until his death in 1641. This work, dated 1634, was painted during an extended visit to the Netherlands in 1634/35. During this period, he also completed a Lamentation similar in style and concept to the present picture for the Church of the "Recollecten" in Antwerp (today in the Museum of Fine Arts, Antwerp). The Munich painting, with its light brushwork and dominant blue tone, reveals the evident influence of Titian.

39 Anthonis van Dyck
(1599 Antwerpen – 1641 London)

Hl. Sebastian

Leinwand, 199,9 x 150,6 cm
Inv. Nr. 607

39 Sir Anthony van Dyck
(1599 Antwerp – 1641 London)

St Sebastian

Canvas, 199.9 x 150.6 cm
Inv. No. 607

Sebastian, ein römischer Offizier, der wegen seines christlichen Glaubens von Kaiser Diokletian zum Tode verurteilt worden war, überstand die Hinrichtung durch Bogenschützen auf wunderbare Weise. Er wurde zu einem der beliebtesten katholischen Heiligen, dessen Martyrium entsprechend häufig dargestellt wurde. Ungewöhnlicherweise zeigt Van Dyck nicht den von Pfeilen durchbohrten Körper, sondern die Vorbereitung zur Marter in einer sehr spannungsreichen Komposition: Aus der Mitte etwas nach links verschoben, steht der mit einem Lendentuch bekleidete Heilige vor einem großen Baum. In der linken Ecke liegt seine abgelegte Rüstung, die rechte Bildhälfte ist mit einer Gruppe Personen, die hinter- und übereinander angeordnet sind, dicht gefüllt. Dem Schergen, der die Beine des Märtyrers mit einem Strick zusammenbindet, folgt ein Bogenschütze, der den Kopf des Heiligen derb niederdrückt, daneben ein römischer Soldat, der Pfeile aus einem Köcher auswählt, den ihm ein Junge darreicht, sowie zwei Soldaten zu Pferde, die von hinten heranpreschen. Zur aktiven Gedrängtheit der rechten Bildhälfte kontrastiert deutlich die ruhige, fast leere linke Seite. Einen weiteren Gegensatz bilden die beiden muskulösen, dunkelhäutigen Schergen gegenüber dem schlanken, glatten, hellhäutigen Körper des Heiligen. Sebastian steht in ruhiger, duldsamer Gelassenheit da und fixiert den Betrachter mit zur Seite gedrücktem Kopf. Er scheint sein Martyrium fast trotzig herauszufordern. Auffällig ist seine Ähnlichkeit mit dem Selbstbildnis Van Dycks in der Alten Pinakothek (Nr. 32).
Der erregten Dramatik entspricht die expressive Malweise, die Verteilung von Licht und Schatten sowie das dunkle, tonige Kolorit. Die Farbigkeit, die von einem dunklen braunen Rot dominiert wird, erinnert an die Spätwerke von Tizian und Tintoretto und deutet auf eine Entstehung des Bildes während Van Dycks Italienaufenthalt, zwischen 1621 und 1627.

Sebastian was a Roman officer who was sentenced to death for his Christian belief by Emperor Diocletian. The execution was carried out by archers, but Sebastian miraculously survived it and became one of the most beloved saints of the Christian Church. His martyrdom was the subject of numerous depictions in the history of art. Van Dyck does not show the usual image of the saint's body pierced by arrows. In a composition full of tension, he depicts the preparations for Sebastian's martyrdom. Pushed somewhat to the left of centre, the martyr, wearing only a loincloth, is seen standing in front of a large tree. In the bottom left-hand corner lies his armour. The right-hand half of the picture is taken up by a number of figures arranged in a tight series of layers behind and above each other. The executioner's henchman can be seen tying Sebastian's legs together with a rope. Beyond him is an archer, who roughly presses down the head of the martyr. A Roman soldier is selecting arrows from a quiver held up to him by a boy. Behind them, two mounted soldiers come galloping up from the rear. The calm, almost empty left-hand side of the picture is strikingly contrasted with the bustling, crowded activity of the right-hand half. A further contrast is created by the two henchmen, whose muscular, dark-skinned bodies are juxtaposed with the lean, pale, smooth-skinned figure of the saint. Sebastian stands there calmly, patiently awaiting his execution, and fixes the observer with his gaze, although his head is being pressed down and twisted to one side. It seems almost as if he would provoke his martyrdom in an act of stubborn defiance. There is a striking similarity between the facial expression of the saint and that of Van Dyck in his self-portrait in the Alte Pinakothek (No. 32).
The dramatic sense of agitation is reflected in the expressive manner of painting, the distribution of light and shade, and the dark, earthy coloration. The dominant dark reddish-brown tone is reminiscent of the late works of Titian and Tintoretto, which suggests that "St Sebastian" was painted during Van Dyck's stay in Italy between 1621 and 1627.

144

40 Anthonis van Dyck
(1599 Antwerpen – 1641 London)

Susanna im Bade

Leinwand, 194 x 144 cm
Inv. Nr. 595

40 Sir Anthony van Dyck
(1599 Antwerp – 1641 London)

Susanna and the Elders

Canvas, 194 x 144 cm
Inv. No. 595

Die Geschichte der Susanna wird im apokryphen 13. Kapitel des Buches Daniel im Alten Testament erzählt. Die schöne, gottesfürchtige Frau des reichen und angesehenen Babyloniers Joachim wurde beim Baden im Garten von zwei Richtern beobachtet. In einem günstigen Augenblick, als Susannas Dienerin sich entfernt hatte, bedrängten sie Susanna. Sie drohten, sollte sie ihnen nicht zu Willen sein, würden sie sie des Ehebruchs mit einem jungen Mann bezichtigen. Susanna verweigerte sich den beiden Ältesten trotzdem und wurde aufgrund der falschen Anschuldigungen zum Tode verurteilt. Doch der Knabe Daniel, der spätere Prophet, hörte Gottes Stimme und erreichte ein zweites Verhör, in dem sich die Verleumder in Widersprüche verwickelten. So überführte er die beiden Ältesten der Falschaussage, die daraufhin gesteinigt wurden, und rettete Susanna.

Das Thema wurde seit dem 16. Jahrhundert ein sehr beliebtes exemplum morale für Keuschheit und Tugendhaftigkeit und bot gleichzeitig als erotisches Motiv eine unbekleidete schöne Frau. Kein Wunder, daß sich diese Badeszene ebenso wie die verwandte Darstellung der „Bathseba im Bade" zu einem Lieblingsthema des 16. und 17. Jahrhunderts entwickelte.

Van Dyck zeigt die drei Hauptpersonen auf sehr engem Raum, lediglich der vom rechten Rand überschnittene Brunnen mit Putto und der links aufragende Baum kennzeichnen den Garten. Susanna hockt auf einem Schemel neben dem Brunnen, ihre Pantoffeln und ihr Schmuck liegen malerisch am Boden verteilt. Die beiden Alten, die sich von der Seite genähert haben, beugen sich bedrängend über die zurückweichende nackte Frau. Der jüngere hebt drohend den Zeigefinger und zerrt gierig am Tuch, mit dem Susanna ihre Blöße zu bedecken versucht, während der ältere – die bis in die Fingerspitzen personifizierte Lüsternheit in Gestik und Mimik – bereits die unbekleidete Schulter betastet. Sein linker Arm schwebt drohend über Susanna, der sich, eingekeilt zwi-

The story of Susanna is told in the apocryphal 13th chapter of the Old Testament Book of Daniel. Susanna was the beautiful and God-fearing wife of Joakim, a wealthy and highly respected Babylonian. She was observed taking a bath in her garden by two elders. When her maidservant left her alone, the elders pressed their attentions on Susanna, threatening to accuse her of adultery with a young man if she refused to comply with their wishes. Susanna nevertheless refused to submit and was sentenced to death on the basis of their false witness. She was saved by the intervention of the youth – and later prophet – Daniel. Having heard the voice of God, he succeeded in obtaining a second hearing of the case, in which the two elders became entangled in contradictions. Daniel thus proved the calumny of the two men, who were thereupon stoned to death, and Susanna was saved.

From the 16th century, this subject was a popular exemplum morale for chastity and virtue. At the same time, it provided an opportunity to paint an erotic picture of a beautiful woman in a state of undress. It is not surprising, therefore, that the scene of Susanna's bath and the related subject of Bathsheba in her bath became two of the favourite themes of 16th- and 17th-century painting. Van Dyck presents the three leading figures in a very tight space. The only details indicating that the scene is set in a garden are the fountain with a putto cut off by the right-hand edge of the painting, and the tall tree on the left. Susanna is seated on a stool next to the fountain. Her slippers and her jewellery lie scattered on the ground in effective visual disarray. The two elders, approaching from the side, lean over the naked woman, pressing their claims on her. Susanna shrinks from them. The younger man raises his finger threateningly and tears lustfully at the robe with which she attempts to cover her nakedness. The older man – in his gestures and facial expression, the personification of lechery – is already touching her bare shoulder. His left arm is

schen Brunnen und den beiden Männern, kein Ausweg bietet.

Mit großem psychologischem Einfühlungsvermögen hat Van Dyck das Thema sexueller Bedrängung zur Darstellung gebracht. Durch den enggefaßten Bildausschnitt und die nahe an den Betrachter herangerückten Figuren wird die spannungsgeladene Aggressivität der Alten und damit die beängstigende Situation Susannas unmittelbar nachvollziehbar.

Das Bild dürfte zu Beginn von Van Dycks italienischer Zeit, d. h. 1621 oder 1622, entstanden sein. Alte Inventare bezeichnen Van Dycks Gemälde mit dem „hl. Sebastian" (Nr. 39) als Pendant zur „Susanna im Bade". Dafür würde neben den übereinstimmenden Bildmaßen und der Verwendung der gleichen, grobstrukturierten Leinwand auch der gegengleiche kompositorische Aufbau sprechen: Kommt bei Susanna die Bedrohung in Form der beiden Männer von links, so drängen sich beim Martyrium des Sebastian die Schergen auf der rechten Bildseite.

raised menacingly over Susanna, for whom there seems to be no escape, trapped as she is between the fountain and the two men.

Van Dyck captures the subject of sexual molestation with great psychological insight. The tight compass of the picture and the way the figures are thrust forward in close proximity to the observer make the threat of aggression posed by the elders, and thus Susanna's terrible predicament, all the more immediate.

The picture was painted c. 1621/22, probably at the beginning of Van Dyck's stay in Italy. Old inventories describe his depiction of "St Sebastian" (No. 39) as a pendant to "Susanna and the Elders". The comparable sizes of the two paintings and the use of the same coarse-textured canvas, as well as compositional symmetries support this theory. In the present picture, the threat to Susanna comes from the two men on the left-hand side of the picture, whereas in the martyrdom of St Sebastian it comes from the executioner's henchmen on the right.

41 Jacob Jordaens
(1593 Antwerpen – 1678 Antwerpen)

Nymphen und Faune
(Allegorie der Fruchtbarkeit)

Leinwand, 250 x 240 cm
Monogrammiert unten links: P. R. Fecit; in der darunter-
liegenden Malschicht die originale Signatur: JoR FECIT
Inv. Nr. 10411

Jordaens „Allegorie der Fruchtbarkeit" zeigt eine gleich-
sam reliefartig dicht gedrängte Gruppe von Satyrn und
Nymphen, die sich um ein Füllhorn scharen und Früchte
von Bäumen pflücken. Von oben schweben Putten mit
einer Blumen- und Früchtegirlande und Fackeln herbei,
ein Flöte spielender Pan und ein Neger schreiten von
rechts heran. Am linken Bildrand öffnet sich ein Landschaftsausblick auf weidendes Vieh an einem Gewässer
und auf weitere Nymphen und Satyrn.

Die Satyrn, bocksbeinige Mischwesen mit Hörnern, sind
wie die Nymphen mit ihren vollen, üppigen weiblichen
Formen Sinnbild der Natur und Fruchtbarkeit. So wird
die Fruchtbarkeit durch Naturgottheiten verkörpert und
nicht durch eine einzelne allegorische Personifikation.
Besonders auffällig ist die neben dem überquellenden
Füllhorn sitzende Nymphe, die aus dem Bild schaut und
den Betrachter in das Geschehen einbezieht. Sie scheint
die Hauptfigur zu sein und könnte als Pomona, die Göttin der Früchte, identifiziert werden.

Die stehende Nymphe links ist mit geringen Veränderungen einem wenige Jahre zuvor entstandenen
Rubens-Bild entnommen, den „Töchtern des Kekrops"
(Vaduz, Liechtenstein-Galerie). Überhaupt ist die ganze
Komposition mit den vielfältigen Körperansichten
und Verschränkungen nicht ohne Rubens' Vorbild
denkbar.

Das Bild entstand wohl um 1617, da seine helle Farbigkeit einem 1617 datierten Gemälde des Künstlers vergleichbar ist. Seine koloristische Wirkung ist besonders
auffällig. Die kühlen Farben in gebrochenen Tönen sind
noch sehr manieristisch. So wird die fast weiße Haut der
Nymphen durch starke grau-blaue und rosa-rote Model-
lierungen belebt. Unvermittelt steht Licht neben Schatten, eine effektvolle Beleuchtung modelliert die Körper
sehr plastisch. Diese starken Kontraste zwischen Licht
und Schatten gehen auf Caravaggio zurück, dessen
Kunst Jordaens, der nie nach Italien gereist war, durch
Antwerpener Maler vermittelt wurde.

---

41 Jacob Jordaens
(1593 Antwerp – 1678 Antwerp)

Nymphs and Fauns
(Allegory of Fertility)

Canvas, 250 x 240 cm
Monogram bottom left: P. R. Fecit; in the layer beneath
this, the original signature: JoR FECIT
Inv. No. 10411

Jordaens' "Allegory of Fertility" presents a dense, almost relief-like group of satyrs and nymphs pressing
round a cornucopia and plucking fruit from the trees.
Putti, bearing torches and a garland of fruit and flowers,
descend from above; while Pan, playing a flute and
accompanied by a dark-skinned figure, advances from
the right. On the left-hand edge of the picture, the view
opens to reveal a landscape with cattle grazing by a pool
of water and more nymphs and satyrs.

Both the satyrs, hybrid creatures with goat-like legs and
horns, and the nymphs, with their voluptuous female
forms, are symbols of nature and fertility. In this picture,
therefore, fertility is represented in the form of natural
deities and not by a single allegorical personification.
Particular emphasis is placed on the nymph seated in the
foreground next to the overflowing cornucopia. By turning her head to look out of the picture, she draws the
observer into the events. She would seem to be the central figure of the painting and can possibly be identified
as Pomona, the Roman goddess of fruit and trees.

The nymph standing on the left was taken with only
minor modifications from Rubens' "Daughters of Cec-
rops" (Liechtenstein Gallery, Vaduz), painted only a few
years earlier. Indeed, the composition as a whole, with
its rich array of bodily views and convolutions, would
have been inconceivable without Rubens.

The picture was painted probably around 1617, since its
bright coloration is comparable to another work by Jordaens dating from that year. The use of cool colours in
broken tones is still very Mannerist. The almost white
skin of the nymphs is enlivened by strong grey-blue and
reddish-pink shading. Light and shadow are directly
juxtaposed, and the bodies acquire their sculptural quality through the effective use of lighting. These bold contrasts between light and shade betray the influence of
Caravaggio. Although Jordaens never went to Italy, he
was acquainted with the work of the Italian master
through other Antwerp painters.

Das Thema scheint Jordaens besonders fasziniert zu haben, denn es existieren mehrere „Allegorien der Fruchtbarkeit" (Bilder in Brüssel, Madrid, London). Die Münchner Fassung nimmt mit ihrer außergewöhnlichen Farbigkeit eine besondere Stellung innerhalb der Gruppe ein. Der Bestimmungsort des Gemäldes ist nicht bekannt, doch dürfte es sich aufgrund des großen Formats um einen Auftraggeber aus dem höfischen Bereich handeln.

The subject of this picture seems to have exercised a special fascination on Jordaens, for there are a number of "Allegories of Fertility" still in existence (in Brussels, Madrid and London). The Munich version, with its remarkably vivid colours, occupies a special place among this group of paintings. The location for which it was originally executed is not known, but in view of the large scale, the client must have been a member of the court.

42 Jacob Jordaens
(1593 Antwerpen – 1678 Antwerpen)

Der Satyr beim Bauern

Leinwand auf Holz, 193,8 x 205 cm
Inv. Nr. 425

42 Jacob Jordaens
(1593 Antwerp – 1678 Antwerp)

Satyr with Peasants

Canvas on wood, 193.8 x 205 cm
Inv. No. 425

Dem großformatigen Gemälde liegt eine Fabel des griechischen Dichters Aesop (6. Jh. v. Chr.) zugrunde, die in den Niederlanden im 17. Jahrhundert weit verbreitet war: Ein Bauer hatte einen frierenden Satyrn mit nach Hause genommen. Beim Abendessen beobachtet dieser, wie der Bauer auf seine Suppe bläst, um sie zu kühlen, obwohl er zuvor auf dem Feld auf dieselbe Weise seine Hände erwärmt hatte. Der Satyr springt daraufhin erschrocken auf, um das Haus zu verlassen. Die mit der Fabel verbundene Moral besagt, sich vor unberechenbaren, doppelzüngigen Leuten zu hüten.

Bei Jordaens findet die Szene in einem schlichten, bäuerlichen Raum statt. Um den Tisch hat sich die Familie versammelt. Die Großmutter sitzt in einem geflochtenen Korbstuhl, hält den Enkel auf dem Schoß, und schaut erstaunt zum aufspringenden Satyrn. Die junge Mutter fixiert den Betrachter, während der Bauer weit über seinen Löffel vorgebeugt verständnislos zum Satyrn blickt. Der kleine Sohn des Bauern bläst in kindlicher Nachahmung des Vaters auf sein Stück Brot – eine Anspielung auf das bei Jordaens beliebte Thema „Wie die Alten sungen, so zwitschern die Jungen".

Es war eine Vorliebe von Jordaens, Genreszenen mit moralisierender Aussage auf humorvolle Weise – bevorzugt nach Sprichwörtern – darzustellen. Mit diesen Themen stand er der Malerei der holländischen Provinzen näher als derjenigen seiner katholischen Malerkollegen in Antwerpen, wobei er jedoch im Gegensatz zu den kleinformatigen holländischen Genreszenen große, repräsentative Formate verwendete.

Die effektvolle Lichtführung mit Hell-Dunkel-Kontrasten verweist auf den Einfluß Caravaggios ebenso wie der starke Realismus und die Untersicht der Darstellung. Die warmen Braun- und Rottöne belegen eine Weiterentwicklung von Jordaens, weg von der kühlen, bunten Farbigkeit des Frühwerks „Nymphen und Faune" (Nr. 41) und verweisen auf die Reifezeit des Meisters, zu Anfang der zwanziger Jahre.

This large-scale painting is based on a fable of the Greek poet Aesop (6th century BC) that was widely known in the Netherlands in the 17th century. A peasant finds a satyr freezing with cold and takes him home. During dinner, the satyr notices how the peasant blows on his soup to cool it, although only shortly before, when they had been out in the fields, the man had warmed his hands in the same way. The satyr thereupon jumps to his feet in bewilderment and flees. The moral of this tale is that one should beware of unpredictable people who blow hot and cold.

In Jordaens' depiction, the scene is set in a simple, rustic room. The family is gathered round the table. The grandmother sits in a wicker chair, holding her grandson on her lap and looking in amazement at the satyr, who is leaping from his seat. The young mother fixes her gaze on the observer, while the peasant, bent forward over his spoon, stares incomprehensibly at the satyr. The peasant's little son puffs on his bread in childlike imitation of his father – a reference to another of Jordaens' favourite themes: "As the old ones have sung, so chirrup the young." (Like father, like son).

Jordaens specialized in humorous interpretations of genre scenes with a moral content, and was particularly fond of proverbs. In this respect, he had more in common with the painters of the Dutch provinces than with his Catholic fellow artists in Antwerp. In contrast to the small scale of most Dutch genre scenes, however, he created impressively large pictures.

The striking lighting of this painting with its chiaroscuro contrasts reveals the influence of Caravaggio, as does the bold sense of realism and the relatively low viewpoint. The warm brown and red tones are evidence of Jordaens' artistic development away from the cool, bright coloration of early works such as "Nymphs and Fauns" (No. 41). The stylistic traits of this picture, painted in the early 1620s, announce the period of the master's maturity.

43 Adriaen Brouwer
(1605/06 Oudenaarde – 1638 Antwerpen)

Der eingeschlafene Wirt

Kupfer, 31 x 24,2 cm
Inv. Nr. 2014

Das Gemälde „Der eingeschlafene Wirt" zeigt im Vordergrund eines Kneipenraumes einen fetten Mann auf einem Faßstuhl schlafend, in der rechten Hand einen Humpen, in der anderen einen Wanderstab als traditionelles Attribut der Gilde umherschweifender Wirtshauspilger. Der Bildtitel ist also irreführend, denn es handelt sich nicht um den Wirt, sondern um einen dicken, faulen Zecher und Prasser. Treffender ist der Titel des 18. Jahrhunderts: „Das Leben der Vollsäufer". So sieht man rechts im Hintergrund eine Zechrunde um einen Tisch versammelt. Einer der Männer ist mit dem Kopf auf seinen Armen am Tisch eingeschlafen, ihm direkt gegenüber übergibt sich ein anderer mitten auf den Tisch, ein dritter liegt am Boden und erbricht sich zur Freude von zwei Schweinen, die so Futter finden.

Alle diese unappetitlichen Folgen übermäßigen Alkoholgenusses werden bereits in einem Holzschnitt von Erhard Schön geschildert, der ein Gedicht von Hans Sachs (1528) über die vier Eigenschaften des Weins und dessen Wirkungen auf die vier Temperamente illustriert. Offenbar kannte Brouwer den Holzschnitt und übernahm von dort die drastischen Auswirkungen des Weines auf den Phlegmatiker. Das in Brouwers Bild auffällig im Vordergrund plazierte Schwein stellt eine weitere Verbindung zum Holzschnitt her, denn in der Zuordnung von Tieren zu den Temperamenten gehört das Schwein zum Phlegmatiker. Auch die Eule, die über dem Schläfer auf dem Fensterladen sitzt, ist ein Symbol für Torheit und Völlerei, Eigenschaften die dem phlegmatischen Temperament zugewiesen werden. Die moralisch-didaktische Absicht des Bildes, die Warnung vor den Auswirkungen der Trunksucht, ist also ganz offensichtlich.

Die Farbgebung auf der Kupfertafel – der einzigen erhaltenen bei Brouwer, der vorzugsweise auf Holztafeln malte – ist in feinen Abstufungen von Brauntönen, fast monochrom, gehalten.

43 Adriaen Brouwer
(1605/06 Oudenarde – 1638 Antwerp)

Sleeping Innkeeper

Copper, 31 x 24.2 cm
Inv. No. 2014

In the foreground of the "Sleeping Innkeeper", a corpulent man can be seen dozing on a barrel chair in a tavern. In his right hand he holds a tankard, in the other a staff, which was the traditional attribute of the pilgrim – and here of the brotherhood of itinerant tipplers who wandered from inn to inn. The title of this picture is, therefore, misleading; for it is not the innkeeper who is depicted, but some fat, lazy reveller and spendthrift. The 18th-century title, "The Life of Drunkards", would be more appropriate. In the background on the right, a round of inebriates is gathered about a table, on which one of them has fallen asleep, his head resting on his arms. Opposite him, another is vomiting on to the table. A third man lies vomiting on the floor, much to the pleasure of two pigs who thus find something to eat.

All these unsavoury consequences of overindulgence in alcohol had already been depicted in a woodcut by Erhard Schön, who had illustrated a poem by Hans Sachs (1528) about the four attributes of wine and its effects on the four temperaments. Brouwer was evidently acquainted with this woodcut and adopted the details to illustrate the extreme effects of wine on a phlegmatic person. The pig placed prominently in the foreground of the picture establishes a further link with the woodcut; for in the association of animals with the human temperaments, the pig is identified with phlegmatic persons. In a similar way, the owl perched on the shutter above the sleeping man is a symbol of folly and gluttony, characteristics that are also associated with the phlegmatic temperament. The moral, didactic intention of the picture is quite clear: to warn of the effects of intemperance. The coloration of this sole surviving copper panel by Brouwer, who painted mainly on wood, is restricted to fine gradations of brown tones in an almost monochrome manner.

Another important aspect of Brouwer's paintings is his scorn for the peasantry. In the 15th and 16th centuries, the depiction of peasants as stupid, coarse people was

Ein weiterer wichtiger Aspekt der Gemälde Brouwers ist der Bauernspott. Die Beschreibung des Bauern als tölpelhafter grober Mensch war während des 15. und 16. Jahrhunderts durch soziale Spannungen und Klassenrivalität entstanden. Es ist eine bekannte Tatsache, daß die auf den ersten Blick lustigen Alltagsszenen der Genremalerei des 17. Jahrhunderts einen tiefergehenden Inhalt haben. Über das vordergründige Amüsement hinaus wollten sie eine ethische Wahrheit vermitteln, die heute nicht mehr so geläufig und erkennbar ist wie damals. Dieses ernsthafte erzieherische Anliegen haben letztlich auch Brouwers Szenen mit trinkenden, rauchenden, spielenden und kämpfenden Bauern.

the outcome of social tensions and class rivalries. The seemingly amusing scenes from everyday life depicted in a lot of genre painting in the 17th century are known to have had a deeper meaning. Over and above the superficial entertainment they provided, they also aimed to convey an ethical truth, which is not as familiar or recognizable today as it was then. These serious educational aims are also present in Brouwer's scenes with drinking, smoking, gambling and brawling peasants.

44 Adriaen Brouwer
(1605/06 Oudenaarde – 1638 Antwerpen)

Raufende Kartenspieler
in einer Schenke

Holz, 33,4 x 49,8 cm
Inv. Nr. 562

In Brouwers späteren Werken trat die moralisch-didaktische Absicht immer mehr zurück und sein Interesse verlagerte sich auf die Schilderung von Affekten, die letztlich im Zentrum seiner Malkunst standen. Unübertroffen gelang es ihm, die Gemütszustände und menschlichen Befindlichkeiten nachvollziehbar zu schildern. Als Themen eigneten sich dafür vor allem die Schlägereien und Streitigkeiten, entstanden aus Trunksucht und Glücksspiel. Anhand solcher Szenen konnte er die Affekte Zorn und Schmerz wirkungsvoll darstellen.

So auch in den „Raufenden Kartenspielern in einer Schenke", wo vier Männer beim Zechen über das Kartenspiel in Streit geraten sind. Die Karten liegen verstreut am Boden. Der links Sitzende hat seinen Dolch vor sich auf dem kleinen Schemel aufgepflanzt und droht mit der erhobenen Faust. Ein anderer holt wutentbrannt zum Schlag mit einem Krug gegen den gemeinsamen Kontrahenten aus und reißt ihn gleichzeitig an den Haaren. Der Angegriffene, auf einem umgekehrten Korb sitzend, zieht mit schmerzverzerrtem Gesicht sein Schwert. Ein vierter versucht dem Schläger in den Arm zu fallen. Meisterhaft hat Brouwer den Höhepunkt der Auseinandersetzung erfaßt. Das Spektakel wird von zwei weiteren Personen neugierig durch eine niedrige Tür beobachtet. Treffend ist der Ort des Geschehens als Spelunke charakterisiert. Liebevoll geschilderte Details, wie der glänzende Tonkrug, ein weißes Tuch und eine Tabakspfeife, sind zu einem Stilleben arrangiert. Das Gemälde ist trotz des deftigen, heftigen Themas überlegt durchkomponiert und fein ausgeführt.

Die Darstellung des Kartenspiels hatte im Zusammenhang mit der christlichen Lasterikonographie eine lange Tradition. Doch ist hier die moralisierende Absicht mit der Warnung vor einer der Todsünden zugunsten von Brouwers Interesse für Zorn und Wut, die er in den Gesichtern zeigt, zurückgetreten.

44 Adriaen Brouwer
(1605/06 Oudenarde – 1638 Antwerp)

Brawling Card Players
in a Tavern

Wood, 33.4 x 49.8 cm
Inv. No. 562

In Brouwer's later works, the didactic, moral intentions recede more and more into the background. His interest shifts to the depiction of human passions, which in the end become the main theme of his painting. He was unsurpassed in the convincing portrayal of human moods and emotions; and the brawls and disputes that were the outcome of drunkenness and gambling proved to be ideal vehicles for his depictions of anger and pain. This is certainly true of the "Brawling Card Players in a Tavern", where four hard-drinking men begin to quarrel over a game of cards. The cards lie scattered about the floor. The man sitting on the left grips his dagger on the little stool in front of him and gestures threateningly with his raised fist. Another angrily raises a jug to hit the common adversary, whom he grabs by the hair. The victim, sitting on an upturned basket, draws his sword, his face distorted with pain. A fourth man attempts to restrain the person wielding the jug. In masterly fashion, Brouwer captures the climax of this dispute. Two further persons observe these events with curiosity through a low door. Appropriately the scene is set in a squalid dive. Lovingly depicted details, such as the shiny earthenware jug, the white cloth and the pipe are arranged in the form of a still life. Despite its coarse, rough subject matter, the painting is worked out to the last detail and executed with great finesse.

The depiction of card-playing had a long tradition in the Christian iconography of vices. Here, however, the usual moralizing aspect, coupled with a warning against committing a deadly sin, gives way to Brouwer's interest in portraying anger and violent passions, which he shows in the faces of the men.

45 Adriaen Brouwer
(1605/06 Oudenaarde – 1638 Antwerpen)

Zwei raufende Bauern
am Faß

Holz, 15,5 x 14,1 cm
Inv. Nr. 2112

In den „Zwei raufenden Bauern am Faß" schildert Brouwer überzeugend Wut, Zorn und Schmerz. Der Ausschnitt ist hier sehr eng gewählt, die beiden Akteure werden nur als Halbfiguren gezeigt. Auf einer Bank vor einem Faß sitzt ein Bauer, der von hinten von einem anderen attackiert wird. Er wehrt den Angriff ab, indem er den Gegner an den Haaren packt und ihn sich gleichzeitig mit dem ausgestreckten Arm vom Leibe hält. Den Oberkörper beugt er weit vom Angreifer weg nach vorn, weshalb er seinen Hut festhalten muß. In den grimassierenden Gesichtern der Raufenden findet die Szene ihren Höhepunkt. Auffällig ist die zurückhaltende Farbgebung der Gewänder, an denen das weiß aufblitzende Hemd, eine kleine gelbe Schleife, eine rote Manschette und eine rote Verschnürung am Hosenlatz Akzente setzen.

Mit der bis dahin ungewöhnlichen Darstellung der Gemütszustände zeigt Brouwer sich auf der Höhe der zeitgenössischen Geistesströmungen. Damals wuchs das Interesse an den Affekten. So gab der Antwerpener Humanist Justus Lipsius 1615 eine Seneca-Gesamtausgabe heraus, in der er das Buch „De Ira" (Über den Zorn) an den Anfang stellte – ein Indiz seiner speziellen Gewichtung. Der Zorn wurde nicht mehr nur als ein vom christlichen Standpunkt aus zu verurteilendes Laster gesehen. Seine Verdammung erfolgte vor allem wegen der den Körper unkontrolliert beherrschenden Leidenschaft, deren Zügelung ein wichtiger Bestandteil der stoischen Lehre war. Ob Brouwer die Seneca-Texte selbst gelesen hatte, ist nicht bekannt, jedoch anzunehmen, da er als Mitglied der Rederijkerkamer (Vereinigungen von Laiendichtern) in Haarlem und Antwerpen eine gewisse literarische Bildung besaß und ihm Senecas Lehre über niederländische Humanistenkreise vermittelt worden sein kann.

45 Adriaen Brouwer
(1605/06 Oudenarde – 1638 Antwerp)

Two Peasants Quarrelling
beside a Barrel

Wood, 15.5 x 14.1 cm
Inv. No. 2112

Anger, rage and pain are convincingly depicted in the "Two Peasants Quarrelling beside a Barrel". Brouwer shows only a small detail here. The two persons are portrayed in little more than half length. A peasant sitting on a bench next to a barrel is being attacked from the rear by another. The peasant attempts to resist this assault by grabbing his adversary by the hair and at the same time holding him at arm's length. Bending the upper part of his body away from the attacker, he is forced to hold his hat on his head with his other hand. The depiction reaches its climax in the grimaces on the faces of the two antagonists. A striking feature of the picture is the subdued coloration of the clothing, against which the bright flash of the white shirt, the little yellow bow, the red cuff and the red lacing to the flies of the trousers stand out.

With this hitherto unusual depiction of the emotional state of the characters, Brouwer shows himself to be fully abreast of contemporary thinking. At that time, there was a growing interest in human passions and emotions. Justus Lipsius, the Antwerp humanist, published a complete edition of Seneca's works in 1615, for example, in which the book "De Ira" (On Anger) was placed at the beginning, providing some indication of the special weight attached to this subject. Anger was no longer seen merely as a vice to be condemned from a Christian standpoint. It was shameful above all because of the uncontrolled physical passions it generated. The bridling of these passions was an important part of Stoic teachings. Although it is not known for certain whether Brouwer had read Seneca's writings, it would not be unlikely. As a member of the Rederijkerkamer (society of lay poets) in Haarlem and Antwerp, he certainly possessed a certain literary education, and he may well have been familiar with Seneca's teachings through Dutch humanist circles.

46 Adriaen Brouwer
(1605/06 Oudenaarde – 1638 Antwerpen)

Rauchende und trinkende Bauern

Holz, 35,1 x 26,5 cm
Inv. Nr. 2062

46 Adriaen Brouwer
(1605/06 Oudenarde – 1638 Antwerp)

Peasants Smoking and Drinking

Wood, 35.1 x 26.5 cm
Inv. No. 2062

Ein Bild wie die „Rauchenden und trinkenden Bauern" fällt unter die von Brouwer als Thema eingeführten Rauchergesellschaften, die sein vertieftes Interesse an menschlichen Gemütszuständen bekunden. Die Mode des Tabakrauchens, damals auch Tabaktrinken genannt, kam mit der Einfuhr dieser Pflanze in den Niederlanden Ende des 16. Jahrhunderts auf. Neben medizinischem Gebrauch fand Tabak vor allem als Genußmittel Verwendung. Da sich die Auswirkungen exzessiven Alkohol- oder Tabakgenusses sehr ähneln, setzte man Tabak mit Alkohol gleich und verrief das Rauchen als Laster, zumal es mit den sozial niedrigsten Schichten – den Seeleuten, Soldaten und Bauern – in Verbindung gebracht wurde.

Das Gemälde zeigt sechs Männer in einer karg eingerichteten Taverne, die das Tabakrauchen zelebrieren. In der geöffneten Tür erscheint ein weiterer Bauer mit zerschlissener, ärmlicher Kleidung, offensichtlich in angetrunkenem Zustand grölend. Über der Tür hängt die Zeichnung einer Eule. Die Figuren sind im Raum verstreut angeordnet, jede für sich im Genuß von Tabak und Alkohol versunken. Entsprechend dem Thema Tabakgenuß hat Brouwer die Physiognomien scharf beobachtet und die unterschiedlichen Reaktionen wiedergegeben. Der Mann im Vordergrund, der dem Betrachter entgegenblickt, sitzt mit übergeschlagenen Beinen und hält genüßlich den Rauch in den Backen zurück, die Augen vor Behagen fast ganz geschlossen. Als Hauptperson im Licht ist er auch farblich hervorgehoben. Seine rote Kappe ist der leuchtende Mittelpunkt und bildet einen Kontrast zu seinem grünen Gewand mit blauem Ärmelumschlag.

"Peasants Smoking and Drinking" belongs to the genre of "smoking society" pictures, which Brouwer himself originated and which reveal his profound interest in human states of mind. The habit of smoking, or "drinking" tobacco as it was then known, came to the Netherlands at the end of the 16th century when the plant was introduced to that country. Tobacco was used for medicinal purposes, but also as a stimulant. Since the effects of excessive indulgence in alcohol and tobacco are similar, the two were set on a par, and smoking was regarded as a vice, especially as it was associated with the lowest classes of society – with sailors, soldiers and peasants.

The painting shows six men in a scantily furnished tavern indulging in the pleasures of tobacco. Another peasant in torn, shabby clothing appears in the open doorway, bawling and evidently in a drunken state. Above the door hangs a drawing of an owl. The individual figures are scattered about the room, each indulging his own craving for tobacco and drink. In this reflection on smoking, Brouwer makes a close study of the physiognomies of the peasants, portraying their different reactions to this intoxicant. The man in the foreground sits with his legs crossed, retaining the tobacco smoke in his puffed cheeks with an expression of profound pleasure, his eyes almost closed in contentment. Seated in the light, and colourfully accentuated, he is the main figure in this scene. His red cap forms the bright highlight of the picture and is strikingly contrasted with his green clothing and blue cuffs.

47 Adriaen Brouwer
(1605/06 Oudenaarde – 1638 Antwerpen)

Das Gefühl

Holz, 23,6 x 20,3 cm
Inv. Nr. 581

Die „Fünf Sinne" wurden im 15. und 16. Jahrhundert gern als Serien dargestellt, mit denen vor der Hingabe an die weltlichen Genüsse gewarnt wurde. Im 17. Jahrhundert wurden die Fünf Sinne in zunächst oberflächlich erscheinenden Alltagsschilderungen verborgen. Es entstanden regelrechte Zyklen, aber es gab auch einzeln herausgelöste Darstellungen des Sehens, Schmeckens, Fühlens, Hörens und Riechens, wie sie bei Brouwer vorkommen.

Für die Darstellung des „Gefühls" als einem der fünf Sinne (vgl. Nr. 48) eignet sich eine Armoperation hervorragend. In diesem Gemälde, das als einziges zu Lebzeiten Brouwers in einer Sammlung nachweisbar ist, wird der Schmerzausdruck zum bestimmenden Thema. Ein Dorfbader sitzt vor einem Patienten und operiert mit angestrengt zusammengekniffenem Mund und konzentriert geöffneten Augen dessen Arm. Dieser verzerrt sein Gesicht vor Schmerz, ein Auge geschlossen, der Mund stöhnend geöffnet. Ein dritter Mann beobachtet die Operation über die Schultern von Operateur und Patient, wobei seine Augen von einem Hut verdeckt werden, um den Betrachter nicht vom Hauptgeschehen abzulenken. Auf dem Tisch im Vordergrund ist aus den Utensilien des Baders – Glasflaschen, Tuch und Kohlebecken – ein Stilleben komponiert.

Brouwers Bild „Das Gefühl" wurde als Teil eines nicht mehr vollständigen Fünf-Sinne-Zyklus' angesehen, zu dem zwei weitere Gemälde in der Alten Pinakothek gerechnet wurden, doch handelt es sich wohl eher um eine eigenständige Tafel.

47 Adriaen Brouwer
(1605/06 Oudenarde – 1638 Antwerp)

The Sense of Touch

Wood, 23.6 x 20.3 cm
Inv. No. 581

In the 15th and 16th centuries, the "five senses" were a popular theme for sequences of pictures containing a warning against indulgence in worldly pleasures. Seventeenth-century depictions of the five senses are embedded in what, at first sight, appear to be superficial everyday situations. Whole cycles of these scenes were created, as well as individual representations of sight, taste, touch, hearing and smell, as in this example by Brouwer, which is his only work known to have belonged to an art collection during his lifetime.

An arm operation is an ideal subject for representing the sense of touch (cf. No. 48). The dominant theme here is the expression of pain. A village barber is seated next to the patient, operating on his arm. The surgeon's lips are tightly pressed together, and his eyes are opened wide in concentration. The victim screws up his face in anguish. One eye is closed; his mouth is open in a groan of pain. A third man watches the operation over the shoulders of the barber and the patient. His eyes are covered by the brim of his hat so as not to distract the observer's attention from the main event of the picture. On the table in the foreground, the barber's utensils have been arranged into a still life consisting of glass bottles, a cloth and a bowl of coals.

Brouwer's "The Sense of Touch", together with two other paintings in the Alte Pinakothek, was thought to belong to a no longer extant cycle depicting the five senses. In all likelihood, however, this panel was painted as an independent work.

166

48 Adriaen Brouwer
(1605/06 Oudenaarde – 1638 Antwerpen)

Dorfbaderstube

Holz, 31,4 x 39,6 cm
Inv. Nr. 561

Bei den von Brouwer häufig gezeigten Operationsszenen handelt es sich letztendlich um Sinnesdarstellungen, die das Gefühl, genauer den Schmerz, veranschaulichen (siehe Nr. 47). Ein sehr schönes Beispiel ist die „Dorfbaderstube", ein Gemälde das in mehrerlei Hinsicht dem „Eingeschlafenen Wirt" (Nr. 43) vergleichbar ist. Auch hier finden sich die Hauptpersonen im Vordergrund, während eine erläuternde Nebenszene im Hintergrund farblich zurückhaltend gestaltet ist. Charakteristisch für Brouwer sind die Innenraumansichten, die nach einem einfachen Schema kastenartig aufgebaut sind. Die untergeordneten Szenen werden in einen nach hinten erweiterten Raumteil verlegt. Ungewöhnlich ist die reiche Raumausstattung mit Gegenständen, die den Ort des Geschehens charakterisieren: Bücher, Flaschen, Töpfe, ein Totenschädel. Im Hintergrund wird ein Mann rasiert, eine Dienstleistung, die man in einer Baderstube zuerst erwartet. Im Vordergrund kniet der Dorfbader vor einem Patienten, an dessen Fuß er mit einem Messer herumbohrt. Seine Gehilfin, die ein Messer über einem Stövchen erhitzt, wendet sich schon einem neuen Patienten zu, der durch die geöffnete Tür hereinblickt. Offensichtlich schmerzt diesen eine blutende Wunde auf der Wange.

Trefflich lassen sich in den Gesichtern die unterschiedlichen Gefühle ablesen. Während der Chirurg die Operation mit höchster Konzentration ausführt, die sich an seinem angespannten Mund offenbart – die Augen werden von der Kappe verdeckt –, zieht der Behandelte mit geschlossenen Augen den Atem schmerzvoll durch den Mund ein. Diese Gruppe ist besonders beleuchtet und durch die Farbgebung hervorgehoben. Als Hauptgruppe des Gemäldes veranschaulicht sie am Beispiel der Operationsszene ein Gefühl, den Schmerz. Brouwers besonderer Beitrag zur Genremalerei seiner Zeit bestand unter anderem in derartigen Darstellungen, die seine Meisterschaft in der Wiedergabe von menschlichen Befindlichkeiten aufzeigen.

48 Adriaen Brouwer
(1605/06 Oudenarde – 1638 Antwerp)

Village Barber's Shop

Wood, 31.4 x 39.6 cm
Inv. No. 561

The surgical operations that Brouwer so frequently painted are in fact depictions of the senses, and in particular the sense of touch or, more precisely, pain (cf. No. 47). The "Village Barber's Shop" is a fine example of this. The painting may be compared in many respects with the "Sleeping Innkeeper" (No. 43). Here, too, the main figures are set in the foreground, whilst a secondary, explanatory scene is painted in subdued colours in the background. Interior views, constructed according to a simple volumetric system are a characteristic feature of Brouwer's work. The secondary scenes are located in a spatial extension to the rear. Unusual in this picture is the wealth of objects used to characterize the location: books, bottles, pots and a skull. In the background, a man is being shaved, a service that might seem more appropriate to a barber's shop. In the foreground, the village barber kneels in front of the patient, probing into his foot with a knife. The female assistant, who is heating another knife over a little stove, turns to look at a new patient peering through the open door. The newcomer is evidently suffering from a painful wound in the cheek.

The feelings of the various parties are beautifully reflected in the expressions of their faces. Whilst the surgeon conducts the operation with the utmost concentration, evident in the tense line of his mouth (his eyes are concealed by his cap), the patient, whose eyes are closed, draws in his breath through his mouth in evident pain. The figures in the foreground are accentuated by the lighting and the coloration. As the principal group in the painting, they serve to illustrate the sense of pain through the experience of an operation. Brouwer's special contribution to the genre painting of his age consisted, among other things, of depictions of this kind, which demonstrate his mastery in representing human feelings.

The "Village Barber's Shop" also reveals Brouwer's virtuosity as a painter. The sketch-like quality of his pic-

„Die Dorfbaderstube" offenbart außerdem die virtuosen malerischen Qualitäten Brouwers, dessen skizzenhaft wirkende Bilder mit ihrer delikaten Farbkomposition und Transparenz den Werken eines Vermeer und Terborch gleichkommen. So ist verständlich, daß Brouwers Gemälde bereits zu seinen Lebzeiten ihre Liebhaber fanden. Der Nachlaß von Peter Paul Rubens verzeichnete 17 Bilder des von ihm hochgeschätzten Künstlerkollegen, und auch Rembrandt besaß Zeichnungen und sieben Gemälde von Brouwer. Die Alte Pinakothek verdankt ihren einmaligen Bestand von 17 Bildern, die zu den Meisterwerken des Künstlers zählen, dem Sammeleifer zweier Wittelsbacher Fürsten.

tures with their delicate colour composition and transparency may be compared with the works of Vermeer or Ter Borch. It is not surprising, therefore, that Brouwer's paintings were greatly admired during the artist's lifetime. The inventory of Rubens' estate included 17 paintings by his highly esteemed fellow artist; and Rembrandt also possessed seven paintings and a number of drawings by Brouwer. The Alte Pinakothek owes its unique collection of 17 of the artist's finest pictures to the passion of two Wittelsbach princes for collecting works of art.

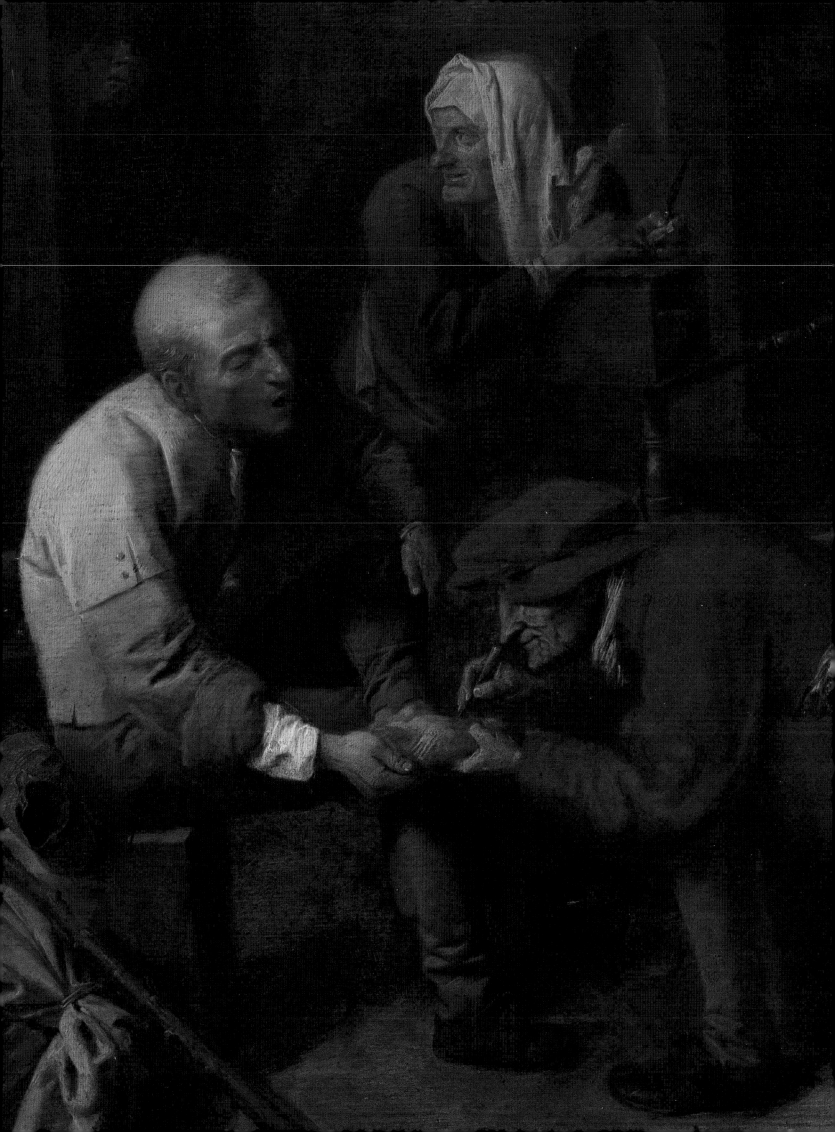

49 David Teniers der Jüngere
(1610 Antwerpen – 1690 Brüssel)

Bauernstube

Holz, 37 x 50,4 cm
Signiert unten rechts: D. TENIERS F
Inv. Nr. 1835

49 David Teniers the Younger
(1610 Antwerp – 1690 Brussels)

Peasant Interior

Wood, 37 x 50.4 cm
Signed bottom right: D. TENIERS F
Inv. No. 1835

Die beiden für diesen Band ausgewählten Bilder David Teniers d. J. sind unter dem unübersehbaren Einfluß Adriaen Brouwers entstanden. So ist auch dieses Gemälde ganz offensichtlich von dessen Kaschemmen mit rauchenden und trinkenden Bauern beeinflußt. Die einzelnen Bestandteile des kargen Interieurs – der offene Fensterladen mit dem einfallenden Licht, das aus Fässern gefertigte Mobiliar, stillebenartig arrangierte irdene Krüge, ein polierter, blitzender Kupferkessel, ein wie zufällig drapiertes weißes Tuch als Farbakzent – sind alles Motive, die von Brouwer her bekannt sind. An dem Stilleben aus Haushaltsutensilien zeigt sich Teniers Meisterschaft in der Beobachtung und Wiedergabe von Dingen des alltäglichen Lebens. Die Personen im Vordergrund sind vertieft in das Rauchen und Trinken: Der eine stopft seine Pfeife, der andere zündet sich seine an und der dritte stößt bereits den Rauch genüßlich mit in den Nacken gelegtem Kopf aus. Der vierte Bauer in dieser Gesellschaft hält Glas und Krug in Händen. Um den Kamin herum sitzen und stehen weitere Personen bei lautstarker Unterhaltung. Ein ebenfalls von Brouwer übernommenes Motiv ist eine Gestalt, die durch die Tür hereinkommt oder hinausgeht, hier eine Frau in der offenen Tür.

Bei dem um 1637–1639 entstandenen Gemälde fällt auf, daß die Figurentypen bereits unverwechselbare Eigenschöpfungen von Teniers sind, der sich seit Mitte der dreißiger Jahre selbständig weiterentwickelte. Unabhängigkeit von seinem Vorbild, dem er in Thematik, Maltechnik und dunkler Farbigkeit nachstrebte, konnte Teniers allerdings erst nach dem Tod Brouwers (1638) erlangen.

The pictures by David Teniers the Younger selected for this catalogue are clearly influenced by the work of Adriaen Brouwer. This painting, too, reveals Teniers' fascination for Brouwer's tavern scenes with smoking, drinking peasants. The individual elements that go to make up the bare interior – the open shutter and the light entering through the window, the furniture fashioned from old barrels, the still life arrangements of earthenware vessels, a gleaming, polished copper pot, a seemingly casually draped white cloth as a bright highlight – are all motifs that are familiar from Brouwer's works. Teniers' powers of observation and his mastery in depicting everyday objects can be seen in the still life arrangement of household utensils. The persons in the foreground are completely absorbed in smoking and drinking. One is filling his pipe, another is lighting his, and the third is already puffing out smoke with obvious pleasure, his head thrown back. The fourth peasant in this group holds a glass and a jug in his hands. Other figures can be seen sitting or standing in front of the fire engaged in loud conversation. A further motif adopted from Brouwer is that of a figure in the act of entering or leaving a room. In the present picture, it is a woman standing in the open doorway.

One striking feature of this painting, dating from c. 1637–39, is that, what were formerly standard figures have now become Teniers' own unmistakable creations. The artist began to develop his own individual style in the mid-1630s, but only after Brouwer's death in 1638 was Teniers able to free himself completely from the influence of the master whose thematic material, technique and dark coloration he had sought to emulate.

50 David Teniers der Jüngere
(1610 Antwerpen – 1690 Brüssel)

Wirtsstube

Holz, 37,3 x 52,8 cm
Inv. Nr. 818

50 David Teniers the Younger
(1610 Antwerp – 1690 Brussels)

Tavern Scene

Wood, 37.3 x 52.8
Inv. No. 818

Die formelhafte Verwendung der einzelnen Bestandteile in Teniers Wirtsstuben wird im Vergleich mit der „Bauernstube" (Nr. 49) deutlich. Fast alle Elemente finden sich hier wieder. In einer kargen Kaschemme sitzen Männer um einen Faßtisch im Vordergrund beim Rauchen und Trinken, eine Gruppe um den Kamin im Hintergrund gibt sich den gleichen Genüssen hin. Eine Gewichtung oder Hervorhebung Einzelner findet nicht statt. So wird die Aufmerksamkeit des Betrachters nicht auf eine Hauptperson gelenkt, sondern die gleichmäßige Verteilung im Raum angestrebt, der auch die Beleuchtung ohne besondere Akzente entspricht. Licht fällt durch eine Fensteröffnung von links sowie durch eine geöffnete Türe rechts hinten, durch die der Wirt mit Schürze verschwindet. Ein Stilleben aus Tonkrügen und Holzscheiten ist am rechten vorderen Bildrand arrangiert, ein weißes Tuch malerisch über einen Holzpflock drapiert und selbst die über dem Kamin aufgehängte Zeichnung mit einem karikierenden Bauernporträt fehlt nicht als Brouwer-Zitat. Der einzige Hinweis auf die negativen Folgen von Rauch- und Alkoholgenuß – bei Brouwer teilweise sehr drastisch geschildert – ist der mit dem Kopf auf seinen Armen schlafende Bauer vor dem Kamin.

Trotz einzelner, häufig wiederholter Elemente und einer etwas spannungslosen Ausgewogenheit der Erzählung erfaßt das Bild, das um 1639/40 auf dem Höhepunkt von Teniers Schaffen entstand, die Atmosphäre in der Schenke genau. Es zeugt von großer künstlerischer Sicherheit und malerischer Delikatesse, die reiche Farbpalette ist gegenüber seinen früheren Werken heller und strahlender geworden.

The use of standard details in Teniers' tavern scenes becomes apparent when this picture is compared with his "Peasant Interior" (No. 49). Almost all the elements of the latter work are to be found here. In a sparsely furnished alehouse, a number of men can be seen in the foreground seated about a barrel table smoking and drinking. In the background, a further group is gathered by the fireplace indulging in the same pleasures. No individual is given special emphasis. Set next to each other, they are all of equal value. The attention of the observer is, therefore, not drawn to any particular person who might represent a central figure. Instead, Teniers seeks to achieve an even distribution of weight in the room, an aim that is supported by the lighting of the picture, which is without special accentuation. Light enters via a window on the left and through the open door in the background on the right. The publican, wearing an apron, is just disappearing through this door. A still life consisting of wooden stakes and earthenware vessels is arranged in the bottom right-hand corner of the painting. A white cloth is draped picturesquely over a wooden rail, and above the fireplace there is a drawn caricature of a peasant that makes conscious reference to Brouwer. The sole allusion to the adverse effects of smoking and drinking – which were often the subject of scathing criticism in similar scenes by Brouwer – is the peasant sleeping in front of the fireplace with his head resting on his arms.

In spite of the repetition of certain set pieces and a somewhat unexciting balance in this depiction, the work, painted c. 1639/40 when Teniers was at the height of his powers, accurately captures the atmosphere of the tavern. It testifies to his sureness of touch and his great sensitivity as a painter. The broad range of colours is brighter and more radiant here than in earlier works.

51 Frans Snyders
(1579 Antwerpen – 1657 Antwerpen)

Vorratskammer mit Diener

Leinwand, 135 x 201 cm
Signiert unten rechts: F · Snyders · fecit.
Inv. Nr. 198

Ein Wildbret-Arrangement aus Rehbock, Hase, Wildschwein und Geflügel ist neben Hummer, Obst und Gemüse auf einem langen, die ganze Bildbreite einnehmenden Tisch, dem Betrachter zum Greifen nahe, ausgebreitet. Hinter dem Tisch steht ein Diener, der Trauben aus dem Korb nimmt und sich dabei nach rechts umblickt, wo ursprünglich eine Frauengestalt stehen sollte, wie eine Vorzeichnung im British Museum, London, belegt. Das Zentrum der Stillebenkomposition auf dem dunkelroten Tischtuch bildet ein toter Rehbock, dessen Kopf über die Tischkante herabhängt und durch ein weißes Tuch hervorgehoben wird. Um ihn herum sind die erlesenen Gegenstände angeordnet, die in ihrem verschwenderischen Überfluß nicht willkürlich, sondern sehr überlegt plaziert sind, wobei die Horizontalen von Tischkante und Tischtuch als gliedernde Elemente dienen. Ergänzt wird das Arrangement durch lebende Tiere, die zusammen mit dem Diener dem Stilleben einen anekdotischen Zug geben: Von rechts pirscht sich eine Katze heran, links schnäbeln Hahn und Henne, und ein Hund kommt neugierig schnuppernd unter dem Tisch hervor.

Das Münchner Gemälde ist ein großartiges Beispiel für den von Snyders entwickelten Typus der mit Delikatessen angefüllten Vorratskammer. Die hier zusammengestellten Köstlichkeiten – alles typische, bei Snyders immer wieder zu findende Requisiten – sind sicher vorrangig dekorativ zu verstehen, dennoch könnte man an die damals so beliebten Fünf-Sinne-Darstellungen denken und hier das Gesicht durch die Katze, den Geruch durch den Hund, das Gehör durch den Rehbock, das Gefühl durch die schnäbelnden Hühner und den Geschmack durch den nach den Trauben greifenden Diener versinnbildlicht sehen.

Das nicht datierte Gemälde kann auf Grund seines warmen, hellen Kolorits und der plastischen Malweise in die Zeit um 1615–1620 gesetzt werden.

51 Frans Snyders
(1579 Antwerp – 1657 Antwerp)

Pantry Scene with Servant

Canvas, 135 x 201 cm
Signed bottom right: F · Snyders · fecit.
Inv. No. 198

An arrangement of game, consisting of a roebuck, a hare, a wild boar and poultry, is laid out together with a lobster, fruit and vegetables in almost tangible proximity to the observer on a table that extends over the entire width of the picture. Behind the table, which is covered with a dark red cloth, stands a servant. He is removing a bunch of grapes from a basket and looks to his right, to where a female figure was originally meant to stand, as a preliminary drawing in the British Museum, London, shows. At the centre of this still life composition, set off against a white cloth, is a dead roebuck, its head hanging over the edge of the table. Various exquisite objects are laid out about the animal. Despite their profusion, they are not arranged at random, but obey a well-considered order. In this respect the horizontal lines of the edge of the table and the tablecloth serve as structuring elements. The arrangement is complemented by living animals that, together with the page, lend this still life an anecdotal quality. A cat stalks in from the right. On the left, a billing cock and and hen can be seen; and from under the table, a dog appears, sniffing inquisitively at the game.

The Munich painting, with its array of exquisite food, is a fine example of the "pantry picture" type that Snyders created within the still life tradition. The delicacies assembled here are standard components of this genre and recur in many of Snyders' works. In this picture, they should certainly be understood primarily in a decorative sense, but there is also a reference to depictions of the five senses that were so popular at that time. Thus the cat would represent "sight", the dog "smell", the roebuck "hearing", the billing fowl "touch", and the servant reaching for the grapes "taste".

The picture bears no date, but its warm, bright coloration and the boldly modelled manner of depiction indicate that it was painted in the years 1615–1620.

52 Daniel Seghers
(1590 Antwerpen – 1661 Antwerpen)
Erasmus Quellinus der Jüngere
(1607 Antwerpen – 1678 Antwerpen)

Blumengirlande um Steinrelief mit der Hl. Familie und Johannes dem Täufer

Kupfer, 79,8 x 61,2 cm
Signiert unten rechts: D. Seghers: Soc^tis JESU.
Inv. Nr. 7079

Diese signierte Kupfertafel ist ein repräsentatives Beispiel für zahlreiche weitere Werke von Daniel Seghers, in denen ein von einem anderen Künstler gemaltes Relief mit einer Blumenrahmung versehen ist. Die aus Stein gehauene Kartusche mit Voluten und Rollwerk rahmt ein geschweiftes Mittelfeld mit einem Steinrelief, auf dem die Heilige Familie samt dem kleinen Johannes dem Täufer dargestellt ist. Die sitzende Maria hält das Kind auf ihrem Schoß. Beide blicken zu Johannes hinunter, dem Josef die Hand aufgelegt hat. Im Hintergrund ist eine bewaldete Landschaft zu erkennen. Ober- und unterhalb des Reliefs schlingen sich je eine Efeuranke um die Kartusche, besteckt mit verschiedenen Blüten, wie Rosen, Pfingstrosen, Tulpen, Schneeglöckchen, Akelei, Nelke, Osterglocke, Hyazinthe und Orangenblüten. Auf der unteren Girlande haben sich Schmetterlinge niedergelassen, die damals als Symbol für die Auferstehung galten. Gegenüber den schmückenden bunten Blüten tritt die Stein imitierende Grisaille-Malerei von Kartusche und Relief in den Hintergrund.
Dieses Gemälde ist wohl identisch mit einem im Inventar Seghers' aufgeführten „...cartel met barreleef van Sr Quelinus op plaet voor den Prins van Nieuwenborch". So läßt sich die Darstellung im Mittelfeld mit dem Stil von Erasmus Quellinus d. J. vereinbaren. Auch die Herkunft des Gemäldes aus Schloß Neuburg an der Donau paßt zur Angabe des Inventars. Außerdem existiert ein Dankesbrief von Philipp Wilhelm, Herzog von Pfalz-Neuburg, geschrieben zu Düsseldorf am 25. Juli 1650, in dem er sich beim Rektor der Antwerpener Jesuiten für die Übersendung eines Gemäldes von Seghers bedankt. Alle diese Indizien sprechen dafür, daß das Münchner Gemälde mit dem in Seghers' Inventar genannten zu identifizieren ist und damit um 1650 entstand.

52 Daniel Seghers
(1590 Antwerp – 1661 Antwerp)
Erasmus Quellinus the Younger
(1607 Antwerp – 1678 Antwerp)

Garland of Flowers about a Stone Relief with the Holy Family and the Infant John

Copper, 79.8 x 61.2 cm
Signed bottom right: D. Seghers: Soc^tis JESU.
Inv. No. 7079

This signed copper panel is a typical example of many works by Daniel Seghers in which a stone relief painted by another artist is surrounded by an arrangement of flowers. The carved cartouche with volutes and scrolls frames a curved central panel consisting of a stone relief depicting the Holy Family and the Infant John. Mary is seated with Jesus on her lap. Both of them are looking down to John, on whom Joseph lays his hand. In the background is a wooded landscape. Above and below the relief, separate strands of ivy twine about the cartouche. The ivy is decorated with roses, peonies, tulips, snowdrops, columbines, carnations, daffodils, hyacinths and orange blossom. The butterflies that have settled on the lower strand of ivy were understood at that time as a symbol of the Resurrection. Alongside the decorative coloured flowers, the grisaille painting of the stone cartouche and the relief recedes into the background.
This picture is probably the same as that listed in Seghers' inventory as "...cartel met barreleef van Sr Quelinus op plaet voor den Prins van Nieuwenborch". The details depicted in the central area are in the style of Erasmus Quellinus the Younger. The provenance of the painting, from Neuburg Palace on the Danube, also fits the description of the inventory. Furthermore, in a letter written in Düsseldorf on 25 July 1650 by Philipp Wilhelm, Duke of the Palatinate-Neuburg, the duke thanks the rector of the Antwerp Jesuits for sending a painting by Seghers.
All this evidence supports the theory that the Munich picture is identical with the one mentioned in Seghers' inventory and was, therefore, painted around 1650.

53 Jan van Kessel der Ältere
(1626 Antwerpen – 1679 Antwerpen)
Erasmus Quellinus der Jüngere
(1607 Antwerpen – 1678 Antwerpen)

Die vier Weltteile: Europa

Kupfer, Mitteltafel 48,6 x 67,3 cm
Signiert und datiert auf dem Bild im Vordergrund:
Jan van Kessel FECIT 1664
Inv. Nr. 1910

Die Darstellung von Europa ist Bestandteil einer vierteiligen Serie der Erdteile, die zwischen 1664 und 1666 entstand. Jeder der damals bekannten Erdteile – Europa, Asien, Afrika, Amerika – wird durch eine große Mitteltafel repräsentiert, die von 16 kleineren gerahmt ist. Die zentrale Tafel zeigt die allegorische Personifikation des Kontinents inmitten stillebenartig arrangierter Gegenstände, die für diesen Erdteil als typisch erachtet wurden. Um die Mitteltafel herum sind 16 Städteansichten angeordnet, wobei im Vordergrund Tiere liegen – entweder nach der Natur, nach Vorlagen oder frei erfunden. Die ungewöhnliche Form der Anordnung und äußeren Gestaltung – jedes der Bilder ist einzeln gerahmt – wurde schon vorher in der Druckgraphik bei Landkarten und Städteansichten verwendet.

Die Mitteltafel zeigt die Personifikation Europas, mit Hermelinumhang und Krone wie eine Königin gekleidet, in einem repräsentativen Innenraum thronend. Ihre Funktion als Trägerin der Kirche verdeutlichen eine Bibel, eine päpstliche Tiara, ein Papstporträt und der Ausblick auf die Engelsburg in Rom. Auch die anderen im Raum verteilten Gegenstände haben eine Bedeutung: Das Füllhorn steht für die Fruchtbarkeit Europas, die Waffen für die Kriegskunst, Staffelei, Palette, Bücher und Globus für Kunst und Wissenschaft, und die Nischenfiguren vertreten die europäischen Königreiche. In negativem Zusammenhang stehen das Trictracspiel, Weinkrug und -pokal, Schmuckschatulle mit Schuldzettel sowie der Tennisschläger, die wohl auf die Laster Trunksucht und Spielleidenschaft verweisen. Abbildungen von Insekten, Tieren, Blumen etc. zeigen die Vielfalt der europäischen Flora und Fauna. Auf einer der Tafeln bilden Würmer und Raupen sogar den Namenszug Jan van Kessels und die Datierung „FECIT 1664".

Die Figuren der Mitteltafel ließ Jan van Kessel vermutlich von Erasmus Quellinus d. J. ausführen. Das von ihm

53 Jan van Kessel the Elder
(1626 Antwerp – 1679 Antwerp)
Erasmus Quellinus the Younger
(1607 Antwerp – 1678 Antwerp)

The Four Continents: Europe

Copper, central panel 48.6 x 67.3 cm
Signed and dated on the picture in the foreground:
Jan van Kessel FECIT 1664
Inv. No. 1910

This representation of Europe belongs to a four-part series depicting the continents of the earth, painted between 1664 and 1666. Each of the continents known at that time – Europe, Asia, Africa and America – is portrayed in a large central panel surrounded by 16 smaller panels. The central panel contains an allegorical personification of the particular continent together with objects regarded as typical of that part of the earth, arranged in the form of a still life. The 16 smaller panels surrounding the central panel present views of important cities, with animals in the foreground, drawn from nature or from zoological works, or sometimes freely invented. The unusual arrangement and outward form of these works (each panel is separately framed) was known in combination with prints of maps and city views.

The central panel here contains a personification of Europe, a female figure, wearing an ermine-trimmed robe and a crown, and seated in state like a queen. Her function as protectress of the Church is indicated by a Bible, a papal tiara, a portrait of the pope and a view through the window to the Castel Sant'Angelo in Rome. The other objects spread about the room are also of significance. The cornucopia represents the fertility of Europe; the weapons, the art of war. The easel, palette, books and globe are symbols of art and science, and the figures in the niches represent the kingdoms of Europe. There are negative symbols, too, such as the tric-trac board (a game similar to backgammon), the wine jug and goblet, the casket of jewels with an IOU, and the tennis racquet, all of which are presumably references to the vices of intemperance and gambling. Depictions of insects, animals, flowers, etc. show the variety of European flora and fauna. On one of the panels, the inscription "Jan van Kessel FECIT 1664" is formed by worms and caterpillars.

The figures in the central panel were presumably exe-

selbst gemalte detailreiche Ambiente, das an Kunst- und Wunderkammern erinnert, steht stark unter dem Einfluß der Allegorien seines Großvaters Jan Brueghel d. Ä.

cuted by Erasmus Quellinus the Younger. The richly detailed setting, painted by Jan van Kessel, is reminiscent of cabinets of art and curiosities and betrays the strong influence of the allegories of his grandfather Jan Brueghel the Elder.

54 Jan Wildens
(um 1585/86 Antwerpen – 1653 Antwerpen)

Landschaft mit abziehendem Unwetter

Holz, 42 x 71,5 cm
Datiert und monogrammiert am Sockel des Obelisken:
1649 IW
Inv. Nr. 5030

Das breitformatige Gemälde zeigt zwischen riesigen, rahmenden Bäumen den Ausblick auf eine Landschaft, über der gerade ein Unwetter niedergegangen ist. Davon zeugen ein greller Blitz, die dunklen, schweren Wolken, aus denen Regen fällt sowie ein doppelter Regenbogen. Vorne öffnet ein Mann das Gatter für sein Pferdefuhrwerk, weiter hinten, durch einen Wasserlauf oder einen Teich vom Vordergrund abgetrennt, sind mehrere Personen zu sehen: Eine Frau mit Kind und Hund, die vor dem Unwetter unter die Bäume flüchten, ein Reiter, ein Hirte mit Schafen, ein Wanderer am Waldrand rechts und eine Person, die unter einem großen Holzkreuz kniet. Als markanter Blickfang dient ein Obelisk, dessen Sockel die Jahreszahl 1649 und des Künstlers Initialen IW trägt. In der Ferne sind eine Windmühle und die Silhouette einer Stadt mit Kirchturm zu erkennen. Durch die Abstufung des Lichts in drei Zonen ergibt sich eine Tiefenwirkung, der Vordergrund ist düster und wird von einem reflektierenden Bachlauf oder Teich vom Mittelgrund abgetrennt. In dieser zweiten Zone ist das Licht heller und zwischen dem Obelisken und dem Waldrand öffnet sich der Ausblick in die Ebene, wo der Blitz alles in helles Licht taucht.

Die Landschaft ist von Jan Wildens nicht nach der Natur gemalt, sondern naturnah-malerisch erfunden, wobei er die aufgewühlte Stimmung mit dem abziehenden Gewitter gut nachempfunden hat. Dieser Atmosphäre entspricht die Farbgebung mit warmen bräunlichen Tönen im Vordergrund.

Das Bild stammt aus der späten Schaffensphase von Wildens, die nach dem Tode von Rubens 1640 einsetzte. Damals versuchte er dessen Nachfolge in der Landschaftsmalerei anzutreten, was ihm jedoch mit seiner etwas trockenen Malweise kaum gelingen sollte.

54 Jan Wildens
(c. 1585/86 Antwerp – 1653 Antwerp)

Landscape with Receding Storm

Wood, 42 x 71.5 cm
Dated and with monogram on the plinth of the obelisk:
1649 IW
Inv. No. 5030

Between large, flanking groups of trees to left and right of this broad horizontal panel is an open view of a landscape. A violent storm has just been raging, as is evident from the livid flash of lightning, the dark, heavy clouds from which rain is still falling, and a double rainbow in the distance. In the foreground, a man is opening a barred gate for his horse-drawn cart. In the middle distance, which is separated from the foreground by a stream or pond, a number of other people can be seen: a woman with a child and a dog who are fleeing from the storm to the cover of the trees; a horseman; a shepherd with a flock of sheep; a wayfarer on the edge of the woods on the right, and a person kneeling at the foot of a tall wooden cross. The obelisk in the middle distance forms a striking landmark in the picture. On its plinth stands the date 1649 and the artist's initials IW. In the distance are a windmill and the outline of a town with a church spire. The division of the scene into three distinctly lit zones helps to create a striking sense of depth. The foreground is dark and gloomy. It is separated by the reflecting strip of water from the middle zone, where the light is brighter. Between the obelisk and the edge of the forest, the view opens to reveal a flat plain, where the lightning bathes everything in a luminous light.

Jan Wildens' landscape is not painted from nature, but is an imaginary scene of naturalistic, picturesque character. The agitated mood in the wake of the thunderstorm is captured with particular sensitivity. The coloration matches this mood with warm brown tones in the foreground.

The picture dates from Wildens' late period, which began after the death of Rubens in 1640. At that time, he hoped to step into Rubens' shoes as a landscape painter, but there was little likelihood of this, in view of Wildens' somewhat dry manner of painting.

55 Lodewijk de Vadder
(1605 Brüssel – 1655 Brüssel)

Landschaft mit Hohlweg

Holz, 32,5 x 51,4 cm
Inv. Nr. 1051

55 Lodewijk de Vadder
(1605 Brussels – 1655 Brussels)

Landscape with Hollow Lane

Wood, 32.5 x 51.4 cm
Inv. No. 1051

Von leicht erhöhtem Standpunkt aus sieht man auf einen breiten, von links kommenden Weg mit drei Reitern und zwei Wanderern. Der Weg mündet in eine sanft hügelige Landschaft mit einem Schäfer, im Hintergrund ist die Silhouette eines Kirchturms zu erkennen. Auffällig ist die steile, sandige Böschung, die den Weg an der linken Seite begrenzt. Auf die Schilderung dieser hellen, sonnenbeschienenen Sandfläche und den Bewuchs des Überhangs mit Büschen, Bäumen und Ranken wird größte Sorgfalt verwendet, während die kleinen Figuren nur Staffage sind. Sandige Hohlwege sind ein charakteristisches und immer wiederkehrendes Motiv in De Vadders Werk. Der Ausblick auf die von Licht durchflutete Landschaft vor weitem Horizont wird gerahmt vom Baumbestand zu seiten des Hohlwegs, wobei sich durch den Sonnenstand starke Schatten ergeben. Mittels dieser kontrastreichen Abfolge von Licht- und Schattenzonen wird Tiefenwirkung erzeugt. Licht und Farbe geben dem routiniert gemalten Bild seine stimmungsvolle Ausstrahlung. Im hauptsächlich von warmen, braunen Tönen dominierten Gemälde steht die dunkle Zone der verschatteten Bäume effektvoll vor einem strahlenden Himmel mit weiß-grauen Wolken. Lichtreflexe spielen in den von der Sonne beschienenen Blättern, mit schnellem, lockerem Pinselstrich gesetzt.

Bei der Landschaft könnte es sich um den Forêt de Soignes handeln. Dieser im Südosten von Brüssel gelegene Wald war bevorzugtes Motiv der ansässigen Landschaftsmaler und scheint auch De Vadder inspiriert zu haben. Seine sensible Naturbeobachtung, die sich vom akademischen Stil gelöst hat, macht ihn zu einem der fähigsten Maler von Waldlandschaften in der Brüsseler Malerei des 17. Jahrhunderts, die für Künstler in seinem Umkreis – Jacques d'Arthois, Ignace van der Stock, Lucas Achtschellinck – vorbildlich wurde.

From an elevated viewpoint, three mounted figures and two wayfarers can be seen on a broad track that enters the picture from the left. The path descends to a landscape of gently rolling hills in which a shepherd sits. In the distance, the silhouette of a church tower can be recognized. A striking feature of this scene is the steep, sandy bank that borders the track on the left. The sunlit surface of this embankment and the overhanging bushes, trees and trailing bines are depicted with the utmost care for detail, whereas the small figures are merely staffage. Sandy defiles and hollow lanes are a characteristic and recurring motif in De Vadder's œuvre. The extensive view of a landscape suffused with light is framed by the trees along both sides of the pass. The position of the sun results in areas of strong shadow, and the alternation of zones of light and shade creates a sense of depth. Lighting and coloration also lend this adroitly painted picture its atmospheric quality. In a work dominated by warm brown tones, the dark zone of the shadowy trees is effectively set against a radiant sky with grey and white clouds. Reflections of sunlight dancing in the leaves are depicted with swift, light brush strokes.

The landscape is possibly a depiction of the Forêt de Soignes south-east of Brussels. It was a favourite location of the local landscape painters and also seems to have inspired De Vadder. His sensitive observation of nature, which has freed itself of academic stylistic traits, makes him one of the most gifted painters of forest scenes in 17th-century landscape art in Brussels. These provided a model for the artists in his circle, including Jacques d'Arthois, Ignace van der Stock and Lucas Achtschellinck.

56 Jan Siberechts
(1627 Antwerpen – um 1703 London)

Viehweide mit schlafender Frau
Leinwand, 107 x 83 cm
Inv. Nr. 2165

56 Jan Siberechts
(1627 Antwerp – c. 1703 London)

Pasture with Sleeping Woman
Canvas, 107 x 83 cm
Inv. No. 2165

Zwei Frauen haben sich am Rande einer Viehweide zum Schlafen hingelegt. Die eine liegt lang ausgestreckt und ganz entspannt an einen Erdwall gelehnt auf dem Rücken, einen Arm unter den Kopf geschoben, das junge Mädchen daneben hat sich in tiefem Schlaf zusammengerollt. Nicht weit davon entfernt und ebenfalls im Vordergrund dösen zwei Schafe nebeneinander. Auf der blumenbewachsenen Weide sind weitere ruhende oder grasende Schafe und Kühe verteilt. Ein Bachlauf begrenzt die Weide, die an seinem Ufer wachsenden Pappeln, Weiden und das Buschwerk heben sich dunkel vor dem hellen Himmel ab und bilden eine Kulisse für die Idylle. Die in sich abgeschlossene, beschauliche Szenerie wird durch keinen Ausblick in die Ferne gestört. Die Wirkung des ruhigen, stimmungsvollen Bildes, in dem die Zeit stillzustehen scheint, beruht auch auf seiner Farbgebung: kühle, zurückhaltende Farben, dominiert von einem Grau-Grün. Die Helligkeit des Mittagslichtes wirkt durch Wolken und Bäume gefiltert. Da hinein setzen die Kleider der beiden Hirtinnen gelbe, rote und blaue Farbakzente. Wunderbar ist der Glanz der beiden Messinggefäße wiedergegeben, Siberechts ständig verwendete Requisiten. In diesem Gemälde schafft Siberechts eine Synthese von Landschafts- und Genrebild, denn die Hirtinnen und Tiere sind nicht auf kleine Staffagefiguren reduziert, sondern in der Intensität der Beobachtung und Wiedergabe der Landschaft gleichwertig behandelt.

Das undatierte Gemälde, das wohl aus der Antwerpener Zeit nach 1660 stammt, stellt durch Komposition, Malweise und Farbigkeit eine Vorwegnahme der französischen Malerei des 19. Jahrhunderts dar.

A woman and a girl have lain down at the edge of a pasture to sleep. The woman is stretched out full length, one arm folded under her head, her body leaning against a bank of earth in a position of complete relaxation. The little girl by her side is curled up fast asleep. In the foreground, not far away, two sheep are dozing next to each other. Scattered over the flowery meadow are other sheep and cows, resting or grazing. The pasture is bounded by a stream, along the bank of which are poplars, willows and bushes that stand out darkly against the light sky, forming a backdrop to this idyll. No distant view intrudes upon the tranquillity of this self-contained, contemplative scene. The peaceful, atmospheric mood of the picture, in which time seems to stand still, derives from the cool, restrained coloration, dominated by grey-green tones. The bright light of midday is filtered by a screen of clouds and trees. Set off against this subdued background are the yellow, red and blue clothes of the two herdswomen. The gleaming surfaces of the two brass vessels are superbly captured. Objects such as these appear regularly in Siberechts' paintings. In this work, the artist achieves a synthesis of landscape and genre forms; for the herdswomen and animals are not reduced to diminutive staffage figures, but are as intensely observed and portrayed as the setting.

Although the picture is not dated, it was painted probably some time after 1660 when Siberechts was in Antwerp. In its composition, technique and coloration it anticipates certain aspects of 19th-century French painting.

BIOGRAPHIEN

Susanne Wagini

Pieter van Avont   Nr. 6
(1600 Mecheln – 1652 Deurne bei Antwerpen)

Der Maler und Kunsthändler Pieter van Avont wurde 1600
in Mecheln geboren. Nach seiner Ausbildung, die er wahr-
scheinlich bei seinem Vater, einem Bildhauer, absolvierte,
wurde er 1620 als Meister in der Mechelner Zunft aufgenommen. 1622 trat er in die Lukasgilde in Antwerpen ein.
Er starb 1652 in Deurne bei Antwerpen, wo er sich gegen
Ende seines Lebens niedergelassen hatte.
Van Avont, der hauptsächlich Figuren und religiöse Historien malte, arbeitete oft mit anderen Künstlern zusammen.
So schuf er in Bildern von Jan Brueghel d. Ä., Lucas van
Uden und Frans Wouters die Figurenstaffage. Zu seiner
Spezialität gehörte die Darstellung der Heiligen Familie, für
die Kollegen die rahmenden Blumen- und Früchtegirlanden
malten.

Hendrick van Balen   Nr. 5
(1575 Antwerpen – 1632 Antwerpen)

Hendrick van Balen wurde 1575 in Antwerpen geboren. Er
soll Schüler bei Adam van Noort, dem Lehrer von Rubens,
gewesen sein. 1592/93 wurde er als Meister in der Antwerpener Lukasgilde aufgenommen und trat offenbar bald darauf eine Italienreise an, deren Nachwirkung in seinen
Gemälden sichtbar ist. Darüber hinaus muß er die Bilder
des Deutschen Johann Rottenhammer, der damals in Venedig tätig war, gekannt haben, denn deren starke Auswir-
kung auf Van Balen ist nicht zu übersehen, und beider
Werke werden häufig verwechselt. Nach seiner Rückkehr
entwickelte sich Van Balen zu einem gefragten Künstler, zu
dessen zahlreichen Schülern u. a. Anthonis van Dyck und
Frans Snyders zählten.
Van Balen, der 1632 in seiner Heimatstadt starb, war auf
kleine Kabinettbilder mit vielfigurigen mythologischen und
biblischen Szenen sowie Allegorien spezialisiert. Bei der
damals üblichen und häufig praktizierten arbeitsteiligen
Zusammenarbeit mit Kollegen wie Joos de Momper und
dem älteren und jüngeren Jan Brueghel war er der Spezialist für die kleinfigurige Figurenstaffage.

Adriaen Brouwer   Nr. 43–48
(1605/06 Oudenaarde – 1638 Antwerpen)

Adriaen Brouwer ist als Maler des Bauerngenres bekannt
geworden. In einer kurzen Schaffenszeit von nur ungefähr
zwölf Jahren entstanden rund 65 Werke, die heute als
eigenhändig anerkannt werden. Mit 17 Gemälden besitzt
die Alte Pinakothek davon den größten geschlossenen
Bestand.
Zum Leben Adriaen Brouwers existieren verhältnismäßig
wenige gesicherte Daten. Er wurde um 1605/06 vermutlich
in Oudenaarde (Flandern) geboren. 1626 ist er in Holland,
sowohl in Amsterdam als auch in Haarlem, bezeugt. Er verließ Holland wieder und kehrte nach Flandern zurück, wo
er seit 1631/32 als Meister in der Antwerpener Lukasgilde
geführt wurde. In dieser Stadt blieb er bis zu seinem frühen
Tod zu Beginn des Jahres 1638.
Seine Fähigkeit, die einfachen, oft derben Freuden des Bau-
ernlebens, wie Trinken, Rauchen, Kartenspiel und den
dabei oft entstehenden Streit, naturgetreu und lebensnah
zu schildern, wird bereits von seinen frühen Biographen
gerühmt. Die künstlerische Herkunft Brouwers ist nicht
genau bekannt, doch war er ohne Zweifel von der flämischen Genremalerei Pieter Bruegels d. Ä. (dem sog. „Bauern-Bruegel") und dessen Nachfolgern geprägt.
Die zumeist kleinformatigen Bilder zeigen virtuose maleri-
sche Qualitäten. Locker, mit dünnem Farbauftrag gemalt
und auf subtile Farbwirkung zielend, fanden die unterhalt-
samen Gemälde bereits früh ihre Liebhaber. Aufgrund der
regen Nachfrage wurden Brouwers Gemälde bereits zu seinen Lebzeiten kopiert und nachgeahmt. Diese im 17. Jahrhundert gefertigten Kopien machen es heute schwierig,
sein Werk abzugrenzen, zumal er sehr selten signierte oder
monogrammierte. Auch eine Chronologie ist nicht ohne
Probleme zu erstellen, da keines seiner Gemälde datiert ist.

Jan Brueghel der Ältere   Nr. 1–6, 21
(1568 Brüssel – 1625 Antwerpen)

Jan Brueghel d. Ä. wurde 1568 in Brüssel als zweiter Sohn
von Pieter Bruegel d. Ä., dem sog. „Bauern-Bruegel", gebo-

ren. Neben seinem Vater ist er das bedeutendste Mitglied der bekannten Malerfamilie. Jan, der den Beinamen „Samt-Brueghel" wegen seines feinen, präzisen Pinselstrichs und der delikaten Leuchtkraft seiner Farben erhielt, war ein sehr vielseitiger Künstler. Er malte Landschaften (See-, Fluß-, Dorf-, Waldlandschaften), mythologische, allegorische und historische Szenen und nicht zuletzt zahlreiche Blumengemälde, die ihm zu seinem zweiten Beinamen „Blumen-Brueghel" verhalfen. Wie auch sein älterer Bruder Pieter ist er von der Malerei des Vaters stark beeinflußt, doch während Pieter d. J. über die kopierende, enge Anlehnung nicht herauskam, entwickelte Jan d. Ä. eine eigenständige Malweise.

Seine Ausbildung absolvierte Jan vermutlich in Antwerpen bei Pieter Goetkindt. Die obligatorische Italienreise führte ihn zwischen 1590 und 1596 nach Neapel, Rom und Mailand. In Mailand lernte er Kardinal Federigo Borromeo kennen, der zu einem wichtigen Gönner und Freund wurde. Nach seiner Rückkehr nach Flandern wurde Jan 1597 in der Antwerpener Lukasgilde aufgenommen. 1606 erhielt er durch den Gouverneur der südlichen Niederlande, Erzherzog Albrecht VIII., und dessen Frau Isabella einen einem Hofkünstler vergleichbaren Status und damit verbundene Privilegien. Mit Peter Paul Rubens und auch anderen befreundeten Künstlern, wie Hendrick van Balen, Frans Snyders, Joos de Momper, Sebastiaen Vrancx und Pieter van Avont, arbeitete er zusammen. Bei Gemeinschaftskompositionen trug jeder seine jeweilige spezielle Begabung als „Fachmaler" bei. Jan Brueghel d. Ä., der Begründer der Antwerpener Kabinettmalerei, starb 1625 hochangesehen und vermögend in Antwerpen. Vor dem Kunsthistorischen Museum in Wien und dem Prado in Madrid besitzt die Alte Pinakothek die größte Sammlung seiner Werke.

Anthonis van Dyck   Nr. 32–40
(1599 Antwerpen – 1641 London)

Anthonis van Dyck wurde 1599 als Sohn eines Textilkaufmanns in Antwerpen geboren. Da sich seine künstlerische Begabung sehr früh zeigte, kam er bereits 1609 im Alter von zehn Jahren zu Hendrick van Balen in die Lehre. In der Zeit von 1618 bis 1620 war Van Dyck – seit 1618 als Meister in der Antwerpener Lukasgilde verzeichnet – in der Werkstatt von Peter Paul Rubens tätig. Dieser schätzte das Talent seines Mitarbeiters sehr und bezeichnete ihn als seinen besten Schüler. Der Ruhm des jungen Malers verbreitete sich rasch, und er wurde 1620 nach England an den Hof König James I. berufen. Von dort aus unternahm er in den Jahren 1621–1627 eine Italienreise, die ihn über Antwerpen, wo er einen längeren Zwischenaufenthalt einlegte, neben Rom und Venedig vor allem nach Genua führte. In dieser Stadt machte er sich als Porträtist des Adels einen Namen. Durch seinen Italienaufenthalt lernte er Werke Tizians und Tintorettos kennen, die ihn sehr beeindruckten und ihre Spuren in seinem Werk hinterließen. Im Herbst 1627 wieder nach

Antwerpen zurückgekehrt, eröffnete Van Dyck eine eigene Werkstatt und wurde 1630 Hofmaler der Statthalterin Erzherzogin Isabella in Brüssel. 1632 zog er erneut nach London, wo er von König Charles I. zum Ritter geschlagen und zum Hofmaler ernannt wurde; als solcher war er vor allem als Porträtist in Anspruch genommen. Reisen 1634/35 und 1640 führten ihn in die Spanischen Niederlande; dort erhielt er als größte Auszeichnung der Antwerpener Lukasgilde die Ernennung zum Ehrenvorsitzenden. In England hatte er 1639 Mary Ruthven, eine Hofdame der Königin, geheiratet. Der seit dem Sommer 1641 gesundheitlich angeschlagene Maler schonte sich nicht und reiste nach Frankreich und in die Niederlande. Im Dezember, wenige Tage nach der Geburt seiner Tochter, starb Van Dyck im Alter von 42 Jahren in London.

Trotz des Einflusses, den Rubens auf ihn ausübte, konnte Van Dyck einen eigenständigen Stil entwickeln. Die Wirkung seiner eleganten Bildnisse ist vor allem in der englischen Porträtmalerei bis zum Ende des 18. Jahrhunderts zu spüren.

Frans Francken der Jüngere   Nr. 10, 11
(1581 Antwerpen – 1642 Antwerpen)

Der 1581 in Antwerpen geborene Frans Francken d. J. ist das begabteste Mitglied einer großen Antwerpener Malerdynastie. Seine Ausbildung erhielt er höchstwahrscheinlich bei seinem Vater Frans Francken d. Ä. Im Jahre 1605 wurde er Freimeister der Lukasgilde, in der er 1614/15 das Amt des Dekans innehatte. Seine enorme Produktivität wurde nicht zuletzt durch die große Werkstatt ermöglicht, die Frans d. J. als Familienbetrieb führte und in der neben seinen drei Söhnen auch seine drei Brüder mitarbeiteten. 1642 starb der bereits zu seiner Zeit hochgeschätzte Künstler in Antwerpen. Die noch heute erhaltenen Gemälde bezeugen seine schöpferische Kraft.

Frans Francken d. J. fertigte vor allem kleinformatige Kabinettbilder. Seine biblischen und mythologischen Historien, Genredarstellungen und Allegorien stattete er mit kleinfigurigen Massenszenen aus. Von besonderer Bedeutung sind die Darstellungen von Galerieinterieurs, die er als eigene Gattung entwickelte.

Abraham Janssen van Nuyssen   Nr. 12
(um 1575 Antwerpen – 1632 Antwerpen)

Abraham Janssen wurde um 1575 in Antwerpen geboren. Ab 1585 war er Schüler bei Jan Snellinck, der Altargemälde, Historienbilder und Teppichkartons fertigte. Zwischen ca. 1598 und 1601 war Janssen in Rom und wurde nach seiner Rückkehr Mitglied in der Lukasgilde von Antwerpen. Der hochgeschätzte Maler, dem große öffentliche Aufträge erteilt wurden, starb 1632 in Antwerpen.

Abraham Janssen ist einer der wenigen flämischen Maler, die vor und neben Peter Paul Rubens die großformatige Monumentalmalerei in Antwerpen pflegten. Seine Themen waren biblische und mythologische Historien sowie Allegorien. Entgegen allgemeiner Erwartung läßt sich nach seinem Italienaufenthalt kein entscheidender Einfluß Caravaggios in seinem Werk beobachten, lediglich dessen scharfe Hell-Dunkel-Kontraste übernahm er. Sein Stil entwickelte sich von einem späten Manierismus hin zu einem Klassizismus, als dessen bekanntester Vertreter in Antwerpen er heute gilt. Seine Gemälde zeichnen sich vor allem durch einen sehr eigenständigen, massiven Figurenstil aus, der bereits von Zeitgenossen treffend als „steenachtig" im Sinne von ausgeprägt plastisch charakterisiert wurde.

Jacob Jordaens
Nr. 41, 42
(1593 Antwerpen – 1678 Antwerpen)

Jacob Jordaens war neben Peter Paul Rubens und Anthonis van Dyck einer der Hauptmeister des flämischen Barock. 1593 wurde er in Antwerpen als das erste Kind eines wohlhabenden Leinenhändlers geboren. Nach seiner Ausbildung bei dem Maler Adam van Noort, bei dem auch Rubens Schüler gewesen war, fand er 1615 Aufnahme als Meister in der Antwerpener Lukasgilde. Der sechzehn Jahre ältere Rubens hatte sichtbaren Einfluß auf Jordaens. Trotz dieses mächtigen Vorbilds gelang es Jordaens jedoch, eine eigene Bildsprache zu entwickeln. Die Themen seiner zahlreichen Gemälde, die zusammen mit seiner großen Werkstatt entstanden, sind sehr vielfältig: biblische und mythologische Historien, Porträts, Illustrationen von Sprichwörtern, Szenen des Volkslebens. Außerdem schuf er eine Serie von Teppichentwürfen mit Darstellungen von Sprichwörtern. Bei diesen profanen Themen macht sich ein holländisch-protestantischer Einfluß bemerkbar. In den dreißiger Jahren hatte er den Höhepunkt seiner Karriere erreicht. Große Aufträge, auch ausländischer Fürsten, wurden an ihn vergeben. Nach dem Tod von Rubens (1640) und von Van Dyck (1641) war er der führende Maler der südlichen Niederlande. Sein gegen 1650 erfolgter Übertritt zum reformierten Glauben beeinträchtigte seine Auftragslage nicht, und als Protestant im katholischen Antwerpen schuf er weiterhin Altargemälde für katholische Kirchen. Nach einer langen, produktiven Schaffenszeit starb er 1678 hochbetagt in seiner Heimatstadt.

Jan van Kessel der Ältere
Nr. 53
(1626 Antwerpen – 1679 Antwerpen)

Jan van Kessel wurde 1626 in Antwerpen als Sohn des Malers Hieronymus van Kessel und der Paschasia Brueghel, einer Tochter von Jan Brueghel d. Ä., geboren. Er ging bei dem Genremaler Simon de Vos sowie bei seinem Onkel Jan Brueghel d. J. in die Lehre. Seine Aufnahme als Meister

in der Antwerpener Lukasgilde fand 1644/45 statt. 1679 ist er in Antwerpen gestorben.
Jan van Kessel malte hauptsächlich Tier- und Blumengemälde kleinen Formats – seltener großformatige Bilder –, wobei die Blumengemälde unter dem Einfluß Daniel Seghers' stehen. Daneben gibt es von ihm Stilleben und Allegorien, wie die Darstellung der Sinne, der vier Elemente oder der vier Weltteile, die sehr stark von Jan Brueghel d. Ä. beeinflußt sind. In den Bildern von Van Kessel, die sich durch eine starke, brillante Farbigkeit auszeichnen, wurden die Figuren zumeist von Künstlerkollegen gemalt.

Joos de Momper
Nr. 9
(1564 Antwerpen – 1635 Antwerpen)

Joos de Momper, 1564 in Antwerpen geboren, entstammte einer namhaften Antwerpener Künstlerfamilie. Sein Vater Bartholomäus, bei dem er seine Ausbildung absolvierte, war Maler und Kunsthändler. Auch Joos de Momper war später im Bilderhandel tätig. Sehr früh, bereits 1581, wurde er als Freimeister in der Lukasgilde aufgenommen. Vieles spricht für eine Italienreise, die in der Zeit zwischen 1581 und 1590, dem Jahr seiner Hochzeit, stattgefunden haben muß. Er starb 1635 in Antwerpen.
Joos de Mompers Rolle in der Entwicklung der Landschaftsmalerei des 17. Jahrhunderts ist bedeutend, sowohl in Flandern als auch in Holland. Er malte hauptsächlich Berglandschaften, die in Komposition und Farbgebung vor allem von Pieter Bruegel d. Ä. und Paul Bril beeinflußt sind. Daneben schuf er auch Dorfansichten, Höhlen- und Grottenbilder sowie Sommer- und Winterdarstellungen. Die belebende Figurenstaffage wurde zumeist von einem Künstlerkollegen gemalt; besonders häufig von Jan Brueghel d. Ä. Die in großer Zahl erhaltenen Gemälde belegen die Produktivität seiner Werkstatt und die Vorliebe seiner Zeitgenossen für derartige Bilder. So lassen sich in vielen Galeriebildern des 17. Jahrhunderts auch seine Landschaftsgemälde finden. Der Wertschätzung durch den Brüsseler Hof verdankt er die Freistellung von Steuern in Antwerpen, ein Privileg, das neben ihm Jan Brueghel d. Ä. genoß.

Erasmus Quellinus der Jüngerer
Nr. 52, 53
(1607 Antwerpen – 1678 Antwerpen)

Erasmus Quellinus, Sohn des gleichnamigen Bildhauers, wurde 1607 in Antwerpen geboren. Wahrscheinlich erhielt er seine erste Ausbildung bei seinem Vater. Sein jüngerer Bruder Artus war einer der bedeutendsten flämischen Bildhauer des 17. Jahrhunderts. 1633/34 wurde Erasmus in der Antwerpener Lukasgilde aufgenommen, vielleicht nach einer Ausbildung bei Peter Paul Rubens, mit dem er bald darauf eng zusammenarbeitete. So war Quellinus an zwei großen Aufträgen neben Rubens beteiligt: 1635 an der Dekoration für den festlichen Einzug von Ferdinand von

Österreich in Antwerpen, der sogenannten Pompa Introitus Ferdinandi, und 1636–1638 an der Ausgestaltung der Torre de la Parada, dem Jagdpavillon von König Philipp IV. bei Madrid. Der vielseitig begabte Künstler war als Maler, Zeichner und Radierer tätig. Er entwarf Buchillustrationen und Titelblätter, schuf neben allegorischen, mythologischen und religiösen Gemälden auch Stilleben und Blumenstücke in Zusammenarbeit mit Jan Fyt, Pieter Boel und Daniel Seghers. Von seiner Hand stammen viele der augentäuscherischen, Stein imitierenden Kartuschenfüllungen für die Blumengirlanden von Seghers. 1656 war er zusammen mit seinem Bruder an der Dekoration des Amsterdamer Rathauses beteiligt. Der Maler, der stilistisch hauptsächlich von Peter Paul Rubens und Anthonis van Dyck beeinflußt war, starb 1678 in Antwerpen.

Peter Paul Rubens   Nr. 13–31
(1577 Siegen – 1640 Antwerpen)

Peter Paul Rubens ist der wichtigste Vertreter nordeuropäischer Barockmalerei. Von ihm besitzt die Alte Pinakothek eine der größten Sammlungen überhaupt. Rubens entstammte einer Antwerpener Patrizierfamilie und wurde aufgrund religiöser und politischer Unruhen 1577 im Exil seiner Familie in Siegen (Deutschland) geboren. Nach seiner Rückkehr nach Antwerpen im Jahre 1589, besuchte er die Lateinschule, wurde für kurze Zeit Page in gräflichen Diensten und schließlich Lehrling bei mehreren Antwerpener Malern. Nach Abschluß seiner Ausbildung 1598 ging Rubens 1600 nach Italien, um die Kunst der klassischen Antike und die italienische Malerei vor allem Michelangelos, Tizians und Tintorettos zu studieren. Als Hofmaler des Herzogs von Mantua fand er schnell Anerkennung. Nach seiner Rückkehr im Jahre 1608 erhielt er sogleich zahlreiche offizielle und private Aufträge in Antwerpen und wurde 1609 Hofmaler der Statthalter in Brüssel. Im gleichen Jahr heiratete er die Antwerpener Patriziertochter Isabella Brant, die ihm drei Kinder gebar und bereits 1626 starb. 1630 schloß er eine zweite Ehe mit der erst sechzehnjährigen Helene Fourment, die in vielen Gemälden der dreißiger Jahre Rubens' Frauentyp schlechthin verkörpert.
Rubens war nicht nur Maler, sondern wurde auch von den Gelehrten seiner Zeit als einer der ihren geschätzt. Außerdem betraute ihn der Brüsseler Hof mit wichtigen diplomatischen Aufgaben bei den Friedensverhandlungen zwischen England und Spanien.
Die frühe Wertschätzung beruht nicht nur auf seiner malerischen Fertigkeit, sondern vor allem auf der Eindringlichkeit seiner Bildsprache, mit der er allegorische oder symbolische Inhalte einfach und prägnant wiederzugeben vermag. Selbstbewußt schreibt er 1621 über sich: „Mein Talent ist so beschaffen, daß noch kein Auftrag meinen Schaffensmut übertroffen hat."

Daniel Seghers   Nr. 52
(1590 Antwerpen – 1661 Antwerpen)

Daniel Seghers wurde 1590 in Antwerpen geboren. Nach seiner Lehrzeit in Holland und später, zurück in Antwerpen, bei Jan Brueghel d. Ä. wird er 1611 als Meister in der Antwerpener Lukasgilde verzeichnet. 1614, vom Calvinismus zum römisch-katholischen Glauben konvertiert, trat er in den Jesuitenorden ein. Nach Empfang der Weihen als Laienbruder 1625 wurde er von seinem Orden für zwei Jahre nach Rom geschickt. Bis zu seinem Tod 1661 lebte und arbeitete Daniel Seghers in Antwerpen.
Neben der Kirche zählten Kaiser, Könige und Fürsten zu seinen Auftraggebern. Ein in Abschrift erhaltenes eigenhändiges Inventar (Abschrift um 1775) stellt eine wichtige Quelle zur Identifizierung seiner Gemälde und ihren illustren Auftraggebern dar.
Daniel Seghers' bevorzugtes Thema waren Blumen, wobei er eine Besonderheit entwickelte: eine Kartusche oder ein Medaillon, das mit Blumengestecken, Kränzen oder Girlanden geschmückt ist. Im Mittelfeld ist entweder ein christliches Motiv dargestellt, was das Gemälde zu einem Andachtsbild machte, aber auch Mythologien oder Porträts. Diese Mittelbilder wurden in der Regel von anderen Malerkollegen, wie Erasmus Quellinus d. J., Gerard Seghers, Abraham van Diepenbeeck oder Cornelis Schut, ausgeführt.
Nach dem Tod seines Lehrers Jan Brueghel d. Ä. (1625) stieg Daniel Seghers zum bedeutendsten Antwerpener Blumenmaler auf. Seine charakteristischen, dekorativen Blumenarrangements von hoher malerischer Feinheit und Qualität fanden großes Interesse und rege Nachfrage.

Jan Siberechts   Nr. 56
(1627 Antwerpen – um 1703 London)

Der Antwerpener Landschaftsmaler Jan Siberechts wurde 1627 als Sohn des gleichnamigen Bildhauers geboren. Wahrscheinlich zunächst Schüler bei seinem Vater, war er später Lehrling bei Adriaen de Bie, einem Porträtmaler aus Mechelen. Im Jahre 1648/49 wurde er als Meister in der Antwerpener Lukasgilde aufgenommen. Ein Italienaufenthalt, der aufgrund südlicher Anklänge in seinen frühen Landschaften vermutet wurde, läßt sich nicht durch Quellen belegen. Bis 1672 war Siberechts in Antwerpen ansässig, um dann, wohl auf Einladung des Herzogs von Buckingham, nach England überzusiedeln. Dort arbeitete er vornehmlich für die Aristokratie bis zu seinem Tod um 1703 in London.
Siberechts frühe Werke weisen Einflüsse der holländischen Italianisanten, Malern wie Jan Asselijn, Nicolaes Berchem, Herman van Swanevelt und Karel Dujardin, auf. Die späteren Antwerpener Bilder der Jahre zwischen ca. 1661–1672 schildern das bäuerliche Landleben ruhig und in idyl-

lischer Verklärung. Charakteristische Themen waren überschwemmte Landstraßen mit zum Markt ziehenden Fuhrwerken und im Wasser watenden Bäuerinnen. In diesen Bildern entwickelte er einen eigenen, selbständigen Stil, unabhängig von der gleichzeitigen Antwerpener Malerei um Rubens. Die seit 1672 in England entstandenen Bilder zeigen hauptsächlich das Landleben und Ansichten der Landsitze des dortigen Adels.

Frans Snyders
Nr. 51
(1579 Antwerpen – 1657 Antwerpen)

Der Stilleben- und Tiermaler Frans Snyders wurde 1579 in Antwerpen als Sohn eines Gastwirts geboren. Seine Ausbildung absolvierte er bei Pieter Brueghel d. J. und wohl auch bei Hendrick van Balen. 1602 wurde er Freimeister in Antwerpen und erst 1608–1609 reiste er nach Italien. Nach seiner Rückkehr begann die engere Zusammenarbeit mit Peter Paul Rubens, aber auch mit Anthonis van Dyck, Cornelis de Vos, Thomas Willeboirts Bosschaert und Jan Boekhorst. Der sehr erfolgreiche Maler hatte einen gewissen Wohlstand erworben und starb 1657 in Antwerpen.
Frans Snyders wurde besonders für seine Tierdarstellungen und die mit erlesenen Delikatessen ausgestatteten Vorratskammern großen Formats berühmt, die als Dekoration von Speise- und Festsälen sehr begehrt waren. Daneben schuf der vielseitige Maler große Marktbilder, Früchtegirlanden, Tierjagden und auch Stilleben kleinerer Formats. Er entwickelte sich zum führenden Spezialisten des autonomen Stillebens in Antwerpen. Diese Gemälde stehen in der Tradition der Markt- und Küchenbilder des 16. Jahrhunderts von Joachim Beuckelaer und Pieter Aertsen, doch ist fraglich, ob Snyders noch die gleiche moralisierende Tendenz verfolgte wie diese. Seine sinnen- und farbenfreudigen Bilder stehen im Gegensatz zur oftmals ausgeprägten Vanitassymbolik der holländischen Stilleben.

David Teniers der Jüngere
Nr. 49, 50
(1610 Antwerpen – 1690 Brüssel)

David Teniers d. J. wurde 1610 in Antwerpen geboren. Er entstammte einer Künstlerfamilie und ging bei seinem Vater David d. Ä. in die Lehre, der vorrangig religiöse und antike Themen malte. Seit seiner Aufnahme als Meister in der Lukasgilde im Jahre 1633 beschäftigte er sich zunächst hauptsächlich mit dem Bauerngenre, wobei er dem Vorbild Adriaen Brouwers folgte. Nach diesem wurde er der wichtigste Vertreter dieses Genres in den südlichen Niederlanden. Von den Gasthausszenen löste sich Teniers in den späteren Jahren und malte vornehmlich Kirmesdarstellungen beziehungsweise friedliche, heitere Landschaften. Diese Werke wurden im 18. Jahrhundert, vor allem in höfischen Kreisen, höher geschätzt als die von Adriaen Brouwer.

Einen Höhepunkt fand seine künstlerische Karriere, als er 1651 zum Hofmaler des Erzherzogs Leopold Wilhelm, dem spanischen Statthalter der südlichen Niederlande, ernannt wurde und daraufhin nach Brüssel umzog. Zu seinen Aufgaben gehörte neben der Tätigung von Ankäufen die Betreuung der bedeutenden Gemäldesammlung. Er fertigte Kopien an, die der Vorbereitung eines druckgraphischen Kataloges der erzherzoglichen Sammlung dienten. Bekannt wurde Teniers auch durch seine dokumentarischen „Galeriebilder", eine eigene Gattung der Antwerpener Malerei seit dem Beginn des 17. Jahrhunderts. Nach dem Tod von Erzherzog Leopold Wilhelm wurde Teniers unter dessen Nachfolger Don Juan d'Austria in seinen Hofämtern bestätigt. Neben den offiziellen Bestellungen auch des europäischen Adels führte er Aufträge für das Bürgertum aus. Als er 1690 in Brüssel starb, war auch das Ende der großen Zeit der flämischen Malerei erreicht.

Lodewijk de Vadder
Nr. 55
(1605 Brüssel – 1655 Brüssel)

Über Lodewijk de Vadder sind nur wenige Nachrichten überliefert. Geboren wurde er 1605 in Brüssel, wo er 1655 auch gestorben ist. Im Jahre 1628 fand er als Meister Aufnahme in der dortigen Lukasgilde, wahrscheinlich nach einer Lehre bei seinem fünfzehn Jahre älteren Bruder Philippe. Dokumentiert ist weiterhin, daß Lodewijk de Vadder Kartons für Tapisserien schuf, wobei er auch mit Jacob Jordaens zusammenarbeitete.
Bekannt wurde De Vadder aber hauptsächlich als Landschaftsmaler der sog. „Brüsseler Schule", die sich neben dem Zentrum Antwerpen um den Hof in Brüssel entwickelte. Kennzeichen dieser Gruppe von Landschaftern ist die Wahl der Orte in der Umgebung von Brüssel und deren realistische Wiedergabe.

David Vinckboons
Nr. 7
(1576 Mecheln – 1632 Amsterdam)

Der 1576 in Mecheln geborene Maler David Vinckboons kam als Kind mit seinen Eltern zwischen 1580 und 1586 nach Antwerpen. David wurde von seinem Vater Philipp, einem Mechelner Wasserfarbenmaler, ausgebildet. Die Familie verließ 1586 Antwerpen aus religiösen Gründen, d. h. um der Verfolgung als Protestanten zu entgehen, und ließ sich in Amsterdam, in den protestantischen holländischen Provinzen, nieder. In dieser Stadt blieb David Vinckboons bis zu seinem Tod gegen Ende 1632.
David Vinckboons war in seiner frühen Schaffensphase stark beeinflußt von dem Landschaftsmaler Gillis van Coninxloo, der ebenfalls 1586 aus Flandern über Frankenthal nach Amsterdam emigriert war und wohl auch als sein Lehrer zu bezeichnen ist. Seine Landschaften staffierte

Vinckboons meist selbst aus, wobei die reich bevölkerten biblischen und weltlichen Szenen – Predigt des Johannes, Kreuztragung Christi, Dorfkirmessen, Bauerndarstellungen, Plünderungen – später zum Hauptgegenstand seiner Bilder werden. Historie, Genre und Landschaft sind bei ihm eng miteinander verzahnt. Seinem flämischen Stil, der auf der südniederländischen Tradition des späten 16. Jahrhunderts fußt, bleibt er auch in Amsterdam treu und kann dort seine Wirkung, vor allem auf das holländische Gesellschaftsstück des 17. Jahrhunderts, entfalten. Die große Beliebtheit seiner Kompositionen belegen zahlreiche Kopien seiner Gemälde und die weit verbreiteten Nachstiche.

Sebastiaen Vrancx   Nr. 8
(1573 Antwerpen – 1647 Antwerpen)

Der Maler Sebastiaen Vrancx wurde 1573 in Antwerpen geboren. Nach der Überlieferung war er Schüler von Adam van Noort, bei dem auch Peter Paul Rubens und Jacob Jordaens gelernt hatten. Von 1597 an unternahm Vrancx eine längere Italienreise, die sich später in Ansichten von antiken Ruinen in seinen Gemälden niederschlug. Nach seiner Rückkehr nach Antwerpen fand er 1600 Aufnahme in der Lukasgilde und war rege am gesellschaftlichen Leben beteiligt: als Mitglied in der Rhetorikerkammer der „Violieren" und der Bruderschaft der Romanisten. Im Jahre 1647 starb er in seiner Heimatstadt.

Vrancx war ein sehr vielseitiger Maler, von dem Genreszenen, wie vornehme Gesellschaften in Parks und Volksfeste, aber auch reine Landschafsdarstellungen bekannt sind. Als junger Künstler beeinflußte ihn Pieter Bruegel d. Ä., wovon vor allem die Illustrationen von Sprichwörtern in dessen Tradition zeugen. Seine heutige Bekanntheit verdankt Vrancx aber zahlreichen militärischen Darstellungen von Schlachten, Überfällen und Plünderungen – Sujets, die,

durch ihn ausgebildet, eine weite Verbreitung fanden. Als Fachmaler für derartige Staffagen arbeitete er gelegentlich mit anderen Künstlern, vor allem Jan Brueghel d. Ä. und Joos de Momper, zusammen.

Jan Wildens   Nr. 54
(um 1585/86 Antwerpen – 1653 Antwerpen)

Der 1585/86 in Antwerpen geborene Landschaftsmaler Jan Wildens trat sehr früh in die Lehre bei Pieter Verhulst ein, wurde 1604 Meister in der Antwerpener Lukasgilde und reiste 1613–1616 nach Italien. Gleich nach seiner Rückkehr arbeitete er im Atelier von Peter Paul Rubens, wo er als Spezialist für Landschaftshintergründe tätig war. Die Zusammenarbeit mit Rubens scheint bereits 1620 wieder beendet gewesen zu sein. Im Jahr 1624, nach dem Tod seiner Gemahlin, war Wildens auch im Kunsthandel tätig. Er starb 1653 in seiner Vaterstadt.
Die wenigen Werke aus der Zeit vor seinem Italienaufenthalt sind gebirgige Überblickslandschaften im Stil u. a. von Jan Brueghel d. Ä. und Joos de Momper. Auf der Italienreise fand eine Entwicklung zu einem Realismus und weiter angelegten, spontaneren Landschaftsschilderungen statt, wobei ihn besonders die Arbeiten von Paul Bril beeindruckten. Daneben lassen sich Einflüsse von Jan Brueghel d. Ä. und Adriaen van Stalbempts erkennen.
Nach dem Tod von Peter Paul Rubens (1640) entstehen eine Reihe von Gemälden, mit denen Wildens stilistisch an dessen späte Landschaften anschließen möchte, ohne jedoch deren leidenschaftlichen, kraftvollen Charakter erreichen zu können. Der Aufbau seiner Landschaften ist einfacher, bühnenartiger und ruhiger.
Neben der Mitarbeit bei Rubens schuf er als Fachmaler auch Landschaftshintergründe für andere Kollegen, wie beispielsweise Jacob Jordaens, Frans Snyders, Jan Boeckhorst und Paul de Vos.

196

BIOGRAPHIES

Susanne Wagini

Pieter van Avont
No. 6

(1600 Malines – 1652 Deurne near Antwerp)

The painter and art dealer Pieter van Avont was born in 1600 in Malines. In 1620, after completing his training, probably as a pupil of his father, who was a sculptor, he was adopted as a master in the Malines guild. In 1622, he entered the Guild of St Luke in Antwerp. He died in 1652 in Deurne near Antwerp, where he had settled towards the end of his life.

Van Avont, who painted primarily small-scale figures and religious history pictures, collaborated frequently with other artists. He executed the staffage in paintings by Jan Brueghel the Elder, Lucas van Uden and Frans Wouters, for example. He also specialized in depictions of the Holy Family, to which his colleagues painted garlands of flowers and fruit.

Hendrick van Balen
No. 5

(1575 Antwerp – 1632 Antwerp)

Hendrick van Balen was born in Antwerp in 1575. He was allegedly a pupil of Adam van Noort, to whom Rubens was also apprenticed. In 1592/93, Van Balen was admitted as a master to the Guild of St Luke in Antwerp. Shortly afterwards, he probably travelled to Italy, for the experiences of such a journey are evident in his painting. He must also have been acquainted with the pictures of Johann Rottenhammer, who was working in Venice at that time, since the German painter exerted an undeniable influence on Van Balen, and the works of the two artists are often confused. After his return, Van Balen rose to become a painter who was much in demand. Among his many pupils were Van Dyck and Frans Snyders.

Van Balen, who died in his home town in 1632, specialized in allegorical depictions and small cabinet pictures of mythological and biblical scenes containing a myriad of figures. In those days, it was not uncommon for painters to collaborate on pictures with other artists. Van Balen frequently worked as a specialist for small-scale figure staffage with painters such as Joos de Momper and the elder and younger Jan Brueghel.

Adriaen Brouwer
Nos. 43 – 48

(1605/06 Oudenarde – 1638 Antwerp)

Adriaen Brouwer is best known as a painter of peasant genre scenes. During his short creative life, which spanned only about 12 years, he executed roughly 65 paintings that are today recognized as the work of the master himself. The 17 pictures in the possession of the Alte Pinakothek represent the largest self-contained collection in the world.

Relatively few details of Brouwer's life are documented. Born c. 1605/06 probably in Oudenarde, Flanders, his presence is recorded in Holland in 1626 – in both Amsterdam and Haarlem. He later returned to Flanders, however, where his name is listed among the masters of the Antwerp Guild of St Luke from 1631/32. He remained in that city until his early death at the beginning of 1638.

His talent for down-to-earth, naturalistic depictions of the simple and often coarse pleasures of peasant life, such as drinking, smoking and playing cards, and the disputes to which these often gave rise, was esteemed by his early biographers. Brouwer's artistic origins are not precisely known, but he was certainly influenced by the Flemish genre painting of Pieter Bruegel the Elder (also known as "Peasant Bruegel") and his circle.

Brouwer's mostly small-scale pictures reveal a masterly technique. Painted with a lightness of touch and a thin application of paint aimed at achieving subtle colour effects, his entertaining depictions soon found many admirers. As a result of the keen demand for his works, Brouwer's paintings were frequently copied and imitated during his own lifetime. The existence of these 17th-century copies makes it difficult today to identify the works he painted himself, especially as he rarely signed them or added his monogram. Since none of his paintings are dated, it is not easy to locate them chronologically either.

Jan Brueghel the Elder
Nos. 1–6, 21

(1568 Brussels – 1625 Antwerp)

Jan Brueghel the Elder was born in Brussels in 1568. He was the second son of Pieter Bruegel the Elder, also known as "Peasant Bruegel". Together with his father, he is the most important member of this famous family of painters. Jan, who was given the nickname "Velvet Brueghel" on account of his fine, precise brushwork and the delicate, luminous quality of his colours, was an extremely versatile artist. He painted many different kinds of landscapes (sea-scapes, riverscapes, village and forest scenes), mythologi-cal, allegorical and historical depictions and large numbers of flower pictures – to which he owes his other nickname, "Flower Brueghel". Like his older brother, Pieter, Jan was strongly influenced by his father's painting. Whereas Pieter Brueghel the Younger did not go beyond an imitative bor-rowing from the work of his father, however, Jan devel-oped his own independent style.

He was probably a pupil of Pieter Goetkindt in Antwerp. In the course of the obligatory journey to Italy, which he undertook between 1590 and 1596, he visited Naples, Rome and Milan. In Milan he made the acquaintance of Cardinal Federigo Borromeo, who became an important patron and friend. In 1597, after his return to Flanders, Jan Brueghel was accepted into the Antwerp Guild of St Luke. In 1606, he was granted a status comparable to that of court painter, with all the privileges pertaining to it, by the governor of the southern provinces of the Netherlands, Archduke Albrecht VIII, and his wife Isabella. On a number of occa-sions, Brueghel collaborated on works with other painters, notably with friends such as Peter Paul Rubens, Hendrick van Balen, Frans Snyders, Joos de Momper, Sebastiaen Vrancx and Pieter van Avont. The contribution each artist made to these joint works depended on his special talents in a particular field. In 1625, Jan Brueghel the Elder, the orig-inator of Antwerp cabinet painting, died in that city, a highly esteemed and prosperous painter. The Alte Pinako-thek in Munich possesses the largest collection of his works. Other major collections are in the Kunsthistorisches Museum in Vienna and the Prado in Madrid.

Sir Anthony van Dyck   Nos. 32–40
(1599 Antwerp – 1641 London)

Anthony van Dyck was born in 1599, the son of an Antwerp textile merchant. His artistic talents manifested themselves at a very early age, and in 1609, when he was only ten years old, he was apprenticed to Hendrick van Balen. From 1618, Van Dyck's name is documented in the Antwerp Guild of St Luke as a master. From 1618 to 1620 he worked in Rubens' workshop. Rubens held the talent of his assistant in high regard and described him as his best pupil. The young artist's fame spread rapidly, and in 1620 he was called to the court of King James I of England. From London, he set out on a journey to Italy in the years 1621–1627. It took him via Antwerp, where he made a longer stop, to Rome, Venice and to Genoa, where he made a name for himself as a por-traitist to the nobility. During his travels in Italy, Van Dyck also acquainted himself with the works of Titian and Tinto-

retto, which made a profound impression on him and left their mark on his own painting. By the autumn of 1627, he had returned to Antwerp, where he opened his own work-shop; and in 1630 he was appointed court painter to the governess, Archduchess Isabella, in Brussels. In 1632, he again moved to London, where he was knighted by King Charles I and granted the position of court painter. In this office, he was largely responsible for portraiture. Journeys in 1634/35 and 1640 took him to the Spanish Netherlands. There he was awarded the highest distinction of the Ant-werp Guild of St Luke, when the members made him their honorary president. In 1639, in England, Van Dyck married Mary Ruthven, a lady-in-waiting to the queen. In the sum-mer of 1641 his health began to decline, but he ignored these warnings and undertook a journey to France and the Netherlands. In December of the same year, only a few days after the birth of his daughter, Van Dyck died in London at the age of 42.

Although his work is evidently indebted to Rubens, Van Dyck developed a style of his own, which is distinct from that of his great mentor. His elegant portraits continued to exert an influence, particularly on English portraiture, down to the end of the 18th century.

Frans Francken the Younger   Nos. 10, 11
(1581 Antwerp – 1642 Antwerp)

Frans Francken the Younger, born in 1581 in Antwerp, was the most talented member of a great family of painters in that city. In all likelihood he was a pupil of his father, Frans Francken the Elder. In 1605, the son became a free master of the Guild of St Luke, and in 1614/15, dean of the guild. His enormous output can be accounted for in part by the large workshop he ran as a family undertaking, in which not only his three sons, but also his three brothers worked. By the time of his death in Antwerp in 1642, he was already a highly esteemed artist. The large number of his extant works is evidence of his creative powers.

Frans Francken the Younger painted mostly small-scale cabinet pictures. His biblical and mythological history paintings, genre scenes and allegories were usually filled with myriad figures. Of special significance are his depic-tions of picture galleries and the paintings contained in them, which he developed into an independent genre.

Abraham Janssen van Nuyssen   No. 12
(c. 1575 Antwerp – 1632 Antwerp)

Abraham Janssen was born in Antwerp around 1575. From 1585 he was a pupil of Jan Snellinck, who painted altar-pieces, historical scenes and cartoons for tapestries. Between c. 1598 and 1601, Janssen was in Rome. After his return, he became a member of the Antwerp Guild of St Luke. Highly esteemed as a painter, he was awarded a number of major public commissions. He died in Antwerp in 1632.

Janssen was one of the few Flemish painters in Antwerp to create works of a monumental scale before and at the same time as Rubens. He painted mainly biblical and mythological subjects and allegories. Contrary to what one might expect, Caravaggio seems to have had no great influence on his work, despite Janssen's stay in Italy. One of the few things the Flemish artist adopted from the Italian was the use of chiaroscuro contrasts. Janssen's œuvre reveals a development from late Mannerism to Classicism. Indeed, he is regarded today as having been the leading exponent of "Antwerp Classicism". His paintings exhibit a highly individual style based on the depictions of powerful, large-scale figures, which his contemporaries fittingly described as *"steenachtig"*; in other words, of a bold, sculptural nature.

Jacob Jordaens   Nos. 41, 42
(1593 Antwerp – 1678 Antwerp)

Together with Rubens and Van Dyck, Jacob Jordaens was one of the great masters of Flemish Baroque painting. Born in Antwerp in 1593, the eldest child of a wealthy linen merchant, he was apprenticed to Adam van Noort, who had also trained Rubens. In 1615, Jordaens was enrolled as a master in the Antwerp Guild of St Luke. Rubens, who was 16 years older than Jordaens, had an evident influence on the latter. In spite of the powerful model the older artist represented, however, Jordaens succeeded in developing his own visual language. His numerous works, executed with the help of a large workshop, cover an extensive range of subjects, from portraits and biblical and mythological history, to the illustration of proverbs and scenes from everyday life. In addition, he made a series of cartoons for tapestries, containing depictions of proverbs. In these profane works, a certain Dutch Protestant influence can be detected. In the 1630s, Jordaens had reached the peak of his career and was awarded major commissions, including a number from foreign princes. After the deaths of Rubens in 1640 and Van Dyck in 1641, he was the leading painter of the southern Netherlands. His conversion to the Reformed Church around 1650 did not affect the volume of commissions he received, and as a Protestant in Catholic Antwerp, he continued to paint altarpieces for Catholic churches. After a long and creative life, he died at a ripe old age in his home town in 1678.

Jan van Kessel the Elder   No. 53
(1626 Antwerp – 1679 Antwerp)

Jan van Kessel was born in Antwerp in 1626, the son of the painter Hieronymus van Kessel and Paschasia Brueghel, a daughter of Jan Brueghel the Elder. Van Kessel was apprenticed to the genre painter Simon de Vos, as well as to his uncle Jan Brueghel the Younger. He became a master of the Antwerp Guild of St Luke in 1644/45 and died in Antwerp in 1679.

Van Kessel was first and foremost a painter of animals and flowers in small-scale pictures. Large-format paintings are relatively rare in his œuvre. His flower paintings were indebted to the work of Daniel Seghers. In addition, he painted a number of still lifes and allegories, such as his depictions of the senses, the four elements, or the four continents of the world known at that time. These reveal the influence of Jan Brueghel the Elder. Van Kessel's pictures are distinguished by their bold and brilliant coloration. The figures in his paintings were usually the work of other artists.

Joos de Momper   No. 9
(1564 Antwerp – 1635 Antwerp)

Born in 1564 in Antwerp, Joos de Momper was the son of a renowned family of artists in that city. His father Bartholomäus, to whom he was apprenticed, was a painter and art dealer. Later, Joos de Momper also dealt in art. In 1581, at a very young age, he was admitted as a master to the Guild of St Luke. Various circumstances suggest that he made a journey to Italy between 1581 and 1590, the year of his marriage. He died in Antwerp in 1635.

Joos de Momper played an important role in the development of 17th-century landscape painting, both in Flanders and in Holland. His landscapes are mainly mountain scenes, which, in their composition and coloration, are indebted in particular to Pieter Bruegel the Elder and Paul Bril. In addition, he painted village scenes and views of caves and grottoes as well as summer and winter scenes. The figure staffage that enlivens many of his works was executed mainly by other artists, especially by Jan Brueghel the Elder. The large numbers of De Momper's paintings that have survived are evidence of the productivity of his workshop and the fondness of his contemporaries for pictures of this kind. His landscape paintings reappear frequently in 17th-century depictions of cabinets of art. The esteem in which he was held by the court in Brussels freed him of the obligation to pay taxes in Antwerp, a privilege enjoyed by Jan Brueghel the Elder as well.

Erasmus Quellinus the Younger   Nos. 52, 53
(1607 Antwerp – 1678 Antwerp)

Erasmus Quellinus was the son of the sculptor of the same name. Born in 1607 in Antwerp, he probably received his initial training from his father. His younger brother Artus was one of the greatest Flemish sculptors of the 17th century. In 1633/34, Erasmus Quellinus the Younger was admitted to the Antwerp Guild of St Luke, perhaps after being a pupil of Rubens, with whom he was to collaborate closely shortly afterwards. Quellinus was involved in two major commissions with Rubens: the festive decorations for the entry of Ferdinand of Austria into Antwerp in 1635 – the *Pompa Introitus Ferdinandi,* as it was called; and the designs for the Torre de la Parada, King Philip IV's hunting lodge near Madrid (1636–1638). Quellinus was a most gifted and versatile artist who worked as a painter, draughtsman and engraver. He illustrated books and title-pages and painted allegorical, mythological and religious works, as well as still lifes and flower pictures in collaboration with Jan Fyt, Pieter Boel and Daniel Seghers. Many of the illusionistic paintings of stone panels framed by cartouches, around which Seghers' garlands of flowers twine, are by Quellinus. In 1656, he and his brother participated in the decoration of the city hall of Amsterdam. The painter, whose style was influenced mainly by Rubens and Van Dyck, died in Antwerp in 1678.

Sir Peter Paul Rubens Nos. 13–31
(1577 Siegen – 1640 Antwerp)

Sir Peter Paul Rubens is the leading representative of north European Baroque painting. The Alte Pinakothek possesses one of the greatest collections of his works in the world. Rubens belonged to a patrician family from Antwerp. He was born in 1577 in Siegen, Germany, where his family was in exile as a result of religious and political unrest. After the return of the family to Antwerp in 1589, Rubens received a classical education, served for a time as a page to a count, and was finally apprenticed to a number of painters in that city. He completed his training in 1598, and in 1600 went to Italy to study the works of Classical antiquity and Italian painting, especially those of Michelangelo, Titian and Tintoretto. As court painter to the Duke of Mantua, his gifts were quickly recognized, and after his return to Antwerp in 1608, he was immediately awarded numerous official and private commissions. In 1609, he was appointed court painter to the governor (stadholder) in Brussels. In the same year, he married Isabella Brant, the daughter of an Antwerp patrician family. Isabella, who bore him three children, died in 1626. In 1630, Rubens married a second time. His new wife, the 16-year-old Helene Fourment, was the subject of many pictures painted by Rubens in the 1630s in which she embodied his ideal female type.

Rubens was not merely a painter. He was esteemed by the scholars of his age as a colleague, and the court in Brussels entrusted him with important diplomatic assignments in the peace negotiations between England and Spain. From 1629 to 1630 he was at the court of King Charles I in England, where he was knighted.

Rubens owed his early recognition not merely to his great facility as a painter, but above all to the powerful visual imagery with which he depicted allegorical and symbolic themes in a simple, yet telling form. Describing his own abilities in 1621, he wrote: "My talent is such that no undertaking, however vast in size or diversified in subject, has ever surpassed my courage."

Daniel Seghers No. 52
(1590 Antwerp – 1661 Antwerp)

Daniel Seghers was born in Antwerp in 1590. After a period of apprenticeship in Holland and later in Antwerp as a pupil of Jan Brueghel the Elder, his name is documented as a master of the Antwerp Guild of St Luke from 1611. In 1614, he converted from Calvinism to Roman Catholicism and entered the Society of Jesus. In 1625, he received orders as a lay brother and was sent to Rome for two years. Up to his death in 1661, Daniel Seghers lived and worked in Antwerp. In addition to the Church, his patrons included the Emperor, kings and princes. A copy of an inventory written in his own hand and dating from c. 1775 represents an important source for the identification of his paintings and the persons who commissioned these works.

Daniel Seghers' favourite subject was flowers, and he developed his own special form of flower painting: a cartouche or medallion decorated with wreaths or garlands of flowers or other arrangements. The central panel usually contains a depiction of either a Christian motif – which makes the painting a devotional picture – or a mythological subject or portrait. As a rule, these central panels were executed by other painters such as Erasmus Quellinus the Younger, Gerard Seghers, Abraham van Diepenbeeck or Cornelis Schut.

After the death of his teacher, Jan Brueghel the Elder, in 1625, Daniel Seghers became the leading flower painter in Antwerp. His characteristic, decorative floral arrangements, which were very popular and much in demand, were of the utmost quality and finesse.

Jan Siberechts No. 56
(1627 Antwerp – c. 1703 London)

The Antwerp landscape painter Jan Siberechts was born in 1627, the son of the sculptor of the same name. Presumably apprenticed to his father at first, he was later a pupil of Adriaen de Bie, a portrait painter from Malines. In 1648/49, Siberechts was accepted as a master of the Antwerp Guild of St Luke. Southern accents in his early landscapes suggest a stay in Italy, although this is not documented. He lived in Antwerp down to 1672, in which year he moved to England, probably at the invitation of the Duke of Buckingham. There, he worked largely for the aristocracy until his death in London in 1703.

Siberechts' early works reveal the influence of the Dutch Italianizers, painters such as Jan Asselijn, Nicolaes Berchem, Herman van Swanevelt and Karel Dujardin. His later pictures, painted in Antwerp between roughly 1661 and

1672, are peaceful, idealized depictions of rustic life. Typical subjects were horse-drawn carts making their way to market along flooded roads, or peasant women wading through water. In these pictures, he developed his own, independent style that was not indebted to the contemporary Antwerp painting of the circle about Rubens. The works Siberechts executed in England after 1672 are mostly depictions of rural life and the country seats of the aristocracy.

Frans Snyders   No. 51
(1579 Antwerp – 1657 Antwerp)

Frans Snyders, a painter of still lifes and animal pictures, was born in Antwerp in 1579, the son of an innkeeper. He was a pupil of Pieter Brueghel the Younger and probably of Hendrick van Balen. In 1602, he became a free master of the Guild of St Luke in Antwerp and travelled to Italy some time later, in 1608–1609. After his return, Snyders began a close collaboration with Rubens, as well as with Van Dyck, Cornelis de Vos, Thomas Willeboirts Bosschaert and Jan Boekhorst. He was an extremely successful painter and acquired a certain wealth. He died in Antwerp in 1657.

Snyders was especially famous for his animal depictions and his large-format pantry scenes, replete with exquisite delicacies. Pictures such as these were greatly in demand to decorate dining-rooms and banqueting halls. In addition, this versatile artist painted large-scale market scenes, garlands of fruit, and hunting scenes, as well as smaller still lifes. He became a leading exponent of the autonomous still life in Antwerp. These pictures belong to the tradition of 16th-century market scenes and kitchen still lifes painted by Joachim Beuckelaer and Pieter Aertsen, but it is doubtful whether Snyders still had the same moralizing intent as these painters. His sensuous, colourful depictions form a distinct contrast to the often pronounced vanitas symbolism of the Dutch still life tradition.

David Teniers the Younger   Nos. 49, 50
(1610 Antwerp – 1690 Brussels)

David Teniers the Younger was born in 1610 of a family of artists in Antwerp. He was apprenticed to his father, David the Elder, who painted mainly religious pictures and themes from Classical antiquity. After his adoption as a master of the Guild of St Luke in 1633, Teniers initially painted peasant genre scenes, following in the footsteps of Adriaen Brouwer. After Brouwer, Teniers was the leading exponent of this genre in the southern Netherlands. In his later years, he moved away from tavern scenes and painted mainly serene landscapes or depictions of kirmes celebrations. In the 18th century, these works were valued even more highly than those by Adriaen Brouwer, especially in court circles.

The high-water mark of Teniers' artistic career was his appointment in 1651 as court painter and curator to Archduke Leopold Wilhelm, the Spanish governor of the southern Netherlands. Teniers thereupon moved to Brussels. His responsibilities included the acquisition of works of art and the superintendence of the archduke's important collection of paintings. In addition, he executed copies for a printed catalogue of the collection. Teniers was also famous for his documentary "gallery pictures", which formed a genre of their own within Antwerp painting from the beginning of the 17th century. After the death of Archduke Leopold Wilhelm, Teniers was confirmed in office by the archduke's successor, Don Juan d'Austria. In addition to official commissions, including a number from the European aristocracy, Teniers also executed works for the middle classes. His death in 1690 in Brussels marked the end of the great age of Flemish painting.

Lodewijk de Vadder   No. 55
(1605 Brussels – 1655 Brussels)

Little is known about Lodewijk de Vadder. He was born in 1605 in Brussels, where he also died in 1655. In 1628, he was adopted by the Guild of St Luke of that city as a master, probably after serving his apprenticeship with his brother Philippe, who was 15 years older. It is documented that Lodewijk de Vadder designed cartoons for tapestries, also in collaboration with Jacob Jordaens.

De Vadder was known principally as a landscape painter of the "Brussels school", which was centred around the court in that city and was the leading school of painting after that of Antwerp. The distinguishing features of this group of landscape painters are the choice of location in the area around Brussels and the realistic nature of their depictions.

David Vinckboons   No. 7
(1576 Malines – 1632 Amsterdam)

Born in Malines in 1576, David Vinckboons moved to Antwerp with his parents between 1580 and 1586 when he was still a child. He was apprenticed to his father Philipp Vinckboons, a water-colourist in Malines. In 1586, the family left Antwerp again for religious reasons – to escape persecution as Protestants – and settled in Amsterdam, in the Protestant Dutch provinces. David Vinckboons remained there till his death towards the end of 1632.

In the early years of his creative life his work was greatly indebted to the landscape painter Gillis van Coninxloo, who had emigrated in 1586 from Flanders via Frankenthal to Amsterdam, and who can also be regarded as Vinckboons' teacher. Vinckboons usually painted the staffage for his own pictures. His later works consist mainly of densely populated biblical and profane scenes, such as John the

Baptist preaching, the Crucifixion, village kirmes festivities, peasant scenes or depictions of looting. Historical themes, genre scenes and landscape are closely related in his œuvre. Even in Amsterdam, he remained true to his Flemish style, based on the late 16th-century tradition of the southern Netherlands; and in his new home, he exerted an influence on the 17th-century Dutch conversation piece. The many copies and engravings of his paintings attest to the great popularity of his work.

Sebastiaen Vrancx   No. 8
(1573 Antwerp – 1647 Antwerp)

Born in Antwerp in 1573, the painter Sebastiaen Vrancx is thought to have been a pupil of Adam van Noort, to whom Rubens and Jacob Jordaens were also apprenticed. In 1597, Vrancx went on an extended journey to Italy, which was later reflected in the views of Classical ruins in his paintings. After his return to Antwerp, he became a master of the Guild of St Luke in 1600 and played an active role in the social life of that city, as a member of the *De Violieren* society of orators and the fraternity of Romanists. He died in Antwerp in 1647.

Vrancx was an extremely versatile painter. His work included genre scenes, depictions of fashionable society in the park and popular festivities, as well as landscapes. As a young artist, he came under the influence of Pieter Bruegel the Elder, as the illustrations of proverbs in the tradition of the older master testify. Today, however, Vrancx owes his fame to his numerous military depictions, including scenes of battle, combat and looting, subjects that in his interpretations found a broad public. As a specialist for staffage of this kind, he also worked with other artists on occasion, notably with Jan Brueghel the Elder and Joos de Momper.

Jan Wildens   No. 54
(c. 1585/86 Antwerp – 1653 Antwerp)

The landscape painter Jan Wildens, born 1585/86 in Antwerp, became a pupil of Pieter Verhulst at a very early age and was accepted as a master in the Antwerp Guild of St Luke in 1604. From 1613 to 1616 he stayed in Italy, and on his return he worked in Rubens' workshop, where he was a specialist for landscape backgrounds. His collaboration with Rubens would seem to have been over by 1620. In 1624, after the death of his wife, Wildens also worked as an art dealer. He died in his home town in 1653.

The few surviving pictures from the time of his stay in Italy are mountainous panorama landscapes in the style of Jan Brueghel the Elder, Joos de Momper and others. During his travels in Italy, his painting underwent a development towards a greater degree of realism and a more expansive, spontaneous form of landscape depiction. He was particularly impressed by the works of Paul Bril. The influence of Jan Brueghel the Elder and Adriaen van Stalbempt can also be recognized.

After Rubens' death in 1640, Wildens painted a series of pictures that sought to take up the late landscape style of that master. They lack the powerful, passionate character of Rubens' works, however. The composition of Wildens' landscapes is simpler, more stage-like and placid.

In addition to his collaboration with Rubens, Wildens also worked as a specialist for landscape backgrounds with other artists such as Jacob Jordaens, Frans Snyders, Jan Boeckhorst and Paul de Vos.

AUSGEWÄHLTE LITERATUR / SELECTED BIBLIOGRAPHY

Alte Pinakothek München. Erläuterungen zu den ausgestellten Gemälden. 2. Aufl. München 1986

Frans Baudouin, Rubens et son siècle. Antwerpen 1972

Christopher Brown, Van Dyck. Oxford 1982

Corpus Rubenianum Ludwig Burchard. Bd. 1 ff., Brüssel 1968 ff.

Klaus Ertz, Jan Brueghel der Ältere (1568–1625). Die Gemälde mit kritischem Œuvrekatalog. Köln 1979

Hans Gerhard Evers, Peter Paul Rubens. München 1942

Zirka Zaremba Filipczak, Picturing Art in Antwerp. 1550–1700. Princeton 1987

Horst Gerson/Engelbert Hendrick Ter Kuile, Art and Architecture in Belgium 1600 to 1800. Harmondsworth 1960

Gustav Glück, Die Landschaften von Peter Paul Rubens. 2. Aufl. Wien 1945

Ursula Härting, Frans Francken der Jüngere (1581–1642). Die Gemälde mit kritischem Œuvrekatalog. Freren 1989

Marie-Louise Hairs, Les peintres flamands de fleurs au XVIIe siècle. 2. Aufl. Brüssel 1965

Rüdiger an der Heiden, Peter Paul Rubens und die Bildnisse seiner Familie in der Alten Pinakothek (= Bayerische Staatsgemäldesammlungen, Künstler und Werke Bd. 4). München 1982

Ders., Die Skizzen zum Medici-Zyklus von Peter Paul Rubens in der Alten Pinakothek (Bayerische Staatsgemäldesammlungen, Künstler und Werke Bd. 7). München 1984

Julius S. Held, The Oil Sketches of Peter Paul Rubens. A critical catalogue, 2 Bde. Princeton 1980

Erich Hubala, Peter Paul Rubens. Der Münchener Kruzifixus (Reclams Werkmonographien zur bildenden Kunst Nr. 127). Stuttgart 1967

Roger A. d'Hulst, Jacob Jordaens. Antwerpen/Stuttgart 1982

Hans Kauffmann, Rubens und Isabella Brant in der Geißblattlaube. In: Bildgedanke und künstlerische Form. Aufsätze und Reden. Berlin 1976, S. 33–49

Gerard Knuttel, Adriaen Brouwer. The master and his work. Den Haag 1962

Erik Larsen, The Paintings of Anthony van Dyck. 2 Bde. Freren 1988

Justus Müller Hofstede, Abraham Janssens. Zur Problematik des flämischen Caravaggismus. In: Jahrbuch der Berliner Museen 13, 1971, S. 208–303

Hella Robels, Frans Snyders. Stilleben- und Tiermaler (1579–1657). München 1989

Wolfgang Schöne, Peter Paul Rubens: Die Geißblattlaube. Doppelbildnis des Künstlers mit Isabella Brant (Reclams Werkmonographien zur bildenden Kunst Nr. 11). Stuttgart 1956

Yvonne Thiéry, Les peintres flamands de paysage au XVIIe siècle. Des précurseurs à Rubens. Brüssel 1986

Yvonne Thiéry/Michel Kervyn de Meerendre, Les peintres flamands de paysage au XVIIe siècle: Le baroque anversois et l'école bruxelloise. Brüssel 1987

Jacques Thuillier/Jacques Foucart, La Galerie Médicis au Palais du Luxembourg. Mailand 1969

Martin Warnke, Peter Paul Rubens. Leben und Werk. Köln 1977

Christopher White, Peter Paul Rubens. Man & Artist. New Haven/London 1987

Ausstellungskataloge/Exhibition catalogues:

Jacob Jordaens. Bearb. von Michael Jaffé. National Gallery of Canada, Ottawa 1968/69

Jan van Kessel d. Ä. (1626–1679). Die vier Erdteile. Bearb. von Ulla Krempel. Bayerische Staatsgemäldesammlungen, Alte Pinakothek, München 1973

Peter Paul Rubens. Bearb. von Justus Müller Hofstede. Kunsthalle Köln 1977

Peter Paul Rubens 1577–1640. Kunsthistorisches Museum Wien 1977

Bruegel – une dynastie de peintres, Palais des Beaux-Arts Brüssel 1980

Adriaen Brouwer und das niederländische Bauerngenre 1600–1660. Bearb. von Konrad Renger. Bayerische Staatsgemäldesammlungen, Alte Pinakothek, Studio-Ausstellung 8, München 1986

Masterworks from Munich. Sixteenth- to Eighteenth-Century Paintings from the Alte Pinakothek. Bearb. von Beverly Louise Brown/Arthur K. Wheelock Jr., National Gallery of Art, Washington 1988, und Cincinnati Art Museum, Cincinnati 1988/89

Peter Paul Rubens: Altäre für Bayern. Bearb. von Konrad Renger. Bayerische Staatsgemäldesammlungen, Alte Pinakothek, München 1990

Anthony van Dyck. Bearb. von Arthur K. Wheelock Jr./Susan J. Barnes/Julius S. Held u. a. National Gallery of Art, Washington 1990/91

David Teniers the Younger. Paintings, Drawings. Bearb. von Margret Klinge. Koninklijk Museum voor Schone Kunsten, Antwerpen 1991

Jacob Jordaens (1593–1678), 2 Bde. Bearb. von Roger A. d'Hulst/Nora de Poorter/Marc Vandenven. Koninklijk Museum voor Schone Kunsten, Antwerpen 1993

Von Bruegel bis Rubens. Das goldene Jahrhundert der flämischen Malerei. Hrsg. von Ekkehard Mai und Hans Vlieghe. Wallraf-Richartz-Museum, Köln 1992 und Kunsthistorisches Museum, Wien 1993

The Age of Rubens. Bearb. von Peter C. Sutton u. a. Museum of Fine Arts, Boston 1993/94